13

War and
social change

War and social change

British society in the
Second World War

edited by .
HAROLD L. SMITH

MANCHESTER UNIVERSITY PRESS

Copyright © Manchester University Press 1986

Whilst copyright in the volume as a whole is vested in
Manchester University Press copyright in the individual
chapters rests with their respective authors and no chapter
may be reproduced whole or in part without the express
permission in writing of both author and publisher.

Published by
Manchester University Press
Oxford Road, Manchester M13 9PL.

British Library cataloguing in publication data
War and social change: British society in
  the Second World War.
  1. Great Britain — Social conditions —
  20th century 2. World War, 1939–1945 —
  Social aspects — Great Britain
  I. Smith, Harold L.
  941.084   HN385

Library of Congress cataloging in publication data applied for

ISBN 0 7190 1777 7 hardback

Phototypeset by
Elliott Brothers & Yeoman, Ltd, Woodend Avenue, Liverpool L24 9JL
Printed and bound in Great Britain by
Biddles Ltd, Guildford and King's Lynn

Contents

III Political ideas and social change

The contributors

Harold L. Smith is Professor of History at the University of Houston, Victoria

Penny Summerfield is Lecturer in the Social History of Education at the University of Lancaster

Daniel M. Fox is Professor of Humanities in Medicine at the State University of New York, Stony Brook

Henry Pelling is Emeritus Reader in Recent British History at the University of Cambridge

Deborah Thom is Senior Research Associate in the Child Care and Development Group (Social and Political Sciences)

John Macnicol is Lecturer in Social Policy at the University of London

Jose Harris is Fellow and Tutor in Modern History, St Catherine's College, Oxford

Jay Winter is University Lecturer in History at the University of Cambridge

John Stevenson is Reader in History at the University of Sheffield

Rory MacLeod advises a Middle Eastern central bank on its foreign investments.

Introduction

The idea that war is a major cause of social change can be traced back at least as far as Aristotle. But current conceptions of the link between war and social change are derived primarily from a generation of scholars whose major works have appeared since 1945. Foremost among these was Richard Titmuss, whose contribution to the official history of the Second World War, *Problems of Social Policy*, secured wide acceptance for the war and social change thesis.[1]

Titmuss believed that public attitudes became more egalitarian during the Second World War, and maintained that this led directly to dramatic changes in social policy. In his view the evacuation at the beginning of the war was of special importance; it exposed chronic social evils, and stimulated public support for new social policies to remedy them. He claimed that the threat of invasion following the retreat from Dunkirk created an unprecedented sense of social solidarity among the British people which found expression in egalitarian policies and collectivist legislation.[2] The introduction of new wartime social services and proposals for reform, such as the Beveridge report, seemed a logical outcome of this change in public attitudes. The Labour victory in the 1945 general election appeared to confirm that a considerable shift in attitudes had occurred during the war, while the post-war Labour government's social legislation was perceived by Titmuss as an attempt to implement wartime thinking on social policy.

Although clearly inspired by Titmuss's theory, even some proponents of the war and social change thesis now find Titmuss's version of it unsatisfactory. Arthur Marwick, who has probably done more than anyone else in recent years to popularise the notion that total wars have been profound forces for social change, has criticised Titmuss's view that war fostered 'social solidarity and therefore social reform' as too

simple an explanation of how the war affected society.[3] Marwick
concedes that the belief that Dunkirk brought about a profound and
lasting transformation of attitudes is a myth.[4] But he insists that the
war and social change thesis remains valid if recast along different lines.

While Titmuss focused on changes associated with innovations in social
policy, Marwick places greater weight on unguided forces which have
brought about alterations in British society. Marwick suggests that there
are four dimensions through which total war affects society.[5] The first
is by the disruption or destruction of pre-war processes and relationships.
As an example he points to the internal population migration stimulated
by enemy bombing raids. The second dimension is the testing of existing
institutions; this forces adaptation in order that a nation be successful
in war. Marwick claims that the British medical system was tested, found
wanting, and therefore replaced by the National Health Service. Third,
total war requires the participation of previously underrepresented groups
in the labour force because of the conscription of large numbers of men
into the armed forces. These groups, including women, derive tangible
benefits from their increased participation in the labour force; the end
to the marriage bar for married women is cited as an example. The fourth
dimension is the psychological effect. Marwick claims that total war is
an emotional and psychological experience 'comparable with the great
revolutions in history'.[6] He suggests that among the upper classes total
war stimulates feelings of sympathy towards the underprivileged, while
encouraging the latter to become more assertive in pressing for egalitarian
social reform. The changes associated with the Second World War were
so far-reaching that Marwick believes the conflict brought about a 'social
and economic revolution'.[7]

However attractive the war and social change thesis may seem, several
historians have expressed reservations. The general histories of the
Second World War by Angus Calder and Henry Pelling concluded that
it would be misleading to view the war from that perspective.[8] Detailed
research studies of the movement for family allowances, the Beveridge
report, the position of women workers, and the issue of equal pay for
women found the war and social change thesis an inappropriate way
of viewing these developments.[9] Even Paul Addison, in an important
book on wartime changes in British politics, noted that these resulted
in 'only very modest changes in society itself'.[10] It is not surprising,
therefore, that the war and social change thesis should be identified as
one of the two prevalent types of 'misapprehension' in current
conceptions of twentieth-century British social history.[11]

This book contains original essays prepared especially for the volume on topics central to the debate about the effect of the Second World War on British society. The chapters fall into three groups: social policy, social structure, and ideas about the proper role of the State. Most of the authors find the war and social change thesis of limited value in interpreting wartime developments.

The essays on social policy draw attention to the considerable continuity between wartime policies and pre-war thinking. After examining the effect of the evacuation of schoolchildren on official attitudes towards reform, John Macnicol concludes that evacuation probably strengthened the existing view in Whitehall that the bulk of those in poverty could not be helped by a Welfare State. Examining the origins of the National Health Service, Dan Fox suggests that by September 1939 a consensus already existed on the need for a national health care system; wartime developments were largely an elaboration of pre-war schemes. John Stevenson arrives at a similar conclusion in considering the vogue for planning which developed during the war. He notes that the planning movement was well established by 1939, and that, despite the impetus which the war supposedly provided, post-war governments continued to function on an *ad hoc* basis while paying lip service to the idea of planning. Rory MacLeod suggests that the apparent wartime consensus in support of a full employment policy was an illusion based on the assumption that the exceptional degree of social solidarity developed during the war would continue after it. Deborah Thom draws attention to the ways in which the war actually hindered educational reform and, through the 1944 Education Act, strengthened traditional social forces. Finally, even though it is often claimed that political attitudes became more radical during the war, Henry Pelling notes that the conflict had a moderating effect on the Labour Party. While it may be useful to speak of an 'Attlee consensus' emerging from the war, this was due as much to a shift to the right by Labour as to a move to the left by the Conservative Party.

The chapters on social structure draw attention to some important areas of change but lend little support to the view that the war was a watershed in British social history. Jay Winter indicates that it further accentuated the decline in mortality rates that was well established before 1939, but concludes that the most fundamental demographic consequence of the war was the striking increase in nuptiality and fertility rates. Penny Summerfield warns against any easy assumption that the war permanently reduced class differences. The conflict did have an equalising effect on incomes, but this proved temporary; with respect to property ownership there is little evidence that the gulf between the middle class and the working class was reduced. In the final chapter in this section I suggest that the war's most important effect on women was to stimulate an increased desire for marriage and family; in this way it strengthened traditional sex roles rather than bringing significant progress towards the emancipation of women.

The third section of the book raises important questions about the consensus on Welfare State policies which Titmuss and Marwick claim the war created. Jose Harris maintains that the wartime consensus on the role of the State was due to emergency conditions which did not survive the restoration of peace. As a result, the Welfare State came into being without the support of a coherent theory of the State or a carefully defined conception of welfare. This eventually left the Welfare State vulnerable to attacks from its opponents.

Notes

1   Richard Titmuss, *Problems of Social Policy*, London, 1950. Also see his *Essays on 'The Welfare State'*, London, 1958.

2   Titmuss, *Problems*, p. 508.

3   Arthur Marwick, 'Total war and social change: myths and misunderstandings', *Social History Society Newsletter*, IX, spring 1984, p. 4.

4   *Ibid.*

5   The clearest explanation of the four dimensions is in Arthur Marwick, 'Problems and consequences of organizing society for total war', in N. F. Dreisziger (ed.), *Mobilization for Total War: the Canadian, American and British Experience, 1914–1918, 1939–1945*, Waterloo, Ontario, 1981, pp. 3–21.

6   *Ibid.*, p. 4.

7   Arthur Marwick, 'Great Britain: society in flux', in A. J. P. Taylor and J. M. Roberts (eds.), *The Twentieth Century*, XIV, London, 1979, p. 1910.

8   Angus Calder, *The People's War*, New York, 1969, and Henry Pelling, *Britain and the Second World War*, London, 1970.

9   See John Macnicol, *The Movement for Family Allowances, 1918–45: a Study in Social Policy Development*, London, 1980, Jose Harris, *William Beveridge*, Oxford, 1977, and 'Some aspects of social policy in Britain during the Second World War', in W. J. Mommsen (ed.), *The Emergence of the Welfare State in Britain and Germany, 1850–1950*, London, 1981, Penny Summerfield, *Women Workers in the Second World War*, London, 1984, and Harold L. Smith, 'The problem of 'equal pay for equal work' in Great Britain during World War II', *Journal of Modern History*, LIII, December, 1981, pp. 652–72.

10   Paul Addison, *The Road to 1945*, London, 1977, p. 14.

11   Michael Bentley, 'Social change: appearance and reality', in Christopher Haigh (ed.), *The Cambridge Historical Encyclopedia of Great Britain and Ireland*, Cambridge, 1985, p. 327.

I Social policy

John Macnicol

The evacuation of schoolchildren

In the social history of twentieth-century Britain the Second World War stands out as a watershed; the sheer scale and magnitude of the events that took place during those crucial six years seems to lend indisputable credibility to the view that modern wars are a major force behind progressive social change.

Yet the term 'social change' is highly problematic. We know that Britain ended the 1940s with a Labour government, a National Health Service, a Keynesian Treasury and an economy that was capable of delivering the magic triumvirate of full employment, low inflation and economic growth. All this would have been unthinkable in the 1930s; though, as Paul Addison has pointed out,[1] there were signs that a progressivist tide of 'middle opinion' was rising gently, nevertheless the speed with which these developments occurred after 1940 must be attributed to the peculiar conditions brought about by the war. Yet, without minimising the very real material and political benefits gained by ordinary working-class people in the 1940s, one must recognise the qualitatively ambiguous nature of these welfare innovations: a National Health Service which greatly benefited working-class women and children but also consolidated the power of an elite of consultants; secondary education for all, but qualitatively differentiated, with selection by and large on grounds of social class, and the independent sector left intact; a comprehensive social security system, but with benefit rates no higher in relation to average earnings than they had been in the 1930s.

Even at this level, evaluation of the war's influence is superficial, because it is limited to political, legislative and institutional innovation. Defined in this way, social change may be quantifiable – but as an historical concept it may tell us little about the experiences of ordinary people. For example, during the Second World War there was a dramatic

increase in the number of children having free or subsidised school meals
in public elementary and grant-aided secondary schools – from 130,000
in July 1940 to 1,840,000 in October 1945. Superficially, this could be
cited as evidence of progressive social change. Yet the First World War
produced exactly the *opposite* result: after an initial rise from 120,000
in 1914 to 600,000 in 1915 the number of children taking meals fell
to 75,000 in 1918 – caused, of course, by the fact that improved
employment opportunities and higher real wages brought about by the
war economy lifted an increasing number of parents above the eligibility
level.[2] A more subtle qualitative measurement would have to discover,
therefore, whether, in terms of the economics of everyday life, ordinary
working-class families in 1914–18 gained more in higher wages, economic
freedom and consequent self-perceived dignity than they lost through
the contraction of the school meals service.

Evaluating war and social change in such experiential terms is further
complicated by the fact that the Second World War brought to the lives
of British citizens a degree of personal disruption that is almost
incalculable – though well captured in some of the literature of the time,
notably Graham Greene's *The Ministry of Fear* (1943). In 1939 less than
half the population left home even for a single night in the year;[3] yet
during the course of the war there were 60 million changes of address
in a civilian population of 38 million.[4] More than in any other period,
there is the problem of aggregating a multitude of personal life-histories.

For example, it has often been argued – most notably by Stanislav
Andreski – that the common shared experience of blitzkreig bombing
brought many civilians into the front line, producing a high 'military
participation ratio' and thus a large amount of social change.[5] Yet the
actual experience of bombing was sharply differentiated. The famous
German raid on Coventry on the night of 14 November 1940 brought
widespread devastation and civilian demoralisation (such that a cordon
had to be thrown round the city, and news from it heavily censored);
likewise, the bombing of the East End of London intimidated its
inhabitants far more than the government dared admit at the time.
However, to many devil-may-care young people London in the blitz was
a place of exhilaration and excitement. Colin Perry has recorded how,
as a carefree eighteen-year-old, he would climb up to rooftops in order
to watch the air raids.[6] Similarly, for one young musician London was
' "Boys' True Adventure" come to life. . . . I couldn't wait for the air
raids. I never had any thoughts of being killed or anything.'[7]

If we consider briefly the effect of bombing on that section of the community that was potentially the most vulnerable – the children – we can see that again the effects varied. Studies and personal observations by teachers, social workers and school medical officers during the war emphasised the children's remarkable ability to maintain emotional equilibrium if they remained in the company of cheerful parents:[8] a typical report by one school medical officer to the Board of Education stated:

I had the opportunity to see several hundred children during the last month. On several occasions I saw them and watched them while bombs were falling in the neighbourhood and air raids were overhead and asked them questions relating to war, sirens, etc. . . . Children have adapted themselves to present conditions of life surprisingly well. . . . Even children who were bombed out of their homes did not seem to suffer in any way. . . . There is no question of shock.[9]

Anna Freud, from her work in the Hampstead Clinic, likewise found that young children could endure the experience of bombing with relative equanimity if in the care of their mothers; sometimes it even appealed to their natural feelings of aggression. However, studies also showed that if bombing was accompanied by evacuation and the destruction of family ties it *did* induce emotional problems; this dual verdict was stressed by the Board of Education after the war, having reviewed the evidence from child guidance clinics.[10]

It must be evident, therefore, that establishing a clear causal link between the intensity of a war and its effect on the social experiences and material conditions of an affected population is highly complex. Even more difficult is evaluating ideological and attitudinal change – for example, the extent to which a war experience forces different groups in the population to alter their perceptions of social problems. Merely documenting legislative and institutional change is not enough: one must examine, in Arthur Marwick's words, changes 'in ideas and in social attitudes and relationships, in how people and classes saw each other, and, most important, in how they saw themselves'.[11] Here this approach will be explored by investigating one particularly appropriate episode in the social history of the Second World War – the evacuation of school-children in the first few months after September 1939.

In the 1930s fears of bombing casualties in a future war led to government plans for the dispersal of the population; dispersal, it was felt, would not only remove civilians from the highly vulnerable urban conurbations where blitzkreig bombing would be concentrated, but would also minimise casualties by spreading the population as thinly as possible. Accordingly, in the late 1930s there was much secret civil defence planning within Whitehall, culminating in the publication of the Anderson report on evacuation in October 1938.[12] Circulars were issued to local authorities; arrangements were made for the billeting of evacuees (involving detailed surveys of available accommodation); those citizens most at risk (principally children, mothers with pre-school children, the elderly, the blind, the disabled) were identified as belonging to the 'priority classes'; and, most important of all, the country was divided into evacuation areas (containing 11 million people, from which 3 million in the priority classes would be removed), reception areas (16 million) which would host the evacuees, and neutral areas (13 million).[13]

During the Munich crisis of September 1938 some rehearsals for evacuation were carried out, and in the following months arrangements were speeded up.[14] Nevertheless, when the first real wave of evacuation took place, on and after 1 September 1939, it was conducted in an atmosphere of haste and confusion. Over the course of several days there was removed to reception areas a total of 826,959 unaccompanied school-children, 523,670 mothers with pre-school children, 12,705 expectant mothers, and 173,000 others in the priority classes.[15]

Evacuees were dispersed to billets over a wide area: for example, London children were spread from Land's End to the Wash, under 476 billeting authorities and 73 education authorities. The scheme only operated because of the assistance given voluntarily by groups such as the Women's Voluntary Service, 17,000 of whose members were mobilised on 1 September. Evacuees frequently began their journey early in the morning at a railway station thronged with crowds of forlorn and confused children, clutching suitcase and gas mask. Exact destinations were kept secret, and rail journeys would be long and slow – with the result that many of the children, already traumatised by separation from their families, arrived at their destinations tired, frightened and lonely. Reception arrangements often went badly: a rural area expecting a few dozen docile grammar-school girls could find itself, at ten o'clock in the evening, invaded by a hundred resentful East End mothers with exhausted and fretful babies. Billeting allocation was frequently chaotic: host families could be hostile; children might be selected according to their good looks and manners; in rural areas, farmers often gleefully snapped up the strongest boys and set them to work on the land.

Most of all, after a few days there began to appear a growing chorus of complaint from hosts about the condition of some of the evacuees. Stories, much enhanced in the retelling, circulated about dirty, lice-ridden children who were ignorant of the basic rules of civilisation: the entire stock of clothing of a girl evacuee from Liverpool might consist of a light cotton dress and a pair of plimsolls; evacuees did not know how to use a knife and fork properly; they displayed an alarming ignorance of the joys of country life, being surprised that apples grew on trees and not in boxes; and, worst of all, their lack of toilet training extended way beyond mere bed-wetting (which, it was alleged, took place frequently) to unimaginable depths of depravity. 'You dirty thing, messing up the lady's carpet. Go and do it in the corner,' said one Glasgow mother to her child, in a story that has passed into the folklore of the Second World War.[16] Typical of this portrayal of the evacuee stereotype was Oliver Lyttleton's recollection:

They duly arrived, some suffering from childish illnesses and one or two from impetigo. I was afraid of infection spreading amongst them, but we did our best and packed them in. I got a shock: I had little dreamt that English children could be so completely ignorant of the rules of hygiene, and that they would regard the floors and carpets as suitable places upon which to relieve themselves. I was still more surprised when some of their parents arrived in motor cars to see them at the weekend.[17]

As we shall see, this sort of reaction was to be highly publicised, both then and after.

By early 1940 there had been a substantial drift-back of evacuees to the cities: something like 80% had returned. There were subsequent waves of evacuation – during the blitz of late 1940, via the Children's Overseas Reception Scheme of the same year (which sent children principally to Canada), and in 1944 when the V1 and V2 rockets arrived – and, of course, roughly 2 million people evacuated themselves by private arrangement in the first months of the war. Evacuation was thus a constant migration of population – on Titmuss's estimate, some 4 million people were dealt with by the government scheme over the course of the war – and in later waves many of the problems of inadequate medical inspection, inappropriate billeting, lack of schooling and so on were overcome. This study will, therefore, concentrate on the first wave of evacuation during the 'phoney war' period because it was this stage that caused most controversy.

Why was evacuation such an important episode in the social history of the Second World War? Two answers immediately suggest themselves. First, it was, after bombing, the most crucial life-event experienced by the civilian population. At a stroke, family ties were disrupted: children found themselves, at an appallingly early age, having to stand on their own two feet in a strange and often hostile environment; parents were suddenly deprived of their offspring. Of course, evacuation was only a part of the enormous social disruption brought about by the war; but subsequent recollections by evacuees, such as those collected by B. S. Johnson,[18] pay eloquent testimony to the lasting effects – both negative and positive – it had on those who endured it, and suggest that qualitatively it was an experience that stood apart from the wider social confusion of wartime.

Second, evacuation has been identified by many writers as an enormously important causal factor in the construction of that wartime reformist consensus that led to the Welfare State legislation of the late 1940s. According to many accounts, middle-class complacency was severely shocked by the evidence of the children's condition: in Newcastle, for example, of 31,000 children registering for evacuation, 13% were found to be deficient in footwear and 21% deficient in clothing; in Scotland, 39% of children turned up in clothing that was 'bad or deplorable'.[19] The shock experienced in middle-class circles was graphically summed up, shortly after the war, by the biographer of the wartime Archbishop of Canterbury:

Who were these boys and girls – half-fed, half-clothed, less than half-taught, complete strangers to the most elementary social discipline and the ordinary decencies of a civilised home? Only one answer was possible. They were the products of the free institutions of which Britons are bidden to think with pride . . . one duty was clear: even the vaguest altruist felt that something ought to be done about it.[20]

And this 'vague altruism' apparently permeated up to the highest levels in government: for example, Neville Chamberlain, who had been a leading figure in the pre-war National Government's denial of the problem of child malnutrition, was so shocked by the stories of the children's condition that he commented to his sister, 'I never knew that such conditions existed, and I feel ashamed of having been so ignorant of my neighbours. For the rest of my life I mean to try and make amends by helping such people to live cleaner and healthier lives.'[21]

The thesis that evacuation was a crucial factor in the creation of a wartime reformist consensus was first suggested by Richard Titmuss: indeed, it was the central theme of his brilliant study of social policy in wartime, *Problems of Social Policy* (1950). Titmuss argued that the social upheavals, sharing of sacrifices and threat of invasion during the first part of the war acted as a catalytic influence on social policy development. Evacuation, and the revelations associated with it, 'dominated social policy for at least the first nine months of the war' and 'aroused the conscience of the nation', leading to a much wider debate on the condition of the people. A crucial turning point was the Dunkirk experience of July 1940: this sharing of danger led to a 'rearrangement of values' among the governing class, such that henceforth they accepted the need for universal social services as reflecting this 'pooling of national resources and sharing of risks'. 'Acceptance of these principles moved forward the goals of welfare,' Titmuss argued: after July 1940 the number of children taking school meals doubled in twelve months and those taking milk in schools rose 50%. The social debate and revolution in attitude engendered by evacuation thus produced a whole string of welfare reforms, from the more liberal administration of National Assistance to the 1944 Education Act. [22]

Some historians of the war have recently expressed serious reservations about the Titmuss interpretation. Arthur Marwick, for example, while agreeing that the evacuation revelations aroused a new sense of social concern 'among an articulate few', nevertheless casts doubt upon the idea that it suddenly dispelled middle-class prejudices about there being a feckless and dirty section of the working class. [23] However, others have been content to accept the message in *Problems of Social Policy*: for example, Peter Gosden, in his detailed study of education in the war, cites Titmuss as the authoritative source on the social consequences of evacuation; [24] likewise, Raynes Minns concludes that the revelations of the children's condition 'made headlines, and once again, as in 1914, when the physical condition of army recruits was found to be so poor, war forced a British government to recognise the extremes of poverty and neglect that survived in our cities, and eventually to act by expanding our welfare services'. [25]

This chapter will, therefore, examine evacuation as an historical episode by addressing three issues: first, why the initial evacuation scheme was such a failure – and whether this failure was caused, as many middle-class observers argued, by the children's behaviour. Second, it will examine, in the light of Titmuss's interpretation, the policy innovations and possible ideological realignments that resulted from the debate over the condition of the children. And finally, it will investigate – as far as possible – how the evacuees themselves perceived the whole business; in other words, to adapt a phrase of E. P. Thompson's, it will try to rescue the children from the enormous condescension of history.

Why, then, did the first scheme fail? In answering this question one is immediately struck by the contrast between, on the one hand, the long history of civil defence preparation, of which the evacuation plan was an important part, and, on the other, the fact that in this planning there was a remarkable lack of attention paid to everyday human problems. For example, as far back as 1923 a sub-committee of the Committee of Imperial Defence had looked into the distribution of doctors, dentists and hospital services in a future war (in effect, tasks that were taken up by the Emergency Medical Service in 1938), and air raid precautions had been discussed within Whitehall since 1924 by the Air Raid Precautions Committee of the Committee of Imperial Defence (which relinquished responsibility for this to the Home Office in 1935).[26]

However, throughout the 1930s these preparations were seriously inhibited by the fact that all civil defence discussions were conducted in an atmosphere of secrecy and pessimism. Secrecy was deemed politically wise because in the pacifist climate of the early 1930s planning for war could be misinterpreted as encouraging war. Thus, for example, Baldwin's responses to questions in the House over Britain's preparedness for war were heavily guarded.[27] Inevitably, this affected the efficiency of the plans that were being drawn up by Whitehall.

Secondly, all participants in such discussions took a very pessimistic view of the likely scale of bombing casualties, and hence considered it pointless to plan in detail. The air raids of 1917–18 had resulted in a casualty ratio of sixteen per ton of German bombs dropped (it was thought that this would be nearer fifty per ton for London), but after the Luftwaffe attacks on Barcelona in March 1938 the figure was uprated to seventy-two per ton.[28] On the basis that 'the bomber will always get through' officials within Whitehall made alarmist predictions that the declaration of war with Germany would be followed immediately by the devastation of cities, epidemics, disruption of food supplies, panic among the civilian population, the breakdown of essential services, and so on. Thus Wing Commander Hodsoll, Secretary of the ARP Committee, gloomily warned his colleagues in November 1936 that 'certain areas have been scheduled as likely to be subject to almost continuous bombing in the event of war',[29] and similar pessimism ran through the 1938 Anderson report on evacuation.

There was some recognition by planners that schools would provide particularly vulnerable targets, especially dangerous because they contained a high concentration of glass. Public opinion would demand that schoolchildren be moved to safe areas; a serious raid on a school would be highly damaging to morale. For example, civil servants collected information and press cuttings on the bombing of a school at

Getalfe, in Madrid, in October 1936, when 70 children were killed in horrific circumstances, and pondered over what would be the effect on public morale if a similar event were to happen in Britain.[30]

However, because of the deeply held pessimism in Whitehall it was considered pointless to make detailed plans for an evacuation that would take place in an atmosphere of panic and confusion; railway timetables would matter little if bombs were raining down. Of course – as Titmuss pointed out – had the Luftwaffe launched an all-out offensive on 3 September 1939, as everyone expected, this scenario would have come about.[31] Indeed, even after the first wave of evacuation had taken place it was the view of the Board of Education that 'if there were any further large-scale evacuation it would probably be a hasty one, occasioned by sudden and serious bombing. Medical examination of each child would then be almost out of the question'.[32] As a result of this pessimism, many important administrative arrangements were settled late in the day – in many cases only after the Munich crisis of September 1938, as in the case of food distribution and transport.[33] By late 1938, in fact, the evident lack of official preparedness was causing concern both to outside bodies like the National Union of Teachers (who frequently complained about it) and to Civil Defence Regional Commissioners: for example, on 28 September 1938 one of them wrote to the Ministry of Health from his headquarters at Maidstone that:

We all arrived on Tuesday to find that the offices were completely unfurnished, without lighting, without telephone and without any equipment of any sort. The result of two days bullying all round is that we have a few tables and two telephones and one borrowed typewriter.[34]

The vagueness of the evacuation plans resulted in neither central nor local government knowing quite what the other was supposed to be doing. For example, on the crucial question of the medical condition of the evacuees, which was to cause so much controversy, the Board of Education believed that local authorities had been adequately warned that pediculosis (head lice) would be a problem and had been given instructions on how to disinfect children by the use of steam baths;[35] also that its memorandum Ev. 4, *Government Evacuation Scheme* (published in May 1939), emphasised that 'the children should be sent away wearing their thickest and warmest footwear'.[36] Yet on the other hand surviving evidence tends to vindicate Richard Padley's accusation, in the Fabian survey of evacuation, that Whitehall used the decentralised local government system to shirk its responsibilities; the Ministry of

Health and Board of Education, he maintained, doled out 'platitudinous' advice via circulars and adopted an attitude of complacency over the possibility of medical problems among evacuee children, such as malnutrition, head lice, impetigo, etc.[37] For example, in December 1938 Ben Smith, MP, wrote to the Board of Education warning that on the evidence of the evacuation rehearsals of September 1938 there would be a sufficient number of ill-clad or poorly-shod children to hinder the successful operation of the scheme; but in reply the President of the Board of Education, Earl de la Warr, blandly denied that this would be so.[38]

Margaret Cole's verdict was that the evacuation scheme had been drawn up by minds that were 'military, male and middle-class'.[39] This was also the view of the other three main independent surveys (of Cambridge, Oxford and Scotland)[40] and of many of the teachers involved; and by April 1940 officials in Whitehall were privately agreeing. Analysing the substantial drift of evacuees back to the danger areas, the Air Raid Precautions Co-ordinating Committee concluded that 'a detailed examination of available materials shows the basic cause to be the failure of the scheme to take account of either the viewpoint or the welfare of those concerned, be they evacuee or host'.[41] The first point to note, therefore, is that many of the disruptions in the first evacuation scheme, which produced so much distress in the children (resulting, in particular, in bed-wetting) were primarily the result of poor civil defence planning.

A brief consideration of the problems encountered in the first months after September 1939 will illustrate this. Firstly, transport arrangements were often chaotic. Having survived the milling crowds at the station platforms (in which they might easily be separated from brother or sister), children often found themselves bundled onto a train, not knowing their destination, and then enduring a long, slow journey in cramped coaches with no corridors or toilets. Leslie Dunkling, who looked back on his evacuation experience as a 'mental minefield', described his journey thus:

Off we went as a tumultuous procession through the streets of West London. In that first hour or so our excitement reached its peak. It was only as the day wore on that we wearied of the journey and began to be afraid. By the time we reached Totnes, in Devon, we had abandoned ourselves to our despair. The younger ones, especially, sat in the church hall howling miserably, waiting to be claimed. We were city mongrels, gathered from the streets, feeling helplessly lost.[42]

William Boyd's excellent survey of evacuation in Scotland showed that out of sixty-eight questionnaire returns giving details of journeys in the first wave, fully one-third spoke of their evacuees not arriving at their destinations until 5 p.m. or later; and it included graphic descriptions of such journeys, including the testimony of one teacher evacuated from Glasgow to Aberdeenshire, whose journey was:

the most depressing, deplorable and disgusting journey I have ever had the misfortune to make. The train took 12½ hours to reach Aberdeen. Half-hours and hours were spent in railway sidings until the line was clear. The journey was a positive nightmare, increased by the darkness of the train (lit by blue lights) and the wretched rainstorm which greeted our arrival at the station. The evacuees were famished when they arrived, having had no food for a matter of 12 hours.[43]

There were innumerable complaints about the billeting and reception arrangements. Billeting allowances were available to cover the cost of hosting an evacuee (for unaccompanied children, 10s 6d per week for the first child, 8s 6d each for subsequent children) and billeting officers had powers of compulsion to utilise appropriate accommodation, but most, being from the locality themselves, preferred to ruffle as few feathers as possible – with the result that on arrival many evacuees found themselves in a scene 'reminiscent of a cross between an early Roman slave market and Selfridge's bargain basement', as one witness put it.[44] Allegations were rife: evacuees complained of cruel and miserly hosts; hosts maintained that many parents had deliberately sent children off in their worst clothes in order to arouse sympathy and gifts of replacement clothing. Defenders of the evacuees pointed out that the exercise had taken place at the end of a particularly hot summer, in which head lice would have thrived, that parents had not been properly informed of how long their children would be evacuated for (and hence despatched them in one day's clothing), or that the first day of evacuation (1 September) was a Friday – the day on which working-class financial resources would have been at their lowest, preventing parents buying extra garments for their children. Some billeting arrangements were equally resented by both sides – as when Roman Catholic children from inner-city Liverpool were sent to staunchly Protestant North Wales, and some were the fault of nobody – as when in Cambridge a Greek head waiter's wife was given a bed inferior to that provided for the wife of an under-waiter.

In some rural communities the role of billeting officer brought out the worst in people, as Evelyn Waugh amusingly recorded in *Put Out More Flags* (1942). Barbara Sothill finds that this duty has:

transformed her, in four months, from one of the most popular women in the countryside into a figure of terror. When her car was seen approaching people fled through covered lines of retreat, through side doors and stable yards, into the snow, anywhere to avoid her persuasive 'But surely you could manage *one* more. He's a boy this time and a very well behaved little fellow.'[45]

But more often the allocation of billets reflected social relations and deferential attitudes in rural society, as when, according to one MP, at Inverary in Scotland 150 women and children were housed in a cold hall, with bedding of dirty mattresses and sacks of straw 'with a broad arrow on them, that had been obtained from the local jail', while near by the Duke of Argyll's castle was left uninhabited.[46] There were protests from parents that reception areas were often close to prime military targets: for example, such areas in Essex were in the flight path of bombers; Dundee, north of the Tay bridge, was an evacuation area, while Newport, south of it, was a reception area. These were but some of the thousands of complaints and allegations made in the autumn of 1939, all adding up to a condemnation of the way billeting had been planned.

There was another problem that provided perhaps the harshest verdict on the government's preparations – the drift-back to the danger areas. Owing to the absence of widespread German air raids, some 45% of unaccompanied children and 80% of mothers with pre-school children had returned by the end of November 1939. By the end of February 1940, out of 3 million people in the priority classes (of which only 1,165,000 had actually taken part in the evacuation) a mere 477,000 remained in the safe reception areas.[47] In educational and governmental circles there was great concern over this: apart from the dangers involved, it meant that – on a National Union of Teachers estimate – some 750,000 children were not receiving formal education in early 1940, since most schools in evacuation areas had been closed. All the Board of Education could do was aim for a minimum of half-time school provision by Easter.[48] Meanwhile, it was feared, children in the cities were running wild like 'street arabs' (as one official put it), without schooling or the protection of the school medical service; there were fears that juvenile delinquency was on the increase as a result. Some attempts were made to stem the tide: in November and December 1939 (in view of the approach of Christmas) the Board of Education and Ministry of Health launched, via the Ministry of Information, a propaganda campaign to persuade parents to keep their children in reception areas. Articles were placed in the press chronicling the joys of country life (and – as will be shown – fruitless attempts were made to demonstrate that the rural environment was having a positive effect on the children's health); talks were given on the radio to parents; special posters were printed; and it was arranged for the Queen to visit certain schools in November to publicise the scheme.[49] All this failed; evacuees voted with their feet, and the drift-back continued. Officials gloomily realised that the inadequate billeting arrangements devised by Whitehall had discredited the scheme, and a propaganda campaign would make little difference. Only when heavy raids on cities began would parents participate willingly in a future evacuation scheme.[50]

But the problems of transport, billeting and the drift-back paled into insignificance compared with the outcry over the alleged medical condition and anti-social behaviour of the evacuees. Immediately after the first wave of evacuation had taken place there was a chorus of outrage from reception areas about some of the evacuees – evidently those from the poorest homes in inner-city areas – who were said to be filthy, verminous, incontinent, ungrateful and thoroughly ill-mannered. In the press, in the House of Commons, in reports to government departments and in popular folklore there emerged the evacuee stereotype – a dirty, lice-ridden and foul-mouthed urchin who wet the bed with monotonous regularity, preferred fish and chips to a proper three-course meal and was about as domesticated as a wildcat; similarly, the evacuee mother appeared as a negligent slut, impossible to live with and having the vocabulary of a Billingsgate fish porter. To their alarm, civil servants began to receive a growing stream of horrifying reports. For example, on 22 September 1939 the Department of Health for Scotland Advisory Committee on Evacuation noted that 'the Billeting Appeal Tribunal in Perth had numerous appeals supported by medical certificates to the effect that the health of the householder would be injured by the presence of evacuees in the home'.[51] Probably the loudest chorus of complaint came from North Wales, where Liverpool children had been billeted: thus Lord Wyndham (Civil Defence Regional Commissioner for Wales) wrote to the President of the Board of Education on 25 October 1939 that:

approximately twenty-five per cent of the children evacuated were in such a filthy condition that they had to be specially treated. These have now been cleaned up, but it took us some time to cope with this disgraceful state of affairs. . . . the condition of these children, and the behaviour of many of the mothers, has completely dissipated the goodwill and welcome accorded to them by the Welsh people, whose hospitality is proverbial.[52]

From other Regional Commissioners came stories of mattresses, bed linen and clothing having to be destroyed, so infested were they with evacuated lice.

What was the actual medical condition of the evacuees? Unfortunately the true picture will never be established, for insufficient evidence survives. Crucially, evacuees in the first wave were never subjected to systematic medical inspection – with the result that allegations thrived, both then and subsequently. So many of the stories were wild exaggerations, inflamed by a number of factors – the 'culture contact' between rural and urban society, personal resentment (particularly if two women were forced to share the same kitchen), the strangeness of the whole situation at the start of a frightening new war, or simply – as Angus Calder put it – the English tendency to confuse manners with morals.[53] Hence, for example, children wet the bed – usually for a very brief period – for a variety of understandable reasons: emotional upset over the strange and terrifying journey, homesickness, fear of their new foster parents – sometimes because a toilet was inaccessible. Yet, as the Cambridge evacuation survey commented wryly, hosts presented this as if it were 'an entirely unknown phenomenon in the past, and that evacuation produced a Niagara all over English and Scottish country beds'.[54]

The surviving evidence is thus both unspecific and contradictory. For example, some of the most condemnatory reports came from a Miss Lily Boys, County Organiser of the Women's Voluntary Service in Lincolnshire, who assisted with the reception arrangements there. She attested in September 1939 that 'universally, householders have been shocked at the disgraceful and disgusting conditions in which a certain portion of the population lives', and that 'the low slum type form the majority of the mothers, some out for what they can get, most of them dirty, many of them idle and unwilling to work or pull their weight'. There had been, according to her, 'an enormous percentage' of dirty and verminous children from Hull, Leeds and Grimsby. Yet, a few days earlier, another observer had monitored the evacuation rehearsals of a comparable group of children – also from Hull – to Lincolnshire and had reported that 'the children were well shod, happy, calm, equipped completely with adequate rucksack or canvas containers'.[55] Irresponsible behaviour was by no means confined to the evacuees. For example, stories of piles of urine-soaked mattresses having to be burned by harassed billeting officers have to be placed alongside evidence that hosts sometimes invented bed-wetting cases in order to claim the extra 3s 6d billeting allowance for additional laundry costs: in Llantrisant, in Wales, the total paid out in such allowances rose from £43 in 1940–41 to a staggering £350 in 1941–42, until there was an official investigation –

whereupon the number of reported cases fell dramatically.[56]

The confusing and contradictory nature of the medical evidence comes over even more clearly when one examines the findings of the later waves of evacuation, for in these the Board of Education and Ministry of Health, anxious not to repeat their mistakes of September 1939, did intervene more actively. Systematic medical inspection took place (the famous 'hair raids'), and more robust instructions were issued to local authorities via circulars (such as the charmingly entitled *The Louse and How to Deal With It*); an official 'Louse Infestation Committee' was even set up to ponder the matter. After May 1940 each evacuee child was medically examined and assigned a record card, on which were entered (in coded form) details of any ailments. From these later inspections, the proportion of children with problems appears to have been low: for example, of four schools in Shepherds Bush, London, sending 670 children to Pontypridd in June 1940, there were 'only one or two with a few nits'; of 300 children being evacuated from Northwold Road Public Elementary School, in the East End, in June 1940, only twenty-five were marked as needing special attention (or 8%), comprising one with scabies, five with nits, eight with eneurisis (bed-wetting) and eleven with 'other conditions'; of 1,211 children going from Stretford (Manchester) schools in the same month, only eighty suffered from vermin or nits, and only fourteen from eneurisis.[57] However, E. F. Mott, Director of Education in Liverpool (whose children were so resented in North Wales), found the proportion of verminous children in three Liverpool schools in poor areas to be 18%, 18% (after inspection) and 30% (an estimate).[58] By and large, these and other regional officers' reports from the second wave of evacuation did not indicate that the outcry of September 1939 was justified; typical of them was the verdict of one officer in October 1940 that 'the general standard of those evacuated is good and 80% of them should offer no difficulty at all in billeting'.[59] Of course, these reports were as biased towards optimism as the nervous hosts of September 1939 were biased towards pessimism; and in the later waves great care was taken by teachers, medical officers and even parents not to repeat the mistakes of the first months of the war.

The most reliable and systematic survey was that carried out by Dr Kenneth Mellanby into pediculosis, and it revealed an incidence that *was* quite high. In December 1939 Mellanby had written to the Board of Education, drawing attention to the sharp difference between pre-war medical inspection returns for pediculosis in children (approximately 10%) and the claims of hosts in the reception areas that it was rife. The

Board decided to sponsor a research project by Mellanby to ascertain the true incidence, given the controversy that was developing. As Dr J. A. Glover put it, 'though I fear the findings would be disquieting it seems to me wiser for the Board itself to discover and publish the true position rather than that others should do so'. Mellanby obtained from thirty-two hospitals in selected rural and urban areas the records of children admitted. He found the rural areas to have a very low incidence of head lice, but for urban children it was indeed quite high, and varied significantly by age and sex. In boys it rose from $11 \cdot 0\%$ in those under one year of age to $44 \cdot 6\%$ in those aged two, then went steadily down to $30 \cdot 8\%$ in those aged eight, and $1 \cdot 6\%$ in those aged eighteen. For girls the distribution was different: $12 \cdot 3\%$ in those under one, up to about 50% almost all through the ages two to twelve; then a fall, but still as high as $12 \cdot 8\%$ at the age of nineteen. On average, therefore, the incidence of head lice in the urban child was about three times higher than had been recorded by school medical officers before the war.[60]

Evacuation did, therefore, provide a sudden and unexpected revelation of the true incidence of head lice, but this was no reflection on the quality of working-class parenthood, as many hosts believed. Mellanby located the causes in environmental and even cultural factors – the greater intermingling of city children, overcrowded dwellings or – in girls – the fashion for 'permanent waves', in which hair would be set and then left uncombed and unwashed for long periods. The marked rural–urban difference in incidence, however, made the louse a symbol of the wider cultural differences between town and country that caused so much resentment on both sides. This was reflected in an interesting phenomenon noticed by Mellanby: many school medical officers in safe *urban* reception areas were insistent that head lice had been virtually unknown in their area until the dirty, verminous and ill-mannered inner city evacuees arrived; they were shocked when confronted with past hospital records for their town showing that this was not so.[61]

The implication in the complaints of many hosts that urban working-class life was degrading was further refuted by the evidence of the effect of evacuation on the children's health. Contrary to what everyone expected, urban children suddenly subjected to the apparently healthy environment of fresh air and green fields did *not* show any marked improvement in health. This was a curious phenomenon that perplexed and exasperated those involved in running the scheme. The initial – and understandable – impression of teachers was that children were thriving on country life. In her interesting and vivid description of the first wave Marjorie Cosens quoted numerous testimonies by teachers to this effect,[62] and some of them even wrote to the Board of Education. For example, in November 1939 the headmaster of Wesley Road School, Willesden, wrote to the Board, claiming that ever since they had been evacuated to Rugby his pupils had shown definite increases in height and weight growth rates.[63] Impressed by such testimony, Kenneth Lindsay (Parliamentary Secretary to the Board of Education) told the House of Commons on 16 November 1939:

The children who have gone to the country are much taller, stronger and better fed, they sleep longer and in every way they are alert and more easy to teach. That is the testimony of teacher after teacher, of Inspectors, of parents and, notoriously, of the children themselves. Among the children of a Woolwich school evacuated to somewhere in Kent the average weight of the boys has increased during the last month by 2½ lb. and of girls by 3½ lb.[64]

Throughout the first months of the war Board of Education officials were desperate to find convincing proof of this, so that it could be used as publicity to stop the drift-back to the danger areas.

However, the Board soon ran into difficulties. It seemed tantalisingly obvious that country life was healthier, but actually proving it was another matter. Obtaining a representative sample of children to study in early 1940 was well nigh impossible: were those children who remained in billets in February 1940 a tiny minority who had enjoyed the evacuation experience, who liked country life, who had kindly hosts, who did not suffer homesickness, or who were being exceptionally well fed by their hosts? The operation of these factors would render the results of any study practically useless, as the Board soon began to find. For example, an investigation into height and weight growth rates was conducted in January 1940 on a group of Manchester children evacuated to Glossop: generally, evacuee children who drank milk regularly grew faster than those who did not, but those who paid for the milk showed faster growth rates than the poorer children who received it free – indicating that social class factors were at work.[65] Much to the disappointment of the Board, surveys conducted in 1940 produced negative results: typical of them was the meticulous investigation, in late 1940, of a group of 1,119 London County Council children evacuated to rural areas; comparing them with an equivalent group of London children in 1938, the study concluded that 'a period of evacuation of several months did not cause any significant difference in the rate of growth of evacuated children'.[66]

Even more puzzling were the results of anthropometric surveys of camp school children made throughout the war. (Camp schools were institutions where children lived communally and attended lessons all the time; though somewhat authoritarian in regime, they at least provided a well balanced diet and regular exercise through organised games.) In 1942, 1943 and 1944 surveys were carried out on camp school children, and to the Board's amazement they indicated that such children actually experienced *retarded* growth rates.[67] Official despair was summed up in a letter from Sir Edward Howarth, Director of the National Camps Corporation (which ran the schools) to N. D. Bosworth Smith of the Board of Education, on 13 August 1942; Howarth had just read the latest report on the children's growth rates and commented:

I have read the report through several times and on each reading find it even more bewildering. It is small wonder that Dr Underwood finds it a 'little disconcerting' as the inference of the inquiry, as far as it has gone at present, would appear to be that it is better for a child to stay in East London sleeping irregular hours in ill ventilated shelters and eating fish and chips than to have fresh air conditions in one of our Camps with regular hours of sleep and plenty of well prepared wholesome food (in which vegetables fresh from the garden play a large part) forming a diet balanced in accordance with the best advice obtainable from the Board of Education and others. . . . On a first reading it seems puzzling that the 'Poorer Growth' camps should be those of five or six of our best camp managers whose experience of diet is exceptional, and that the 'Good Growth' camps should include two Managers whose catering has constantly to be reviewed as not up to our standard.[68]

Thus did ordinary children confound the experts. The only explanation that officials could come up with was that, since children grew fastest during school holiday periods, the constant attendance at a camp school inhibited development: the regime of organised games, for example, caused children to burn up too much energy.[69] As the new President of the Board of Education, R. A. Butler, put it, in delightful contrast to his officials' rather ponderous concern, 'Children are human and if they run about too much don't put on weight. School discipline always has this effect on one.'[70]

Clearly, therefore, children preferred the inner-city environment and family life in which they had been born and reared. Yet within Whitehall there was a marked reluctance to accept the implications behind such evidence; officials tended to fall back on the convenient explanation that the 'problem evacuees' revealed in September 1939 were a product of poor-quality home life among some sections of the working class rather than highly exaggerated cultural differences or poverty. Far from there being a 'rearrangement of values', as Titmuss believed, officials tended to cling stubbornly to entrenched attitudes.

This was clearly illustrated by official reaction to the charge, made in the first months of the war, that the revelations of head lice, impetigo, scabies and general uncleanliness were proof that the school medical service had serious deficiencies: clearly, such conditions had been markedly under-recorded in medical inspections before the war. Both the Board of Education and Ministry of Health were acutely sensitive on this issue, given the controversy that had raged in the 1930s over the issue of child malnutrition and ill health. In February 1940 the Chief Medical Officer at the Board of Education, Sir Arthur MacNalty, outlined to Sir Maurice Holmes (Permanent Secretary at the Board) his response to such criticisms. Essentially he held to the line taken by the Ministry of Health in the 1930s: the school medical service was primarily educational, and had never been designed as a complete child health service, nor as an agency to relieve poverty as such – indeed, it operated within strict terms of reference set down by Parliament; systematic medical inspection of evacuees would have been impossible in the conditions of panic and devastation forecast by all civil defence planners before the war; many of the evacuees' problems, such as bed-wetting, had cleared up quickly. Finally, MacNalty absolved the school medical service from prime responsibility for the condition of the evacuees: while acknowledging the 'unexpectedly high incidence of pediculosis and bad habits among school children' that had been revealed, he favoured the following analysis:

The root cause of these conditions lies in the home. They mean that slum clearances still lack completion; that low standards of living still persist, and that the lessons taught in the school and clinic, and good social habits, do not always survive the pressure of bad home circumstances when young people have passed from supervision.

Holmes agreed that it was in 'the homes of the children' that 'the source of the trouble so often lies' and concluded that 'the problem of the dirty school child is not one which could be solved by any enquiry into the School Medical Service'.[71] This, in short, was a commitment to the time-honoured strategy of educating the parents into better habits rather than an acceptance of the need for a universalist Welfare State.

If one looks at one particular example of policy-making – the expansion of free or subsidised milk to children – one sees another striking demonstration of official reluctance to alter traditional patterns of thinking. This is an interesting case to examine, of course, because in

Problems of Social Policy Titmuss presented it as a clear example of a policy change engendered originally by the social debate on evacuation, and then given sudden new urgency by the 'decisive' influence of Dunkirk in July 1940; a marked change in government thinking – a new acceptance of the milk-in-schools scheme as a universalist social service rather than a relief measure tainted with Poor Law associations – took place 'five days after the evacuation of the British Expeditionary Force from Dunkirk'. [72] As a result, the number of children taking milk in schools on any one day rose from 2,479,000 in February 1941 (57·6% of those attending school) to 3,428,000 in February 1944 (76·3%). Yet the surviving evidence suggests a very different interpretation to that offered by Titmuss – and one which, interestingly enough, was summarised in *The Health of the School Child, 1939–45*, published in 1947. [73]

Space does not permit a full account of the highly complex arrangements for providing milk to schoolchildren that developed out of the 1934 'milk-in-schools' scheme. Essentially, there had grown up in the 1930s a system of subsidies which enabled milk to be bought cheaply by local education authorities for distribution (free or at minimal cost) to children. While recognising the undeniable (if somewhat over-stressed) value of milk in a child's nutritional development, the Board of Education and Ministry of Health also appreciated that greater milk consumption would be a way of reducing the surplus stocks then being held by producers. The 1934 milk-in-schools scheme was thus closely bound up with wider questions of production targets, availability of supply and price fixing, supervised by the Milk Marketing Board.

Briefly, the wartime expansion took place for three reasons. First, expansion was being planned prior to the outbreak of war, and the events of 1939–45 were simply a natural continuation. A White Paper of July 1937 had stated it to be the government's aim further to reduce the price of liquid milk to local authorities in order to improve distribution; throughout 1938 there were discussions within the Board of Education, [74] and in July 1939 a Milk Industry Act was passed.

Second, milk in schools became part of wider wartime rationing and food policy. During the first year of the war, evacuation, the closure of schools and other disruptions threw the milk distribution system into some disarray. (The result was a marked fall in the number of children taking milk in schools – from an estimated daily average of 2,500,000 in 1938–39 down to 2,100,000 in July 1940). Even in December 1940 – well after the Durkirk turning-point identified by Titmuss – the

Ministry of Food was uncertain whether expansion was possible because of the continuing 'precarious' supply situation.[75] However, in mid-1940, just about the time of Dunkirk – but quite unconnected with it – expansion of the milk supply to children took on a new urgency as the Ministry of Food belatedly worked out a national food policy for an island race threatened by the submarine. Accordingly, on 12 June 1940 Lord Woolton, Minister of Food, despatched a memorandum to the Food Policy Committee of the War Cabinet in which he identified three groups in the population to whom food distribution should be improved: workers in factories ('if we are to obtain the maximum production over a long period of time from them'), people on low incomes and 'children of school age and under and nursing mothers whom, on grounds both of humanity and of racial preservation, it is essential we should protect against malnutrition'.[76] These 'social capital' arguments may have been what Titmuss meant when he argued that major wars increase governmental concern for women and children, and produce social policies to protect them.[77] But the context in which they were voiced by Lord Woolton was the much wider concern about the nutritional status, and hence the efficiency and morale, of the *whole* population – in other words, arguments of utility rather than social justice; unequal shares would have meant starvation for some – hardly the best recipe for a united war effort. By mid-1941, therefore, it was the prevailing view within the Board of Education that the milk-in-schools scheme was 'an essential part of our war food policy and not mainly a scheme to increase milk drinking and use up a surplus of liquid milk';[78] by that time, for example, the Ministry of Food was assuming, for rationing calculation purposes, that each child was receiving five-sixths of a pint of milk per day.[79] Expansion was further spurred on by the reduction in the meat allowance in school canteens that the Ministry of Food was forced to introduce in 1941, owing to problems of supply. The milk ration for children was increased specifically to compensate for the nutritional shortfall in school meals that would otherwise have occurred; civil servants realised there would be a public outcry if the meat reduction took place and nothing was done to make up for it.[80]

Wartime expansion of milk consumption took place for a third reason that related more to specific practical problems than to a new attitude on the part of policy-makers: simply, the disruptions of wartime made it virtually impossible to implement the pre-war means test criteria, such as the definition of a 'necessitous' child eligible for free milk, or the distinguishing of those children receiving cheap milk for the under-fives under section 2 of the 1939 Milk Industry Act. Means testing was expensive, clumsy and time-wasting. With children constantly moving between evacuation and reception areas, endless administrative problems arose. By February 1940 Board of Education officials were realising the futility of trying to operate pre-war means tests: for example, it might be difficult to trace the parents of an evacuated child. The London County Council had found that it simply was not worth trying to recover the cost of milk from the 25% of London parents whose income was high enough to make them liable for the full billeting contribution, since 'the few pounds they had succeeded in recovering over a period of several months were far less than the cost of its collection'.[81] For these three reasons, therefore, the Board of Education Circular No. 1567 of late 1941 announced the government's aim of increasing milk consumption among schoolchildren to as near 100% as possible.

Within Whitehall, therefore, there *was* surprise and concern that evacuation should have revealed so many symptoms of inner-city poverty, but the reaction of officials to these revelations was to seek their cause in working-class *mores* rather than to swing round to support for increased State intervention to raise living standards. This analysis was held, in a much more robust form, by quite a substantial section of middle-class opinion – particularly within the voluntary social work profession. When considering the long-term effects of the social debate on evacuation, therefore, we must recognise that, as well as helping to construct an ideological climate favourable to welfare legislation, it also boosted a conservative, behaviouristic analysis of poverty that viewed the root cause of the children's condition as family failure, poor parenting and general social inadequacy. Thus for the Women's Group on Public Welfare, in their study of evacuation, *Our Towns* (1943):

The effect of evacuation was to flood the dark places with light and bring home to the national consciousness that the 'submerged tenth' described by Charles Booth still exists in our towns like a hidden sore, poor, dirty and crude in its habits, an intolerable and degrading burden to decent people forced by poverty to neighbour with it.

Within this group are the 'problem families', always on the edge of pauperism and crime, riddled with mental and physical defects, in and out of the Courts for child neglect, a menace to the community of which the gravity is out of all proportion to their numbers.[82]

And, having provided a generally pessimistic account of the evacuee children's condition, *Our Towns* drew the conclusion that what was needed was primarily a reform of the education system that would 'lay the foundations for community life and expose the schools to the pressure of middle-class standards and requirements', with an emphasis on 'training for future wives'.[83] Likewise, in reviewing *Our Towns*, the journal *Social Work* argued that two things stood out about its analysis of the evacuation experience – 'our failure to educate our girls as *home-makers*, in spite of seventy years of compulsory education, and our failure to provide our people with the raw material for home-making'.[84]

This interpretation was also shared by most of the speakers in a House of Lords debate on 5 May 1943. Lord Geddes introduced a motion on 'the shock of public opinion in the reception areas caused in September 1939', calling for the government to work for 'positive health' among the people. Geddes had just read *Our Towns*, and clearly its analysis fitted in with his observations of the evacuees, for he praised it warmly. The evacuee mothers, he maintained, 'seemed quite unable to do very much for themselves. They were quite obviously without any effective social traditions. They did not know how to cook'; their culinary skills extended only to bread and jam or bought fish and chips. They were, he said, 'cultural orphans', and 'the children just did not know at all how to keep a house clean. They were like untrained puppies or untrained kittens; they messed in the corner of any room'. Something was very wrong, 'not on the medical side, because that was not too bad, but on the teaching side and on the disciplinary side'. Other Lords (including the Archbishop of York and Lord (Cosmo) Lang, ex-Archbishop of Canterbury) were also strongly in agreement with *Our Towns*: Lang, for example, maintained that:

many of the children came from homes where the houses were decent, where the wages were good, and where, apparently, the state of the children was not due to any real defect in the conditions under which they were living but simply to the heedlessness, the shiftlessness, the carelessness and the ignorance of the mothers.[85]

Reading accounts of evacuation by more conservatively-minded social commentators, one repeatedly encounters this analysis. For example, John A. F. Watson, chairman of the South East London Juvenile Court, commented on one woman's account of dealing with 'problem' evacuees that:

the behaviour of some of these children, their habits and their language, will leave the average reader aghast. And the cause is manifest in every sordid glimpse we gain of their parents and their homes . . . the enduring lesson to be learned from this painful wartime experiment is that the primary aim of education must be to produce not merely cleverer children, but in the next generation wiser parents.[86]

Evacuation, in short, marks the conceptual transition from the 'social problem group' of the inter-war years to the 'problem family' of the 1940s and 1950s. The latter was less crudely hereditarian in emphasis and – in keeping with the Keynesian optimism of the 1940s – less pessimistic, in that problem families were seen as amenable to character reform through intensive social work intervention.[87] But many argued that evacuation had revealed more clearly than ever the existence of a degraded 'underclass', and in the late 1940s and 1950s several inconclusive but much-publicised surveys were conducted into the precise numerical incidence of problem families in Britain. Until its ideological crisis of the 1960s the social work profession was deeply influenced by the 'problem family' concept, and many commentators dated the origins of this interpretation to the evacuation revelations of September 1939.[88]

Finally, after so much emphasis on the views of middle-class adults, what of the children themselves? They saw evacuation through very different eyes. B. S. Johnson's collection of memoirs records the great variety in the treatment meted out by hosts – from kindness and generosity to unimaginable cruelty – and how, above all, the behaviour of inner-city children that so horrified Women's Institute moralisers was frequently a natural and adaptive response to the emotional trauma of family separation and to the strangeness of country life.[89] The Oxford, Cambridge, Fabian and Scottish surveys were all very sympathetic to the children, and tried hard to present their perspective. They found that the vast majority of bed-wetting cases cleared up very quickly, especially if treated sympathetically.[90] They vividly recorded the perplexed reactions of evacuees, from one woman's uneasy comment, 'there's too much grass about', to the London boy who was horrified that milk should come from a dirty cow and not a clean bottle.[91] Oxford was 'full of forbidding old ladies' who hovered behind lace curtains, waiting to report children who played in the street too noisily. London children in Oxford missed the warmth and communality of East End street life; as one girl put it:

I cannot do as I like in the house. I must also come in when I am told and sit down and eat my meals properly and not run out into the street with a slice of bread in my hand.[92]

Evacuation, in fact, revealed the essential *solidarity* of working-class family life – quite the opposite of what many middle-class observers maintained. The most common reason for children returning to the danger areas was homesickness for parents and relatives, or parents worrying endlessly about them. Revealingly, the Oxford survey found that, of 217 unaccompanied evacuee children, fully 87% received at least one letter per week and/or a quarterly visit from their parents. And only a derisory 3% said they would want to live in Oxford after the war.[93] This sort of first-hand evidence from the children reveals how utterly distorted were the verdicts of groups such as the National Federation of Women's Institutes when, after citing highly selective and impressionistic reports from their local workers – which tended to repeat *ad nauseam* the 'fish and chips' allegations and held the evacuee mother up to ridicule – they concluded:

Real affection between foster parents and the child is the general rule. . . . Almost without exception, if any comment is made it includes a reference to the immense improvement in the health and manners of the children and to their gains in weight. . . . There are hardly any reports of home sickness and many accounts of how the children cried bitterly when they were removed by their parents.[94]

This chapter has tried to show – in the space available – how complex was the evacuation experience. It was an episode that affected the children in many different ways, but running through the diversity of experience was the trauma of family separation and the culture shock of coping with a new environment. These difficulties were greatly exacerbated by poor civil defence planning. A minority of the children – the exact proportion cannot be established – displayed symptoms of the poverty and deprivation that had been quite commonplace in the 1930s, and significantly under-recorded by government reports; these medical and social symptoms horrified many hosts in the reception areas precisely because they seemed to epitomise wider rural–urban cultural differences. In a sense, evacuation did provide a shock to public consciousness and a 'throwing together of social classes' (though it must be remembered that most hosts, like most evacuees, were working-class). However, it is difficult to find evidence that this brought about fundamental ideological shifts on the part of different groups – notably, within Whitehall. Evacuation required the help of a large number of middle-class voluntary workers in the rural areas who, perhaps more than any other section of the population, had very fixed ideas of social propriety; it was this lobby that propagated the wildly exaggerated and inaccurate stories of the evacuees' condition. In short, the social debate on evacuation probably served to *reinforce* existing analyses of working-class poverty rather than to change them: for conservative social observers, it confirmed their view that the bulk of the problems were caused by an incorrigible underclass of personally inadequate 'cultural orphans' for whom a Welfare State could do little. Evacuation thus shows us that the ideological consensus of wartime, so stressed by Titmuss and some historians, was something of a myth.

Notes

1   Paul Addison, *The Road to 1945*, Jonathan Cape, London, 1975, ch. 1.
2   *The Health of the School Child: Report of the Chief Medical Officer at the Ministry of Education for the Years 1939–45*, HMSO, London, 1947, p. 23.
3   A. J. P. Taylor, *English History, 1914–1945*, Penguin Books, Harmondsworth, 1979 edn, p. 383.
4   Sheila Ferguson and Hilde Fitzgerald, *Studies in the Social Services*, History of the Second World War, United Kingdom Civil Series, HMSO and Longmans, London, 1954, p. 4.
5   Stanislav Andreski, *Military Organisation and Society*, Routledge, London, 1954.
6   Colin Perry, *Boy in the Blitz*, Leo Cooper, London, 1972.
7   Kitty Grime, *Jazz at Ronnie Scott's*, Robert Hale, London, 1979, pp. 15–16.
8   For example, Memorandum by H. R. V. Ball (HMI), 'Children's Reactions to the War', 13 November 1940, PRO ED 50/206.
9   Testimony by Dr J. Gavronsky, Board of Education Memorandum, 'Nervous Strain in Children', 1941, PRO ED 50/206.
10 Anna Freud, 'Special experiences of young children, particularly in times of social disturbance', in Kenneth Soddy (ed.), *Mental Health and Infant Development*, I, Routledge, London, 1955, pp. 141–60; Dorothy Burlingham and Anna Freud, *Young Children in War-time in a Residential War Nursery*, Allen & Unwin, London, 1942, pp. 29, 31, 41; *The Health of the School Child, op. cit.*, pp. 70–5.
11 Arthur Marwick, 'People's war and top people's peace? British society and the Second World War', in Alan Sked and Chris Cook (eds.), *Crisis and Controversy: Essays in Honour of A. J. P. Taylor*, Macmillan, London, 1976, p. 159.
12 *Report of the Committee on Evacuation*, July 1938, Cmd 5837. The committee was established on 24 May 1938 and reported on 26 July, but publication was delayed until 27 October because of the Munich crisis.
13 Ministry of Health, Memorandum Ev. 4, *Government Evacuation Scheme*, May 1939.
14 Memoranda in PRO MH 101/1–3.
15 Richard Titmuss, *Problems of Social Policy*, History of the Second World War, United Kingdom Civil Series, HMSO and Longmans, London, 1950, p. 103.
16 Originally this appeared in Titmuss, *Problems of Social Policy, op. cit.*, p. 122. It has been cited by several writers: for example, Angus Calder, *The People's War*, Panther, 1971 edn, p. 683.
17 Quoted in P. H. J. H. Gosden, *Education in the Second World War: a Study in Policy and Administration*, Methuen, London, 1976, p. 13.
18 B. S. Johnson (ed.), *The Evacuees*, Gollancz, London, 1968.

19   Titmuss, *Problems of Social Policy, op. cit.*, p. 115; William Boyd (ed.), *Evacuation in Scotland: a Record of Events and Experiments*, University of London Press, Bickley, Kent, 1944, p. 57.

20   F. A. Iremonger, *William Temple*, Oxford University Press, London, 1949, pp. 569–70.

21   Quoted in Addison, *The Road to 1945, op. cit.*, p. 72.

22   Titmuss, *Problems of Social Policy, op. cit.*, pp. 114, 506–17.

23   Arthur Marwick, *War and Social Change in the Twentieth Century*, Macmillan, London, 1974, pp. 156–7; Marwick, *Class: Image and Reality in Britain, France and the USA since 1930*, Collins, London, 1980, p. 219.

24   Gosden, *Education in the Second World War, op. cit.*, p. 164.

25   Raynes Minns, *Bombers and Mash: the Domestic Front, 1939–45*, Virago, London, 1980, p. 18.

26   Memorandum, 'Review of the E.M.S., 1923–May 1940: Sir John Hebb's Report', PRO MH 101/1.

27   *H. of C. Deb.*, 5th Ser., Vol. 270, 10 November 1932, col. 633; and Vol. 292, 30 July 1934, cols. 2335–6. This latter statement by Baldwin was during a debate on a motion censuring the government for its failure to do more on disarmament.

28   Titmuss, *Problems of Social Policy, op. cit.*, pp. 4, 14.

29   Memorandum of 2 November 1936, SRO ED 24/1.

30   Memoranda in SRO ED 24/1.

31   Titmuss, *Problems of Social Policy, op. cit.*, pp. 21–2.

32   E. N. Strong to J. A. Glover, 15 November 1939, PRO ED 50/206.

33   *Minutes of the Evacuation Sub-committee of the Committee of Imperial Defence*, SRO ED 24/3.

34   J. K. Hawton to A. N. Rucker, 28 September 1938, PRO HLG 7/60.

35   Memoranda in PRO ED 10/245.

36   Ministry of Health, *Memorandum Ev. 4, op. cit.*, p. 7.

37   Richard Padley and Margaret Cole (eds.), *Evacuation Survey: a Report to the Fabian Society*, Routledge, London, 1940, pp. 36, 57–8.

38   Ben Smith to Earl de la Warr, 21 December 1938, and reply by de la Warr, 13 January 1939, PRO ED 50/204.

39   Padley and Cole, *Evacuation Survey, op. cit.*, p. 4.

40   Susan Isaacs (ed.), *The Cambridge Evacuation Survey*, Methuen, London, 1941, p. 38; Barnett House Study Group, *London Children in Wartime Oxford: a Survey of Social and Educational Results of Evacuation*, Oxford University Press, London, 1947; Boyd, *Evacuation in Scotland, op. cit.*

41   Memorandum of A.R.P. Co-ordinating Committee, 12 April 1940, PRO HLG 10/247.

42   Johnson, *The Evacuees, op. cit.*, pp. 73, 75.

43   Boyd, *Evacuation in Scotland, op. cit.*, pp. 55–6.

44   Titmuss, *Problems of Social Policy, op. cit.*, p. 111.

45   Evelyn Waugh, *Put Out More Flags*, Penguin, Harmondsworth, 1982 edn, p. 79.

46   *H. of C. Deb.*, 5th Ser., Vol. 351, 14 September 1939, cols. 810–1.

47   Memorandum of A.R.P. Co-ordinating Committee, 12 April 1940, PRO HLG 10/247.

48   Memorandum, 'Education of Children in Wartime', *c.* early 1940, PRO ED 10/247; statement by President of the Board of Education, 'Conference on Evacuation', 22 January 1940, PRO HLG 7/89.

49   Memoranda in PRO ED 10/246. This propaganda campaign was organised by Professor John Hilton.

50   Memorandum, 'Conference on Evacuation', *op. cit.*

51   Department of Health for Scotland Advisory Committee on Evacuation, *Minutes of 10th Meeting*, 22 September 1939, SRO ED 24/7.

52   Lord Wyndham to Earl de la Warr, 25 October 1939, PRO ED 10/246.

53   Calder, *The People's War, op. cit.*, p. 49.

54   Isaacs, *The Cambridge Evacuation Survey, op. cit.*, p. 47.

55   Memorandum by Lily Boys, 'Women's Voluntary Services for Civil Defence, Preliminary Report on Evacuation of Children and Others to Lindsey (Lincs.)', 13 September 1939, PRO HLG 7/74; Memorandum by E. J. Davis, 'Hull Evacuation', 28 August 1939, PRO HLG 7/74.

56   Memoranda in PRO HLG 7/162.

57   Reports of June 1940, PRO ED 50/206.

58   E. F. Mott to Board of Education, 17 June 1940, PRO ED 50/206.

59   Report by F. L. Edwards, 22 October 1940, PRO HLG 7/75.

60   Memorandum by Kenneth Mellanby, 'Suggestions for an Investigation on the Prevalence of Lousiness in Britain', December 1939; J. A. Glover to Mellanby, 6 December 1939; Memorandum by Mellanby, 'The Incidence of Head Lice in England', 1940, PRO ED 50/196. Mellanby's report was also published in *The Medical Officer*, 1 February 1941.

61   Mellanby to Glover, 16 March 1940, PRO ED 50/196.

62   Marjorie Cosens, 'Evacuation, a social revolution', *Social Work*, 1, 3 January 1940, pp. 165–82.

63   P. Ellison to H. Viant, 17 November 1939, PRO ED 10/246.

64   *H. of C. Deb.*, 5th Ser., Vol. 353, 16 November 1939, col. 908.

65   H. C. Stone (Hulme St Mary's Boys' School) to J. G. Woolham (Acting School Medical Officer, Manchester), 16 January 1940, and other memoranda of January and February 1940 in PRO ED 50/211.

66   Memorandum, 'The Effect of Evacuation upon the Height and Weight of Schoolchildren', 1 November 1940, PRO ED 50/211.

67   These reports, containing detailed statistical evidence, are in PRO ED 50/211.

68   Howarth to Bosworth Smith, 13 August 1942, PRO ED 50/211.

69   Memorandum by E. R. Bransby, 'The Wartime Growth of Children', 6 October 1944, PRO ED 50/211.

70   Margin comment by Butler, on note by Bosworth Smith, 4 June 1943, PRO ED 50/211.

71   MacNalty to Holmes, 16 February 1940, and Holmes to the President of the Board of Education, 16 February 1940, PRO ED 50/196.

72   Titmuss, *Problems of Social Policy, op. cit.*, pp. 509–11.

73   *The Health of the School Child, op. cit.*, ch. 2.

74   Memorandum, 'Note of Conference: Milk', February 1938, PRO ED 50/231.

75   L. G. K. Starke (Ministry of Food) to N. Bosworth Smith, 31 December

1940, PRO ED 50/229.

76 *War Cabinet Food Policy Committee: Meals and Food Supplies for Factory Workers, Children and Poor Families. Memorandum by the Minister of Food*, 12 June 1940, PRO ED 50/215.

77 R. M. Titmuss, 'War and social policy', in *Essays on 'the Welfare State'*, Allen & Unwin, London, 1958, p. 84.

78 H. Ramsbotham (Board of Education) to Lord Woolton (Ministry of Food), 26 May 1941, PRO ED 50/229.

79 E. D. Marris (Board of Education) to L. G. Duke (Ministry of Health), 8 June 1941, PRO ED 50/229.

80 Memoranda in PRO ED 50/190 and 191.

81 Memorandum by E. D. Marris, 'Draft Letter about School Milk for Evacuee Children', 28 July 1943, PRO ED 50/229. Marris even felt it would have saved a lot of trouble to give free milk to all evacuated children from the very start of the war. Marris to Duke, 8 June 1941, PRO ED 50/229.

82 Women's Group on Public Welfare, *Our Towns, a Close-up*, Oxford University Press, London, 1943, p. xiii.

83 *Ibid.*, pp. 106, 108.

84 *Social Work*, 2, 8 April 1943, p. 326.

85 *H. of L. Deb.*, 5th Ser., Vol. 127, 5 May 1943, cols. 365–95. I am grateful to Dr Charles Webster for this reference.

86 Introduction by John A. F. Watson, in Norah Baring, *A Friendly Hearth*, Jonathan Cape, London, 1946, pp. 6–7.

87 See, for example, Tom Stephens (ed.), *Problem Families: an Experiment in Social Rehabilitation*, Pacifist Service Units, Liverpool, 1947.

88 For a thoughtful discussion see A. F. Philp and Noel Timms, *The Problem of 'the Problem Family'*, Family Service Units, London, 1957.

89 Johnson, *The Evacuees, op. cit.*

90 See, for example, John Bowlby, 'Psychological aspects', in Padley and Cole, *Evacuation Survey, op. cit.*, p. 188.

91 Boyd, *Evacuation in Scotland, op. cit.*, p. 71; Barnett House Study Group, *London Children, op. cit.*, p. 66.

92 Barnett House Study Group, *London Children, op. cit.*, p. 34.

93 *Ibid.*, pp. 41, 101.

94 National Federation of Women's Institutes, *Town Children through Country Eyes: a Survey on Evacuation, 1940*, National Federation of Women's Institutes, Dorking, 1940, p. 15.

Acknowledgements

I wish to thank the trustees of the University of London Central Research Fund for awarding me a small grant which made research in the Public Record Office, Scottish Record Office and other archives possible.

Daniel M. Fox

The National Health Service and the Second World War: the elaboration of concensus

During the first four decades of the twentieth century a consensus emerged in Britain about which health services should be available to whom, when, where and how. This consensus was strengthened by events during World War II and became law as the National Health Service Act of 1946. Consensus about health policy was possible because members of important groups in medicine and politics had similar beliefs about the significance of the recent history of biomedical science for human welfare in the future. On the basis of these beliefs, they criticised existing services and devised proposals to organise and finance them in the future. Beliefs about equity and rational public administration, strengthened by events during the war, reinforced the consensus about the implications of medical science for the organisation of health services. Because conflicts about health policy within and among various groups were about means rather than ends, they were resolved by negotiations and mutual accommodation.

This interpretation of the origins of the National Health Service seems, at first, to contradict what most scholars have written. Asserting that the NHS was created as the result of half a century of ideas and events reduces the importance accorded to World War II by such scholars as Richard Titmuss[1] and Arthur Marwick[2] and challenges the emphasis placed on the Labour government elected in 1945 by Paul Addison[3] and, to a greater degree, Kenneth Morgan.[4] Insisting that the history of health policy was different from that of other social services because it was profoundly influenced by beliefs about medical science appears to contradict the views of, among others, Bentley Gilbert[5] and Ian Gough.[6] Moreover, emphasising the significance for policy of beliefs about medical science seems to diminish the importance accorded to the quest for equity and administrative rationality by, for example, Brian

Abel-Smith,[7] Harry Eckstein[8] and Rudolf Klein.[9] Reducing bitter conflicts about doctors' pay and the role of local authorities to disputes within a consensus attributes less importance to the clash of civil servants, politicians and leaders of interest groups than it was accorded by such scholars as Eckstein, Paul Addison, John Pater[10] and A. J. Willocks.[11]

My interpretation of the origins of the NHS is not, however, radically revisionist. Most historians of the NHS agree that a consensus about what was wrong with health services and how, in general, to reorganise them began to emerge after World War I. They agree that, in the years between the wars, expenditures on health services increased, from all sources, in large measure as a result of optimism about the effectiveness of medical care. Most scholars acknowledge, moreover, that by the end of World War II civil servants, politicians and leading doctors concurred about many of the details of a national health service.[12]

I differ from other scholars mainly in emphasising the similarity of the health policies adopted by Western nations in the middle decades of the twentieth century. Most historians describe the NHS as a unique British institution, very different from the health services of other countries. What they interpret as fundamental differences I regard as variations on a theme. Each country in Western Europe and North America has mandated or encouraged the creation of graded hierarchies of hospitals and physicians organised in geographic regions and has subsidised its citizens' access to these regional hierarchies. From an international perspective, the history of health policy is the story of how almost universally held beliefs about the proper organisation of medical services and the benefits of increasing citizens' access to them were refracted by particular political cultures.[13]

National health policies were similar because they were responses to enthusiasm about the recent progress of medical science and anticipation that it would continue uninterrupted in the future. This interpretation of recent history was accepted and reinforced by the popular and professional media in each country and was cited in documents about reorganising health services. According to this view of history, medical scientists had been spectacularly successful in discovering the causes of and cures for disease since the second half of the nineteenth century. Moreover, their methods of inquiry promised continuing progress in the future.

The advance of medical science and the dissemination of its findings seemed to occur according to an orderly pattern. Fundamental discoveries were made in laboratories, which were usually associated with medical schools or teaching hospitals. These discoveries were translated into procedures which were tested in teaching hospitals and then transmitted down a hierarchy of institutions and practitioners. The task of officials of public and philanthropic organisations in each country was to create and systematise these hierarchies and make their benefits more accessible to citizens of all social classes.

During the half-century after World War I these beliefs became the basis of health policy in Western countries and even in China and India.[14] The beliefs justified large investments in the supply of services – in hospitals, medical schools and scientific research – as preconditions to improving the health of individuals. Philanthropy, government appropriations and entrepreneurial investment contributed – in varying amounts in each country – to a surging supply of health services during this half century.

According to the dominant beliefs, moreover, the supply of services had to be organised according to a rational pattern and made accessible to people of every social class. Institutions and practitioners should be arrayed in levels, according to their technical sophistication, so that patients could be referred to the proper place. Hierarchies of services were organised, usually in geographic regions based on medical schools, in a variety of ways: in some countries by law, others by voluntary action, still others by a combination of regulation and exhortation. Since access to the services arrayed in regional hierarchies was assumed to produce healthier, longer-lived and more productive citizens, it was subsidised in every country; either direct or through social insurance or through employee benefits or by some combination of fiscal tools.

The history of health policy in the United States, which has often been described as 'lagging behind' Britain and other countries, illustrates how beliefs about medical science penetrated political cultures in the twentieth century.[15] From about 1910 to about 1945 the United States, like Britain, achieved a consensus on health policy. In both countries hospitals proliferated, even in the worst years of the Great Depression. In both, teaching hospitals were accorded esteem and extraordinary resources. Both countries increased their investment in scientific research. In both, the roles of generalist and specialist doctors were more precisely differentiated. During World War II, as officials and leaders of interest groups in Britain negotiated over what became the NHS, their counterparts in the United States created a national hospital policy which rewarded regions in which hierarchies of institutions of varying sophistication were organised. National policy, moreover, reduced the cost of medical care for most people by exempting health insurance provided by employers from corporate and personal income taxes. By 1946 Britain and the United States had created new health policies which were based on strikingly similar assumptions.

Richard Titmuss on the origins of the NHS

Interpreting the history of the NHS as a British variant on an international theme contradicts the thesis Richard Titmuss argued in his scholarly polemic, *Problems of Social Policy*, and in subsequent essays.[16] I am troubled by three aspects of Titmuss's history of the origins of the NHS: his uncritical belief in the progress of medical science, his attribution of causal significance to collective civilian experience in World War II, and his nationalism. Titmuss assumed that the progress of medical science created imperatives for policy. For him medical progress was a fact, not a belief about events. Since the implications of scientific progress were self-evident, they were ignored or resisted by politicians and civil servants only as a result of class prejudice, ignorance or incompetence.[17] To Titmuss, the national solidarity which emerged in response to unprecedented danger during World War II provided the impetus for Britain to adopt a proper policy to make medical science available to its citizens without direct cost to them. Titmuss later called the NHS 'this most unsordid act' of social policy.[18] Such a policy was, he believed, uniquely British: an example of collective values and sensitive political institutions which were superior to other countries'. The United States, for example, whose political economy Titmuss loathed because of its reliance on markets, could not establish a similar policy.[19]

Titmuss's great theme, which he repeatedly stated or implied, was discontinuity between pre-war and wartime social policy. Post-war health policy, he asserted, was created between 1940 and 1944. The most dangerous period of the war, in 1940 and 1941, was the 'most fruitful for social policy'. Politicians and civil servants were pulled by events into thinking about post-war health policy. The organisation of hospital services into hierarchies in geographic regions was a wartime expedient: 'a new idea', a 'new principle'. According to Titmuss, 'in total war the troubles of individuals often multiplied until they became matters of national concern, while the demands of humanity pointed, just as often, in the same direction'.[20]

However, Titmuss seemed, at times, to be troubled by his own thesis.

In a book written during the war he had accepted R. H. Tawney's view that 'in the long run the world reaps in war what it sows in peace'.[21] In *Problems of Social Policy* he frequently acknowledged the pre-war origins of wartime innovations in health policy. Describing the influence of previous wars on social policy, he admitted that wartime innovations 'were not new ideas'. Instead 'the momentum of war spread and quickened a trend toward social altruism and crystallized within the nation demands for social justice'.[22] Although Titmuss sometimes implied that the experience of the Second World War was unique, he never explicitly repudiated this earlier interpretation.

Like Tawney, whose enthusiastic review of *Problems of Social Policy* helped it to achieve success,[23] Titmuss wanted his scholarship to influence social action. In his eagerness to encourage a more enlightened 'collective conscience' about the misery of many people in Britain, Titmuss sometimes contradicted evidence he presented elsewhere, whether consciously or unconsciously we cannot know. He called attention to his doubts, however. Towards the end of the book, for example, he even undercut his fundamental premise, wondering 'if the conception of a collective conscience has any reality . . .'.[24] Titmuss's book, though an unreliable guide to the history of the NHS, is a model of compassion and scholarly integrity, and one of the best historical narratives in English of the past century.[25]

The history which follows describes the continuity of pre-war and wartime events in the shaping of British health policy. In addition, it describes the consistency of British policy with transnational beliefs about the proper organisation of health services. The sources for the narrative are manuscripts which were not available to Titmuss, printed documents, and a rich secondary literature. Titmuss's masterpiece remains, however, an important reminder that many people in Britain in the 1940s felt a sense of discontinuity between the war and pre-war years and that this feeling reinforced the national consensus about proper social policy.

British health policy, 1911–29

During the second and third decades of this century the emphasis of discussion and action about public policy for health shifted from general measures to alleviate the economic effects of illness among the poor and the working class to specific proposals for organising and financing personal health services for the British people. National Health Insurance was introduced in 1911 as a strategy to maintain income for sick workers.[26] But the emphasis of NHI rapidly shifted from income to services. By the end of World War I the purpose of health insurance had been subtly but decisively redefined.[27] It was now a programme for providing medical care rather than for preventing sick workers from becoming paupers.

This change in the priorities of health policy, begun gradually in the administration of NHI after 1911, was accelerated by events at home and abroad during the war. At home the central government sought to improve and extend the medical services provided by local authorities in order to maintain the productivity of civilian workers when half the doctors were in military service.[28] The achievements of medicine at the front were widely celebrated. Death rates from contagious diseases and from infections related to wounds were lower than in previous wars, as a result, many experts concluded, of both scientific knowledge and the way services were organised. Emergency surgery in field and base hospitals had never been so successful. Moreover, military experience increased the number of doctors who were familiar with new medical technology and improved the co-ordination of the people and resources required to use it. In addition, as *The Times* commented, 'The war taught the public the value of so-called teamwork and the need of applied science in medical treatment'.[29]

By 1918 social policy in Britain was compartmentalised. Income, services and improving the environment were conceived as parallel rather than competing strategies to improve the health and welfare of citizens. Advocates of new policy for medical services assumed that others would promote proper policy for income, nutrition, housing and sanitation. Their concern was increasingly limited to medical care: to translating the results of advancing science into properly organised and accessible services.

People who disagreed about many issues of medical care policy agreed that services should be organised in hierarchies of institutions and practitioners within geographic regions. Each interest group – general practitioners, consultants, hospital trustees, Medical Officers of Health and civil servants – justified hierarchical organisation from its own perspective. In the years between the wars, debates about equity of access to services, about the proper roles of local authorities and voluntary associations and about how to pay doctors were conducted in a context of agreement about the overall organisation of medical services. The assumptions which made this agreement possible gradually came to determine the allocation of resources within the health sector.

The consensus that hierarchical regionalism should be the basis of health policy was stimulated by events immediately after the war. As Chancellor of the Exchequer, David Lloyd George had guided the shift in the priority of public policy for health from maintaining workers' incomes to providing medical services. As Prime Minister he presided over another major change in policy: from providing services to the poor and the working class to specifying which services in what configuration should be available to everyone. His principal agent in this change of policy was Christopher Addison, a former medical school dean who in 1918 became the first Minister of Health. Addison's goals for health policy were expressed most clearly by Lord Bertrand Dawson, a prominent academic physician who, as a major-general, had organised military medical care in France during the war. Addison and Dawson, in lectures, public speeches and official reports, emphasised that how services were organised was the starting question for public policy. Providing money to maintain income or to finance access to service was, for them, a subordinate issue.[30]

Addison and Dawson articulated an approach to policy which was endorsed by every interest group concerned with health affairs and by leaders of the Conservative, Liberal and Labour parties. Throughout the 1920s the British Medical Association, the Society of Medical Officers of Health and leaders of voluntary hospitals repeatedly asserted that the basis of proper policy for medical care was the organisation of hierarchies of institutions in geographic regions.[31] A partial exception to the consensus was the Royal Commission on National Health Insurance, which reported in 1926. Although the commission endorsed regional co-ordination leading 'towards a unified health service' as the proper framework for the eventual expansion of compulsory insurance, it reasserted the pre-war purpose of health policy, arguing that priority in spending national resources must be given to improving the 'economic condition'. A minority report, however, asserted that medical services should be accorded priority.[32]

The major legislation affecting medical care at the end of the 1920s, the Local Government Act of 1929, revealed the strength of the consensus about the proper way to organise services. The Act permitted local authorities to convert Poor Law infirmaries into public general hospitals. The Minister of Health, Neville Chamberlain, anticipated that the new law would lead to the creation of 'one single health authority in each area', managing a co-ordinated hierarchy of public and voluntary hospitals and medical services.[33]

Health policy in the '30s

In the decade before World War II the most controversial questions about public policy for medical care in Britain were when and how, not whether, more medical care, subsidised with public funds and organised in regional hierarchies, would be provided for more people. There was widespread agreement that medical services were inefficiently organised and inequitably distributed. The logic of medical science was combined with considerations of efficiency and equity in discussions about the proper provision of medical services. Leaders of medical interest groups and officials of local government strengthened their commitment to organising medical care in hierarchies within geographic regions. A few centrist intellectuals tried to stimulate debate about how priority should be apportioned among measures to promote the general welfare – especially better nutrition and higher wages – to prevent illness, and to medical services. But these discussions had little influence on either policy or public opinion.

Innovations in the organisation of medical care during the 1930s occurred primarily in hospitals. The consensus of opinion that had persisted for more than a decade justified giving hospitals the highest priority in the allocation of resources for medical care. Hospitals, graded by the sophistication of their staff and technology would be central institutions in the regional hierarchies into which members of every interest group believed medical services should be organised. Local authorities in London and the larger county boroughs established hospital in-patient and ambulatory services which served increasing numbers of people – including many members of the middle classes. Voluntary hospitals provided services to more paying patients from all social classes. These services were financed mainly by pre-payment plans, by private insurance and by direct subsidies from employers, unions and local government. The income of the voluntary hospitals exceeded their expenditure in the decade before the war.[34]

The priority accorded expenditure on hospital care was endorsed by spokesmen for the major medical interest groups: the British Medical Association, the Royal Colleges of Medicine and of Surgery, the Society of Medical Officers of Health and the Socialist Medical Association. Debate about proper policy for health in the 1930s was a struggle for territory rather than an argument about priorities. Doctors in private practice and leaders of voluntary hospitals resented, as they had for many years, competition for patients by the clinics and hospitals of local government. Medical Officers of Health resisted pressure from voluntary hospitals for subsidy from local authorities. But these conflicts were about money and control rather than about what should be done to reduce deaths and relieve suffering.

The strength of the consensus on health policy was evident in the proceedings of a Voluntary Hospitals Commission established in 1935 by the British Hospitals Association. Before any witnesses were heard, most of the members of the commission had agreed among themselves that the voluntary and municipal hospitals should be integrated in regional councils. The spokesman for the BMA asserted that the public and voluntary institutions in each region should share a joint medical staff. Lord Dawson, speaking for the Royal College of Medicine, declared that all hospitals should be governed by a single national authority because the municipal hospitals had 'financial resources' while the voluntaries had 'medical knowledge'. Leaders of the Socialist Medical Association urged public grants to promote regional integration of hospitals and advocated that part-time consultants on hospital staffs receive a 'definite honorarium' rather than salaries or fees.[35]

A handful of centrist reformers, most of them outside medicine, dissented from this consensus. In the mid-1930s these reformers tried to analyse the costs and benefits of particular policies in order to encourage national social planning. Two groups within this small and unstable coalition of business leaders, professionals and public officials addressed policy for medical care: The Next Five Years and Political and Economic Planning. The Next Five Years group accorded priority in health policy to improved nutrition rather than medical services.[36] Political and Economic Planning struggled with the implications of choosing among priorities in its massive *Report on the British Health Services*, published in December 1937.[37]

The PEP report first challenged, then hesitated about and finally affirmed the consensus that public policy for medical care should be curative, hierarchical and implemented through regionalisation. At the beginning of the report its anonymous authors demanded 'first, better use and improved arrangement of existing services, second, the expansion of measures for improving nutrition . . . third, the provision of general practitioner services for dependants of insured persons . . . and fourth, increased research . . . on industrial and social causes of ill-health'. Nevertheless, the authors repeatedly endorsed specialisation and co-ordination as priorities in medical care. The 'goal to be aimed at' in 'any extension of health insurance' was 'a completely planned health service combining a general practitioner and nursing service, the specialist and hospital services'. Because hierarchy was the inevitable result of 'technical efficiency', medical services should be regionalised and 'graded'. By the end of the report the high priority accorded to nutrition was replaced by a weaker statement that nutrition policy should 'probably' have a 'prior claim on any funds available for extending the health services'.[38]

PEP concluded its report with an equivocal statement about priorities. On the one hand the authors recognised that according primacy in policy to personal health services encouraged 'too large resources to be allocated to cases which stir pity and too little for constructive and preventive purposes'. On the other, the authors asserted that 'finance' was the 'main limiting factor' to adopting all PEP's priorities. Making more money available would postpone the necessity to choose among priorities for policy. The PEP report thus reinforced the consensus. Its reasoned case for tolerating ambiguity about priorities was applauded by the medical and general press.[39]

The emergence of a national hospital policy, 1939–42

By the late 1930s there was no important dissent from the consensus that the basis of public policy for health should be hierarchies of hospitals in geographic regions. As support grew for the organisation of hospital hierarchies among doctors, officials of local authorities and voluntary hospital leaders, advocates of it within the Ministry of Health became more aggressive. In 1936 the Chief Medical Officer of the Ministry doubted whether 'public opinion' would 'approve' the administration by local authorities of specialist services 'based upon hospitals'.[40] By mid-1983, however, the consensus among interest group leaders about the proper organisation of hospitals became the basis of civil defence policy when the Ministry established an Emergency Hospital Service. Within newly established regions, hospitals were graded and co-ordinated by staff of the Ministry. Consultants were paid full-time salaries and distributed among these regions.[41]

The Emergency Hospital Service was immediately regarded as the basis of a post-war national hospital service. By September 1939 civil servants were elaborating plans to create a national hospital system after the war. The implications of the wartime reorganisation of hospitals for post-war policy were frequently discussed outside the Ministry by leaders of medical and hospital interest groups, by PEP and, most important, by the Nuffield Provincial Hospital Trust, which was established in 1939 to advocate the co-ordination of voluntary hospitals on a regional basis. The Minister and civil servants encouraged the Trust to stimulate public discussion of post-war hospital policy.[42]

Planning for a post-war national hospital service was a major concern of the Ministry in 1941. The Minister told a committee of the War Cabinet that 'we now had for the first time in our history a hospital service sufficient to meet the needs of a population as a whole'.[43] The Permanent Secretary told his colleagues that 'reversion to the pre-war hospital world would probably be impossible at the end of the war'.[44] In response to a parliamentary question on 9 October 1941 the Minister declared the 'objective of the Government to ensure that by means of a comprehensive hospital service appropriate treatment shall be readily available to every person in need of it'. This service would be administered by local authorities 'in close co-operation with the voluntary agencies'. The service must, however, 'be design[ed] . . . with reference to areas substantially larger than those of individual authorities'.[45] Questioned about policy for a 'general national health service', the Minister insisted that the 'hospital service must be considered first'.[46] Within the Ministry, however, the scope of planning for post-war policy had already expanded to include what the new Chief Medical Officer called 'all medical services' in a meeting with representatives of the Nuffield Trust.[47]

Although the government had announced that a post-war hospital service would be controlled by local authorities, civil servants continued to work closely with the Nuffield Trust, which represented the interests of the voluntaries. Prominent leaders of local government complained in public and in private about the Trust's influence. Charles (later Lord) Latham, for example, told a newspaper that he suspected a plot by 'fifth columnists against democrats . . . to steal the people's municipal hospitals'.[48] Nevertheless, the Ministry and the Trust had agreed in the summer of 1941 to co-sponsor surveys of hospital facilities throughout Britain. Within a few months the Trust's enthusiasm for organising *ad hoc* regional councils and its desire for 'speedy publication and local discussion' of the surveys created more antagonism among officials of local government than the Ministry was willing to ignore. The Permanent Secretary informed the Trust that the 'Government was not committed to any form of regional body'. The conclusions of each survey 'would be conveyed to the local authorities and representatives of voluntary hospitals concerned' by the Ministry on a schedule it determined.[49]

The surveys reinforced the consensus among civil servants and the medical community about the substance of post-war policy. Though not officially published until 1945, the conclusions of the surveyors were discussed informally and were supported by every faction in medical and general politics. The surveyors agreed on the need to create regions which transcended the boundaries of local authorities, to redistribute consultants from the large cities, to 'control . . . the range of work in cottage or general practitioner hospitals', and to reorganise 'provision for the chronic sick'.[50] Each of these issues was contentious when the surveys began. By 1945, when they were published, considerable planning and negotiation between civil servants and representatives of interest groups had occurred. The surveys, begun to provide a basis for policy, were later regarded by the Ministry as 'justification' of it.[51]

Conflict within consensus, 1941–45

Agreement about the general outlines of post-war policy did not, however, eliminate sharp conflict over its details. Each faction within the medical profession and among the laymen who governed hospitals either as officials of local authorities or as members of voluntary hospital boards engaged in protracted arguments with each other and with officials. Although most of the arguments occurred in closed meetings, they erupted occasionally in the reports of committees and commissions and in the press.

About one issue, however, there was no controversy. The consensus about organisation that had developed since the last war would be the basis of the new National Health Service: medical care would be conceived as a hierarchy based on hospitals which were arrayed according to their sophistication in regions and were linked with the services provided to individuals by both local authorities and autonomous general practitioners.

A Medical Planning Commission, organised by the BMA in 1941 to resolve conflict within the profession, issued an interim report in 1942 urging the 'grouping of hospitals' in hierarchies as a prerequisite to making 'all necessary services' available to everyone. A month before the coalition government announced its commitment to a post-war hospital policy the MPC's Hospital Committee 'approved in principle the regionalisation of medical services, including both hospital and personal services'.[52] After the announcement the Deputy Chief Medical Officer assured the MPC committee privately that support for hierarchical regionalism from the medical profession was more important to the Ministry than its public assurances of local authority control.[53] As his chief commented a short time later, the priority of the Ministry was to maintain support for the consensus on regional hierarchies among doctors, even at the expense of telling the exact truth. Doctors' 'continued existence as a series of isolated units', he explained, 'is in the interests neither of themselves nor of the public they serve'.[54]

Although the BMA officially rejected the MPC's interim report, most of its members agreed with the report's priorities for reorganising hospital and medical services after the war. The Association tabled the report mainly because it recommended that general practitioners be paid full-time salaries. In addition, a few general practitioners worried that organising services in rigid hierarchies could exclude them completely from hospital practice. But most GPs, the BMA's public opinion polls indicated, overwhelmingly favoured the provision of free hospital care in institutions managed by regional boards independent of local authorities.[55]

A few months later a group called Medical Planning Research, consisting of 200 doctors under the age of forty-five, endorsed hierarchical regionalisation in the context of wider social reform. Like the abolition of poverty and the redistribution of wealth, the reorganisation of medical care was a pressing post-war obligation. A medical service based on 'key hospitals' should be 'available for everyone'.[56]

The doctors who spoke for the Fabian Society and the Socialist Medical Association also gave priority to the creation of regionalised hierarchical medical services. The Fabians told Sir William Beveridge's committee looking into post-war social insurance that the first requirement for a 'healthy nation' was 'that our doctors are constantly versed in current medical knowledge' through their participation in regional networks. Leaders of the SMA told Beveridge that the 'advantages of modern medical science' could only be diffused by 'changes in the method of organising medical care'.[57]

Beveridge's report, *Social Insurance and Allied Services*, which was published at the end of 1942, reflected and amplified the consensus within the medical profession about post-war health policy. Beveridge declared that he agreed with the report of the Medical Planning Commission. Moreover, achieving 'positive health' should take precedence over other uses of 'public and personal resources'. Medical care should be 'comprehensive', 'free' and limited only by the needs of each person.[58]

Beveridge was inconsistent about policy for medical care. On the one hand he wanted the State to provide a free, comprehensive health service. On the other, he repeatedly declared that he only wanted the State to guarantee citizens' entitlement to what he called 'basic' doctor and hospital services which would be paid for by compulsory insurance. Moreover, payment for services by 'previous contribution' was 'better even than free service supported by the taxpayer' because, having paid, people would demand their entitlement.[59]

Beveridge's inconsistency was a result of his deference to medical experts whose views on social policy were fundamentally different from his. Leaders of the medical profession and senior officials of the Ministry, reflecting the consensus that had emerged since World War I, were committed to an optimum standard in public policy for medical care. They believed that whatever doctors prescribed when they practised in their proper place in a regional hierarchy was the correct standard of care. Unlike the doctors, Beveridge repeatedly endorsed a policy of entitlement to a minimum set of services. A guaranteed minimum requires that explicit limits be set in order to allocate scarce resources equitably – perhaps even that treatment sometimes be withheld. Like the doctors, however, Beveridge assumed that it would be unethical for care to be withheld consciously from individuals.

To avoid self-contradiction, Beveridge reasoned that, in time, the minimum would become the optimum. As the standard of living rose, and citizens had access to services of ever-increasing effectiveness, their need for medical care would decline. They would demand fewer services and doctors' ethics would compel them to provide less treatment. Beveridge assumed, therefore, that the cost of health services would remain stable between 1945 and 1965 while the cost of other social insurance would increase by 50%. Health costs would be stable because of 'a reduction in the number of cases requiring' treatment.[60]

Between 1943 and 1945 civil servants negotiated with interest groups to obtain their concurrence with policies that would embody the consensus articulated in Beveridge's report. Although agreement on fundamentals made a national health service possible, it could not resolve long-standing conflicts about authority and the control of resources. Doctors and voluntary hospital officials were eager to limit the power of local authorities over the proposed hospital regions. The local authorities were equally adamant in defending their role. Moreover, there were conflicts within the interest groups: large voluntary hospitals against smaller ones; London and other large cities against local authorities which had made less expensive commitments to medical care; and consultants against general practitioners within the medical profession. Each of these groups pressed its case in numerous meetings with civil servants in 1943 and 1944.

As a result of these negotiations, a White Paper on post-war health policy, issued by the government in 1944, described a broad consensus among officials and interest groups. The White Paper emphasised the pre-war origins of the proposed post-war health policy, reciting the history of proposals for regionalisation since the report of Lord Dawson's Consultative Council in 1920. As a result of this history, the White Paper insisted, there was agreement that the new health service 'will provide for everyone all the medical advice, treatment and care they may require'. The government proposed to organise services in regions which met medical rather than political criteria: each region should be large enough 'to allow most of the varied hospital and specialist services being organised within its boundaries'. Hospital management was, however, designed to satisfy political criteria; to make doctors, local authorities and voluntary hospitals even-handedly unhappy. The hospitals would be managed by joint authorities – combining counties and county boroughs – which would contract for services with voluntary hospitals. Doctors and voluntary hospitals could choose whether or not to participate in the service. Consultants and the medical staff of local authority health centres would be salaried; general practitioners would continue to be paid by capitation.[61]

Publication of the White Paper initiated another series of negotiations between the ministry and interest groups. Early in 1945 the coalition government accepted draft legislation for submission to Parliament when the war ended. The Conservative, Labour and Liberal parties accepted the principles in the White Paper and the subsequent compromises on details negotiated between the Ministry and the interest groups. The doctors believed that their concern about money and autonomy had largely been resolved: the BMA, the Royal Colleges and the Society of Medical Officers of Health endorsed the draft legislation. The British Hospitals Association and King Edward's Hospital Fund for London believed that voluntary interests could adequately be protected on the joint boards that would plan services for hospital regions. Most of the local authorities were satisfied with their role in regional planning and administration and in the governance of municipal hospitals.[62]

Disagreement had, however, been compromised rather than resolved. In spring 1945 leaders of each interest group and their advocates within the civil service were prepared to express their preferences again if a new government reopened discussions about policy. Barely suppressed conflict was most evident among doctors. Consultants, represented by the Royal Colleges, were eager to preserve the independence of teaching hospitals, diminish the role of local authorities and eliminate general practitioners entirely from hospital practice. As Lord Moran, speaking for the Royal College of Physicians, told the Minister, every doctor 'should be part of a great University service'.[63] The leaders of the BMA were caught between their distaste for Moran's hierarchical imperialism on the one hand and their suspicion of local authorities on the other. They feared that the price of GPs' freedom from regulation by local government could be their subordination to consultants.[64]

Conflict was less intense outside the medical profession because leaders of the major interest groups assumed that the compromises they had negotiated would soon be submitted to Parliament. Officials of local authorities worried mainly about the details of future relationships between voluntary and municipal hospitals and their medical staffs.[65] Moreover, they believed that their interests were protected by the Permanent Secretary, his principal deputies and the Chief Medical Officer. Similarly, voluntary hospital leaders, confident that they had retained independence and gained a perpetual subsidy, focused their attention on 'how best can . . . a comprehensive service be organised and administered'.[66] Neither local authority nor voluntary hospital leaders apparently knew that senior officials within the Ministry – including the Chief Medical Officer and a future Permanent Secretary – had been convinced by the experience of the Emergency Medical Service that hospitals should be nationalised and then administered in 'natural' (that is, medical rather than local government) regions.[67]

During the election campaign of 1945 each of the political parties took a position on the organisation of a health service that was designed to attract support among the medical and hospital interest groups. The Conservatives, with Lord Moran strongly influencing his patient, Prime Minister Churchill, accepted the agreements worked out by the Ministry after the White Paper was published. When Labour left the coalition the government made additional concessions to doctors. Liberals wanted local authorities to have 'general control' of voluntary hospitals in loosely organised regions. The Communists advocated 'hospital committees', with membership to include 'all grades of health workers', to administer both regions and individual institutions. Labour wanted to move gradually to 'public control' through a 'unified system of admissions' to hospitals.[68]

After Labour's election victory, how doctors would be paid under the new national health service appeared to be the most controversial issue. Throughout the war Labour health spokesmen outside the government had repeatedly advocated that general practitioners be paid by salary rather than by capitation or fees. Labour's public position on medical care policy was expressed mainly by the Socialist Medical Association, which, since its inception, had advocated a full-time salaried medical service. But the leaders of the SMA had indicated repeatedly in previous years that they regarded salaried general practice as a much lower priority than either universality of access or hierarchical regionalisation. Moreover the leaders of the party, absorbed in the affairs of the coalition government for six years, had not yet taken a public position on the shape of the new health service.

The Labour government had very few choices to make about the proposed national health service in the summer of 1945. The party's health policy had evolved over a generation, beginning with an endorsement of the organisation of hospitals in regional hierarchies after World War I. Its dominant individuals, Clement Attlee, Ernest Bevin and Herbert Morrison, had participated in confidential discussions about post-war health policy as members of the War Cabinet. The new Minister of Health, Aneurin Bevan, was briefed by civil servants who had been managing an Emergency Hospital (later called Medical) Service for six years and actively planning a post-war health service for five.

The new government was, however, obligated to examine the agreements about post-war policy which had been negotiated with medical, hospital and local government interest groups. The government took few political risks in pausing to assess the agreements negotiated since 1944. Labour owed nothing to the leaders of the medical and voluntary hospital associations. Leaders of the large municipal authorities had no political home outside the Labour Party and no reason to expect the party to harm them. Moreover, reassessment was appreciated by several groups within Labour. The Socialist Medical Association, pleased that most consultants wanted to be salaried under the new service, as they had been during the war, pressed again for a salaried general practitioner service. The Trades Union Congress bristled at the traditional condescension of voluntary hospitals' governers and was indifferent to the administrative concerns of local government officials.

Most members of the general public were apparently not interested in the issues of auspice and autonomy that bothered doctors and hospitals. Forty-two per cent of the respondents in a widely publicised poll were prepared to see voluntary hospitals 'taken over' by either local or national government. More important, opinion polls indicated that, although the public wanted a free health service, it accorded it a lower priority than either new housing or full employment. [69]

The government's reconsideration was rapid and was limited to issues of implementation rather than of purpose. The new government was eager to create a national health service that embraced the goals of hierarchy, equity and efficiency. The new service would, all interest groups and parties had agreed since before the war, assert the centrality of general practice and preventive medicine but allocate resources on the assumption that hospitals were the most important component of national policy for health services. The few dissenters from this policy were ignored; like pacifists during the war, they were dismissed as misguided.

After a generation of discussion, beliefs about the priorities of a national health service were widely shared. The primary goal of health policy had changed in less than forty years from preventing poverty by replacing lost income to alleviating physical distress and then to providing all citizens with the means of care and cure. Prevention, once conceived mainly as measures to improve the general welfare – environmental regulation, nutrition, housing and income – had been redefined to include discrete services – inoculation, examination, and education, for example – provided by professionals to individuals. Hierarchy in the organisation of services was assumed to be an inevitable result of scientific and technical change. Hierarchical relationships should be administered through regional organisations of doctors, hospitals and supporting services. When financial and geographical barriers to access by patients were removed or reduced, priorities for allocating resources within a national health service would be determined by the efficient application of the findings of medical science to the needs of individuals.

By 1945 these priorities were regarded as self-evident. They were shared by politicians and officials in central and local government, doctors, hospital leaders, the press and, according to the polls, by the general public. Moreover the consensus among experts about how medical care should be organised and what services should receive priority was translated into policy at a time when citizens' impatience to achieve a better standard of living and a more equitable distribution of the nation's resources had been revealed in the results of the election of 1945.

The National Health Service, in a narrow sense was created by Cabinet decisions in the autumn and winter of 1945 and by legislation enacted in 1946. In a more important sense the NHS Act of 1946 was the culmination of decades of increasing agreement about how medical care ought to be organised and distributed. A similar service would have been created in 1945 by either the Conservative or the Liberal parties. The experience of national solidarity in wartime most likely hastened agreement on the details of a national health service, but it did not influence the substance of the consensus about its organisation and priorities. In creating the National Health Service the government acted on its mandate to press for increased equity by implementing the beliefs about the proper organisation of medical care that had emerged during the previous generation.

The consensus as law and legacy

A year after the end of the war in Europe the House of Commons debated the government's Bill to establish the National Health Service. The debate was a public recitation of widely shared beliefs about the growing effectiveness of scientific medicine. The civil servants had advised the Minister to begin the debate by discussing the need for comprehensive medical care – for prevention, clinics, general practitioners and a graded hierarchy of hospitals. But Bevan rejected their advice.[70] For him, both as a private person and as a politician, hospitals were the proper focus of a National Health Service. The cost of hospital care created 'financial anxiety'. Hospitals were 'unevenly distributed'; they lacked a 'plan' or 'system'; their facilities were 'inadequate' and many were 'too small'. The best hospitals were those which were large and operated according to the principles of modern science: 'I would rather be kept alive in the efficient if cold altruism of a large hospital,' Bevan declared, 'than to expire in a gush of warm sympathy in a small one.'[71]

Bevan proclaimed the government's commitment to the fundamental assumption of pre-war discussions of a national health service: hospitals should dominate regional hierarchies of service. 'Hospitals,' he insisted, 'are in many ways the vertebrae of the health system. . . .' They should be arrayed in regional units of a thousand beds, each unit linked 'as the conclusion has always been reached . . . with the medical school'. Doctors must have an effective voice in managing these regional hierarchies: they required 'full participation in the administration of their own profession'.[72]

Bevan, like most participants in the politics of health, believed that the progress of medical science justified the centrality of hospitals and specialised doctors in the new national health service. But Bevan had to reconcile this belief with his socialism and with his responsibility as a Minister. The services administered through regional hierarchies might not be equitably distributed and their managers might try to escape accountability to the Ministry. Bevan acknowledged these problems and placed them on the national political agenda when he spoke in Parliament in May 1946. Doctors, he declared, must somehow be subordinate to 'lay control'. Citizens, whom Bevan called 'the users' of health services, would be responsible for co-ordinating – in Bevan's words, for maintaining 'continuity' – among the services of general practitioners, hospitals and local authorities.[73]

The National Health Service created in 1946 and inaugurated two years later transformed enthusiasm about the recent progress of medical science into public policy. This transformation began before World War I, accelerated as a result of events during and after that war, and became the consensus among members of influential groups in the 1920s and 1930s. During World War II the consensus about how medical care should be organised which had emerged in the previous quarter-century was the basis of the Emergency Medical Service and of planning for a post-war national health service. By the end of the war there was broad political agreement about the purpose and organisation of the new health service.

Once the NHS was created, politicians and leaders of interest groups found it increasingly difficult to avoid answering difficult practical questions in order to preserve a consensus based on an interpretation of history. Such problems as how to allocate scarce resources equitably among hospitals and regions and how to ensure professional accountability to lay authority were postponed by the consensus of 1946. Each future crisis over any of these problems would, however, be resolved by a compromise, because the disputants agreed that providing medical care to individuals through institutions and practitioners which were arrayed in regional hierarchies was self-evidently the proper policy. Only if this consensus began to erode would there be any fundamental change in the National Health Service.

Notes

1   Richard Titmuss, *Problems of Social Policy*, London, 1950, *passim*.

2   Arthur Marwick, *War and Social Change in the Twentieth Century*, London, 1977, p. 161. *cf.* Henry Pelling, *The Labour Governments, 1945–51*, New York, 1984, p. 102.

3   Paul Addison, *The Road to 1945*, London, 1975, p. 239.

4   Kenneth O. Morgan, *Labour in Power, 1945–1951*, Oxford, 1984, pp. 22, 154.

5   Bentley B. Gilbert, *British Social Policy, 1914–1939*, Ithaca, N.Y., 1970, pp. vii, 308.

6   Ian Gough, *The Political Economy of the Welfare State*, London, 1979, pp. 70–1.

7   Brian Abel-Smith, *The Hospitals, 1800–1948*, Cambridge, Mass., 1964, pp. 440 ff.

8   Harry Eckstein, *The English Health Service*, Cambridge, Mass., 1958, pp. 45, 86 and *passim*.

9   Rudolf Klein, *The Politics of the National Health Service*, London, 1983, *passim*.

10   John E. Pater, *The Making of the National Health Service*, London, 1981, *passim*.

11   Arthur J. Willocks, *The Creation of the National Health Service*, London, 1967, *passim*. Willocks generally follows Eckstein and Titmuss in interpreting the origins of the NHS.

12   Most of the secondary sources acknowledge, though with varying emphases, the pre-war consensus about the proper organisation of a national health service. Notable examples include: Eckstein, p. 109; Gilbert, p. 308; Klein, pp. 6–7, 26, 27; Almont Lindsay, *Socialized Medicine in England and Wales: the National Health Service, 1948–1961*, Chapel Hill, N.C., pp. 24–5; and Pater, 45, 85, 173. Abel-Smith, pp. 404–24, 440–57, provides considerable data about pre-war agreement, but remains an advocate of the Titmuss thesis. For Titmuss on the pre-war concensus, see below, n. 25. The history of the NHS popularised among health professionals uncritically embraces the thesis that the Second World War brought about the ideas for as well as the possibility of the NHS. Two recent examples: Barbara Stocking, 'The management of medical technology in the United Kingdom', in J. David Banta and Kerry Britten Kemp (eds.), *The Management of Health Care Technology in Nine Countries*, New York, 1982, p. 12, and John Lister, 'Private medical practice and the National Health Service', *New England Journal of Medicine*, CCCXI, 1984, pp. 1057–8.

13   These generalisations and those in the following paragraph are discussed at length and documented in *Health Policies, Health Politics: the Experience of Britain and America, 1911–1965*, Princeton, N.J., 1986.

14   I cite sources for India and China because of the surprise this point may elicit. For India: Conrad Seipp (ed.), *Health Care for the Community: Selected Papers of Dr. John B. Grant*, Baltimore, Md, 1963, *passim*. For China, in addition to Grant's essays, see AnElissa Lucas, *Chinese Medical Modernization: Comparative Policy Continuities, 1930's–1980's*, New York, 1982, pp. 9–10, 20.

15   For an analysis of the historiographic problems which have contributed

to scholars' emphasis on the differences between the history of health policy in Britain and the United States see Daniel M. Fox, 'The decline of historicism: the case of compulsory health insurance in the United States', *Bulletin of the History of Medicine*, LVII, 1983, 597–610; and *id.*, 'The application of history to social policy', *Journal of Social History*, 1985, XVIII, 349–64.

16   Titmuss, *Problems, passim*. A useful summary and analysis of Titmuss's thought is David Reisman, *Richard Titmuss: Welfare and Society*, London, 1977.

17   Titmuss was convinced that 'As knowledge increased of the causal factors in disease, and as advances in the natural sciences began to penetrate the practice of medicine, it became clearer that action meant social action and . . . collective responsibility'. ('Health' in Morris Ginsberg, ed., *Law and Opinion in England in the Twentieth Century*, London, 1959, pp. 304–5.) Margaret Gowing, 'Richard Morris Titmuss, 1907–1973', *Proceedings of the British Academy*, LXI, 1975, p. 410, says that, for Titmuss, '. . . the National Health Service Act of 1946 was not the apex of "welfare state" benevolence but the consequence of the advance of scientific knowledge and of popular awareness of issues of health and disease'.

18   Richard Titmuss, *Commitment to Welfare*, London, 1968, p. 203.

19   Titmuss's distaste for market economies and for the United States in particular was expressed in many essays and in his final book, *The Gift Relationship*, Harmondsworth, 1979; *cf.* Hilary Rose, 'Rereading Titmuss: the social division of welfare', *Journal of Social Policy*, X, 1981, pp. 485, 488.

20   Titmuss, *Problems*, pp. 508–9, 502–3, 473 and *passim*.

21   Richard and Kathleen Titmuss, *Parents' Revolt: a Study of the Declining Birth Rate in Acquisitive Societies*, London, 1942, p. 117.

22   Titmuss, *Problems*, p. 54.

23   R. H. Tawney, 'The war and the people', *New Statesman and Nation*, XXXIX, 1950, p. 454–6, *cf.* Robert Pinker's introduction to Reisman, pp. xii–xiii.

24   Titmuss, *Problems*, p. 501. *Cf.* Reisman, pp. 33, 38.

25   Titmuss makes a curious use of primary sources which exaggerates the inadequacies of pre-war hospitals and understates the continuity of pre-war and wartime events. He uses the hospital surveys published in 1945 as sources for his descriptions of conditions in 1940 and 1941. The surveyors, however, exaggerated the inadequacy of facilities because they measured them against arbitrarily high standards. Although Titmuss was supposed to have had privileged access to contemporary documents, moreover, it is possible that he did not see the manuscripts now available to scholars in the Public Record Office. On the other hand, it may be that Titmuss was so committed to his interpretation that he saw no need to use evidence which suggested continuity between pre-war and wartime opinion about how to organise health services.

26   The standard source for the history of national health insurance is Bentley B. Gilbert, *The Evolution of National Insurance in Great Britain*, London, 1966. Gilbert's interpretation that Lloyd George was primarily interested in income rather than in services was challenged, unpersuasively, by Frank Honigsbaum, *The Struggle for the Ministry of Health*, Occasional Papers in Social Administration No. 37, London, 1970. Documentary evidence of Lloyd George's priorities is in a paper titled 'Insurance scheme', printed 'for the use of the Cabinet' in March

1911 and found in the William Braithwaite papers, British Library of Political and Social Science, box 11.51. British historical memory later inverted the priorities of 1910. Thus Political and Economic Planning, *Report on the British Health Services*, London, 1937, claimed that 'Not only was National Health Insurance planned to provide medical services but its object was also to give sick people financial assistance during their incapacity'.

27   On the shift from income to services as priority in policy: Lucy Masterman, *C. F. G. Masterman: a Biography*, London, 1939, pp. 242, 252, 264; *cf.* Francis M. Mason, 'Charles Masterman and national health insurance', *Albion*, 1978, X, pp. 54–75; and documents quoted in Bernard M. Allen, *Sir Robert Morant: a Great Public Servant*, London, 1934.

28   Frank Honigsbaum, *The Division in British Medicine*, New York, 1979, p. 101.

29   Our Medical Correspondent [Robert McNair Wilson], 'Health centres for all; the State and the doctors', *The Times*, 16 May 1919.

30   I have documented these points in considerable detail in *Health Policies, Health Politics*. Useful sources include: Kenneth and Jane Morgan, *Portrait of a Progress: the Political Career of Christopher, Viscount Addison*, Oxford, 1980; Honigsbaum, *The Struggle: Christopher Addison, Four and a Half Years: a personal diary from June 1914 to January 1919*, 2 vols, London, 1934; Major General Sir Bertrand Dawson, 'The future of the medical profession', *British Medical Journal*, 1918, ii, 23–6, 56–60; and Ministry of Health, Consultative Council on Medical and Allied Services, *Interim Report on the Future Provision of Medical and Allied Services*, London, 1920, Cmd 693.

31   For Conservative-Unionist support: Waldorf Astor, *The Health of the People: a New National Policy*, London, 1917. For Labour policy: 'Labour Party conference resolutions on public health', March 1929, JSM/PH/125/1. The Labour Party, Memorandum prepared by the Advisory Committee on Public Health, 'The organization of the preventive and curative medical services and hospital and laboratory systems under a ministry of health', London, July 1919, JSM/PH/50, Labour Party Archives. For BMA positions: British Medical Association, Hospitals Committee, documents 1922–23, BMA Registry, Vol. 2073; Ministry of Health Committee, documents 1920–21, BMA Registry, Vol. 2000. For Medical Officers of Health: 'The report of the consultative council', *Public Health*, 1920, XXXIII, pp. 155, 157. For voluntary hospitals: five reports of the Voluntary Hospital Committee (later Commission) reports were published between 1921 and 1925).

32   *Report of the Royal Commission on National Health Insurance*, London, 1926, Cmd 2596.

33   Chamberlain declared his commitment to a 'single health authority' in a memorandum of 19 November 1924 to the Cabinet; quoted in Keith Feiling, *The Life of Neville Chamberlain*, London, 1946, pp. 450–60. He made his commitment explicit during the second reading of the Local Government Bill of 1929. His remarks in the House were quoted in the Ministry's *General Circular on the Local Government Act, 1929*, London, 1929, p. 8.

34   Abel-Smith, *passim.*; *cf.* Vivienne Walters, *Class Inequality and Health Care: the Origins and Impact of the National Health Service*, London, 1980, pp. 51–3.

35   Proceedings, Voluntary Hospitals Commission, 1937, British Hospitals

Contributory Schemes Association Papers, British Library of Political and Social Science. I provide more elaborate documentation for the views of the BMA, the MOHs and the medical left in *Health Policies, Health Politics*.

36   *The Next Five Years: an essay in Political Agreement*, London, 1935.

37   The background of the report and evidence of the difficulty of writing it can be reconstructed from documents in the PEP papers, box WG14/2-15/3, British Library of Political and Social Science.

38   PEP, pp. 26, 222, 337.

39   PEP, pp. 408, 414. For the impact of the report see Kenneth Lindsay, 'PEP through the 1930's: organization, structure, people', in John Pinder (ed.), *Fifty Years of Political and Economic Planning*, London, 1981, pp. 9-31.

40   'Memorandum on provision of specialist services by the C.M.O.', MH 80/24 Public Record Office.

41   C. L. Dunn, *The Emergency Medical Services*, I, London, 1952, *passim*. Titmuss, *Problems, passim*.

42   The documents which form the basis of these assertions include: A. MacNalty to E. J. Maude, 'Proposed national hospital service', 21 September 1939; A. N. Rucker to E. J. Maude, 'Proposed national hospital service', 29 September 1939, MH 80/24, PRO, BHA, Provisional Central Council, 5 December 1939. British Hospitals Contributory Schemes Papers; PEP cited in Pater; miscellaneous letters and clippings in MH 77/25, PRO; and Sir E. Farquahar Buzzard, 'Post-war hospital policy', *The Lancet*, 1941, i, pp. 155-6.

43   War Cabinet, Lord President's Committee, 15 October 1941, MH 80/34, PRO.

44   The quote is John Pater's paraphrase (pp. 28-9) of a document he noted as in MH 77/26. I did not locate the document. It may be what Maude believed and said; it is, however, a stronger statement than what he wrote in other documents during these months.

45   Hansard, *Parliamentary Debates*, House of Commons, 5th Ser., Vol. 374, 9 October 1941, cols. 1116-20.

46   Instructions to Minister for Parliament, 9 October 1941, MH 77/22, PRO.

47   'Hospital regionalisation', 6 February 1941 (quoting Wilson Jameson, with corrections in his hand), MH 80/24, PRO.

48   Charles Latham, 'The case for public control', *The Star*, 1941; clipping in MH 77/25, PRO.

49   Minutes of a meeting between E. J. Maude and W. M. Goodenough (Nuffield Trust), 12 March 1942, MH 77/19, PRO. A chronological file of pertinent documents is in MH 80/34, PRO.

50   M. F. McNichol to W. Jameson, 13 April 1944; MH 77/24, PRO.

51   J. Pater to E. J. Maude, 5 May 1946, MH 77/25, PRO.

52   Hospitals Committee minutes, Medical Planning Commission, 4 September 1941, Vol. 2075, BMA Registry.

53   Minutes, Hospitals Committee, Medical Planning Commission, 18 November 1941, Vol. 2075, BMA Registry.

54   Honigsbaum, *The Division*, 185.

55   BMA, Annual Representative Meeting, 'Medical Planning Commission', *British Medical Journal Supplement*, 1, 26 September, 10 October 1942, ii.

56   Medical Planning Research, 'Interim General Report', *The Lancet*,

Supplement, 21 November 1942, ii, pp. 599–622.

57   Joan Simeon Clarke, 'National Health Insurance', in William A. Robson (ed.), *Social Security*, London, 1943; *cf.* D. Stark Murray, *Health for All*, London, 1942, 7, 45.

58   Sir William Beveridge, *Social Insurance and Allied Services*, London, 1942, Cmd 6404, pp. 8, 14, 120, 159.

59   *Ibid.*, pp. 11, 12, 120, 159, 160–1. *Cf.* T. H. Marshall, *Social Policy in the Twentieth Century*, London, 1975, p. 100, who distinguished between a 'social security system . . . with its guarantee of a minimum and the NHS, with its promise of the optimum'.

60   Beveridge, pp. 104–5, 161.

61   Ministry of Health and Department of Health for Scotland, *A National Health Service*, London, 1944, Cmd 6502.

62   There is vast documentation of the negotiations following publication of the White Paper. Much material is in MH 80/27, MH 77/30B, MH 80/33, PRO. The *British Medical Journal* and *The Lancet* reported many of the discussions. Eckstein, Pater and Honigsbaum, *The Division*, have useful accounts of events.

63   Moran's comment was made a year later in Consultant Services Committee, *A Consultant Service for the Nation*, London, 1946, p. 21. But he apparently said much the same thing to the Minister and to Churchill in spring 1945: see draft election manifesto attached to Cabinet minutes on the NHS, 6 June 1945, MH 77/30A, PRO: 'The whole service must be so designed that in each area the growth is helped and guided by the influence of a university.'

64   Eckstein and Honigsbaum, *The Division*, have excellent accounts of general practitioners' behaviour.

65   Minutes of meetings with local authority leaders are in MH 77/30B, PRO.

66   Address of the President, Annual General Meeting, 21 September 1944, British Hospital Contributory Scheme Association papers.

67   The history of this decision and of Hawton's role in it is described in Pater, pp. 178–9.

68   James M. Mackintosh, *The Nation's Health: Target for Tomorrow*, Vol. 5, London, 1944, summarised the proposals of each party.

69   British Institute of Public Opinion, *The Nation's Health*, London, 1944, p. 26. A highly flawed survey commissioned by the Beveridge committee in 1942 found, according to its modern interpreter, that 'from the point of view of the working-class consumer, it was health that was the first priority of future social reform'. Nevertheless, 'there was little coherent conception of what should take' the place of the 'exiting system' and 'no evidence to suggest that grass-roots opinion was harbouring any wider vision of more far-reaching social revolution'. José Harris, 'Did British workers want the welfare state? G. D. H. Cole's survey of 1942', in Jay Winter (ed.), *The Working Class in Modern British History: Essays in Honour of Henry Pelling*, Cambridge, 1983, pp. 203, 214.

70   'Suggested contents of second reading speech', n.d., 1946, MH 80/30, PRO.

71   Hansard, *Parliamentary Debates*, House of Commons, 5th Ser., Vol. 422, 30 April, 1 May 1941, cols. 43–6.

72   *Ibid.*, cols. 46, 47, 50, 52.

73   *Ibid.*, col. 30. Lord Hill told Gordon McPherson in an interview, 26 April

1978, 'I asked Nye where was the co-ordination between the three parts [of the NHS] and he said the patient was'. I am grateful to Rudolf Klein for this source.

Acknowledgements

Besides the source of note 73 I am grateful to Rudolf Klein for many other acts of kindness during my research on the history of the NHS. I also acknowledge the penetrating criticism and extraordinary generosity of Charles Webster. Klein and Webster were indispensable guides to the history of the NHS. I have, perhaps perversely, rejected much of their advice in asserting my interpretation of the NHS's origins.

John Stevenson

Planners' moon? The Second World War and the planning movement

On 4 January 1941, with the Battle of Britain only just won and the blitz still raging, Edward Hulton's *Picture Post* published a special edition under the headline 'A Plan for Britain'. Between the advertisements for Brylcream and Bile Beans was set out a forty-page prospectus for a 'new Britain', consisting of a series of short articles putting forward proposals for a fresh approach to employment, social security, town planning, architecture, the countryside, education, health, the medical services and leisure. Contributors included Thomas Balogh, Maxwell Fry, A. D. Lindsay, Julian Huxley and J. B. Priestley. In an editorial foreword the need for this prospectus was explained. The previous war had ended with the country unprepared for the transition from war to peace: 'The plan was not there. We got no new Britain, and we got no new Europe.' In contrast, 'this time we can be better prepared . . . this is a time for doing the thinking, so that we can make things how we want them to be'.[1] These proposals, with their aspirations for the future, put forward in a popular picture magazine, illustrate strikingly an important theme in British wartime politics. The ideas carried in the individual features, including an end to mass unemployment, a planned economy, a comprehensive system of social security and health care, a clean sweep of all that was old-fashioned and squalid in housing and the urban legacy of the industrial revolution, and many more, represented a virtual glossary of progressive views current in the Britain of the 1930s and its contributors a fair cross-section of the high-minded and socially concerned individuals who had been advocating these and similar ideas well before the outbreak of war. But the war was here the occasion for their collective expression, at a time when, with the threat of invasion passed, debates about the future shape of British society were becoming a major ingredient in political discussion. *Picture Post* was in no doubt about their justification: 'Our plan for a new Britain is not something outside the war, or something *after* the war. It is an essential part of our war aims. It is, indeed, our most positive war aim. The new Britain is the country we are fighting for.'[2]

Expressed in this way, 'A Plan for Britain' was symptomatic of a mood of collectivist enthusiasm which seemed to find its opportunity in the shared perils and challenges of the early years of the war. The growth of what Paul Addison has called 'Attlee consensus' clearly drew upon the kind of ideas represented in the *Picture Post* issue.[3] Clearly many of the schemes and proposals outlined there were to find full or partial implementation in the Butler Education Act, the creation of the Welfare State and a National Health Service, the New Town and National Parks Acts, and the nationalisation of basic industries. The drive towards greater State intervention and a more collectivist solution to the nation's pre-war problems has been properly identified as part of the legacy of the 'people's war'. In this consensus, 'planning' formed a major if somewhat ambiguous ingredient. In some areas it was an end in itself, notably in the field of town and environmental planning, in others the means by which changes should be brought about, essentially through well thought out rationalisation and reorganisation, or, more broadly, as a global commitment to the future – the only way of ensuring that desirable social and economic changes could be brought about. While 'planning' in these various guises seemed to find its moment in the Second World War, it also drew upon a long evolution of social and political thought which stretched back to before the Great War. The rise of State intervention in the social sphere prior to 1914 has been acknowledged as marking the beginnings of the process of greater involvement which was to find expression in the Second World War. Social investigation by the late Victorian and Edwardian pioneers laid out the contours and dimensions of social problems, such as poverty, in ways which suggested solutions. The burst of social legislation prior to 1914 was possible only within a context in which the most obvious social evils of the day, such as the poverty caused by old age, sickness and unemployment, had been identified and shown to be amenable to State action.

The Great War, with the enormous challenges it posed to the assumptions of *laissez-faire* liberalism, took the role of the State a great deal further. By its end the State had assumed greater control than ever before of the nation's economy and manpower resources. Control of the munitions industry and its related establishments was soon followed in other sections of industry. By a process which almost seemed inevitable the State found itself directing a major part of the country's industries, and controlling or licensing most of the remainder. Government 'controllers' to deal with shipping, labour, food, food production and national service greatly extended the control of government. Following munitions, shipbuilding and ship repairing, virtually all transport by rail, sea or canal, flour milling, agriculture, collieries and the chemical industry had become part of a network of control. Intervention and planning of resources became necessary in almost every sphere. The introduction of conscription was not only crucial to obtain the manpower resources necessary but also to plan a total war economy. If conscription represented a major presumption upon the values of Edwardian Britain, so too did the growing battery of controls over licensing hours, house rents, rationing and information. By the latter years of the war, the experience of government direction and the evident need to recompense the sacrifices of the home population encouraged the desire to carry wartime controls into lasting social reform and post-war 'reconstruction'. The impact of the war was put forcibly by Seebohm Rowntree in 1918:

The war has torn the scales from our eyes, and forced us to see things as they really are, and by the light of this clearer vision we have come to regard many conditions as intolerable which before had only seemed inevitable . . . As a nation, however, we acquiesced in this state of things. We were so familiar with it that its evils failed to impress us. Even in our progressive and sanguine moods, the utmost that we hoped for was a very gradual and a very tentative improvement. But the war changed all this. We have completely revised our notions as to what is possible or impossible. We have seen accomplished within a few brief months or years reforms to which we should have assigned, not decades, but generations. I do not believe for a moment that in the future we shall allow millions of our fellow-countrymen, through no fault of their own, to pass through life ill-housed, ill-clothed, ill-fed, ill-educated.[4]

Significantly, 'reconstruction' implied planning for the future. A Reconstruction Committee was formed in March 1916 which was turned in July 1917, under the impact of growing labour unrest and the first Russian revolution, into the Ministry of Reconstruction. The Ministry worked through a series of committees which investigated demobilisation, labour, unemployment pay and housing. Its reports provided a series of blueprints for post-war society. A committee under J. H. Whitley proposed the establishment of joint industrial councils made up of representatives of employers and workers, operating on national, district and works level to resolve peacefully industrial disputes. Reports on housing, drawing upon the experience of model estates built before the

war and during it for special groups such as munition workers, paved
the way for the massive scheme of 'homes fit for heroes' inaugurated
by the post-war coalition government.[5] Similarly, attention was turned
to education: the Board of Education Report for 1917–18 declared that
the War 'has certainly brought a clearer and wider recognition of the
value of education, and, while showing the defects and shortcomings
of our system, has produced the resolution to improve it'.[6] Amongst
a broad section of opinion, not only vote-seeking politicians, the idea
of 'reconstruction' with its blueprints for the future tapped currents of
social thinking which antedated the war, but now sustained by the
example of the role of the State in managing the war effort. It was
William Beveridge who hailed a revolution in public administration: 'We
have . . . under the stress of war, made practical discoveries in the art
of government almost comparable to the immense discoveries made at
the same time in the art of flying'.[7] The effect on attitudes towards
greater State intervention and the role of planning has been summed
up by Rodney Barker:

By the closing years of the war the pacific complement of all this military
collectivism was the preparation for social reconstruction with the onset of peace,
carried out by the state and pursued with the assistance of its own investigative
committees. Once lodged in the realm of 'common sense' and sustained by
'practical' measures, state collectivism looked less and less like contestable belief,
and became increasingly the broad starting point for argument, rather than its
disputed conclusion.[8]

But plans for post-war reconstruction were to bear only limited fruit.
Although the promise of a 'land fit for heroes to live in' secured a victory
for Lloyd George and his coalition government in 1918, it was soon to
find its promises increasingly hard to fulfil as the post-war boom petered
out and Britain moved into the years of the Slump. Even before the
'Geddes axe' cut a swathe through the ambitious post-war housing
programme and halted the further extension of welfare provision in such
areas as education, a certain faltering in the reconstructivist drive was
evident. The Ministry of Reconstruction, the only potential co-ordinating
body for post-war plans, was dismantled in June 1919, just when it should
have been at the peak of its activities.

None the less, the spirit which had animated plans for post-war
construction did not die away in the interwar years. In part at least, the
conditions which frustrated their fuller implication also provided the
justification for renewed efforts to improve social conditions. There was
a continuing output of serious social investigation which had as its aim

the accurate delineation of social problems and implicitly or explicitly to indicate solutions. A. L. Bowley's study of 1925, *Has Poverty Diminished?*, was able to compare conditions in five towns in the early 1920s with those immediately prior to the war and, while showing the improvements that had taken place, demonstrate the still significant causes of poverty. *The Social Survey of Merseyside* and *The New Survey of London Life and Labour* were under way by the late 1920s. In the mid-1930s Seebohm Rowntree was in a particularly strong position to comment authoritatively on changes in living conditions when he repeated his 1899 enquiry in York. The rise of unemployment led to its own set of enquiries, initially into the condition of the depressed areas and eventually, more in the '30s than in the '20s, into the problems of the unemployed themselves. Housing and the slum problem, town and country planning, population and family policy, nutrition and public health all come under detailed scrutiny.[9] The intellectual thrust of many of these enquiries was towards a more 'scientific' study of society, building upon the empirical traditions of the social enquiries of the late Victorian and Edwardian era. The use of the 'street survey' and the 'random sample' went hand in hand with the attempt to measure deprivation through the use of 'poverty lines', standards of 'minimum needs', 'overcrowding' indices, and objective standards of health and adequate nutrition. Malcolm Muggeridge wryly but perceptively noted, 'Facts were wanted about everyone and everything – cross-sections of society, symptomatic opinions and observations, detailed investigations and statistics'.[10] The purpose of these studies varied widely; many felt constrained by their academic background to make only guarded recommendations, in an area fraught with political implications. Other writers, such as Seebohm Rowntree, were much less guarded, putting forward solutions to family poverty and circulating new ideas about how they could be reconciled with the economic needs of industry. Socialist writers like the Coles clearly saw rational diagnosis as an indictment of a wasteful social system. Inevitably, in time, some of the progressive ideas being put forward seeped into public consciousness. Many pressure groups set themselves the task of sedulously winning over influential opinion to their view of the future. For example, the Family Endowment Society, led by Eleanor Rathbone, argued strongly for a system of family allowances, enlisting the support of people like William Beveridge and Seebohm Rowntree for a measure which was widely recognised as a major step towards eliminating poverty.[11] A similar course, however, was being pursued by the varied groups pressing for such things as nursery schools, a national health service, 'new towns' and National Parks.

But while the advocacy of many of these proposals drew upon long-term developments in social and political thought, it was the economic situation in the inter-war years which forced many to address the question of how the endemic problems of overcapacity in basic industries, structural unemployment and the evident failure of *laissez-faire* to preserve national prosperity could be overcome. Even by the end of the 1920s there were the beginnings of calls for a more directly interventionist role by government and some deliberate trade and industrial policy for the future. When the depression worsened after the Wall Street crash, the fringe voices of 'unorthodox' economists and politicians were joined by increasing numbers of people who looked to new ways of solving the country's problems. High on this agenda was economic planning. In *Reconstruction*, published in 1933, Harold Macmillan wrote, ' "Planning" is forced upon us . . . not for idealistic reasons but because the old mechanism which served us when markets were expanding naturally and spontaneously is no longer adequate when the tendency is in the opposite direction'.[12] Although *laissez-faire* was by no means discarded in the 1930s and the dead hand of economic orthodoxy, particularly in fiscal matters remained strong, there were signs of change in the stance of government in some areas. As Angus Calder has noted, there was a formidable catalogue of reorganisation and rationalisation carried out either by the government or with its encouragement. By the outbreak of the war the State had reorganised the railways into four companies where there had been 130 before; nationally owned corporations had been created in broadcasting and air passenger transport; a national grid for electricity supply had been created and a national supply industry organised; agriculture had been rescued from the doldrums by regulation of its prices and quota systems; while encouragement had been given to sometimes savage reductions of capacity in shipbuilding, textiles and mining. Calder has called this an 'irreversible break' with the past, and the preparations from the mid-'30s for a future war showed the extent to which the lessons learned in the Great War were applied even before hostilities broke out.[13] The 'shadow factory' schemes, begun in 1936, showed the determination of the government to control vital war production from the outset. The rubicon of conscription, crossed so painfully and reluctantly in 1916, was accepted as a necessity from the start of any future war. The Military Training Act of 1939 effectively introduced conscription in peacetime for the first time in Britain's history. While the government remained wedded to budgetary orthodoxy, it was by 1938 allocating over a quarter of the budget to defence, prefiguring the even greater commitments after war's outbreak.

Outside government, what has been called a 'young man's consensus' was developing on the necessity of greater State intervention in both the economic and the social sphere. These views crystallised in pressure groups such as Political and Economic Planning, established in 1931, and the *Next Five Years* Group, formed in 1934. Covering a broader range than the single-issue groups, they presented reports and analyses on a wide range of economic and social issues which generally looked forward to the legislation of the 1940s. The list of those involved in PEP during the 1930s and early 1940s included the banker Basil Blackett, businessmen such as Laurence Neal and Israel Sieff, the scientist Julian Huxley, the educational pioneer and National MP Kenneth Lindsay, architects and town-planning enthusiasts such as Maxwell Fry, Raymond Unwin and Ernest Simon, the anthropologist Tom Harrisson, academics such as Alexander Cairncross, John Maynard Keynes and William Beveridge, and sympathetic MPs such as Harold Macmillan and Sir Arnold Wilson. Major reports were produced on housing, social services, the health services, the press and the location of industry. Its shorter *Broadsheets*, over 150 of which had been produced by 1940, provided discussion on a wide range of topics of economic and social concern. PEP had a strong technocratic outlook, drawing most of its support and research groups from managers, academics and other experts. Its General Secretary, Max Nicholson, has summed up the thrust of much of its work as being: to supersede piecemeal treatment of public policy by co-ordinated policies founded on 'fact-based' and 'research-based' programmes; reliable decision-making based upon accurate and comprehensive forecasting; and the implementation of policy through democratic principles.[14] The *Next Five Years* Group tended towards a less technocratic style. Its members again included many of those involved in progressive causes between the wars, especially in education and the social services, including Seebohm Rowntree, H. G. Wells, Siegfried Sassoon, R. C. K. Ensor, H. A. L. Fisher, G. P. Gooch, J. A. Hobson and William Temple. Again, the proposals of the *Next Five Years* Group anticipated many of the developments of the 1940s, such as a National Development Board, greater public investment in housing, the co-ordination of social services to achieve a 'National Minimum', the expansion of secondary education, and town and country planning. The young Harold Macmillan was especially active in the group, eventually taking charge of it and its periodical *New Outlook*. The views he expressed in *The Middle Way*, published in 1938, pointing towards a managed economy and the expansion of welfare services to achieve a national minimum, came close to expressing the essential ingredients of what both PEP and the *Next Five Years* Group wanted in the way of a change of direction by the National Government. Macmillan, with a few other radical Tories, such as Robert Boothby, Julian Amery and Duncan Sandys, represented a strand of Conservative thinking which already accepted much of the argument of 'middle opinion'.

In spite of only a short period of minority government the Labour Party in the 1920s had also developed some ambitious long-term policies. Following the debacle of 1931, the trade unions came to play an increasingly important part in shaping Labour policy. Ernest Bevin, for example, in his pamphlet *My Plan for 200,000 Workers*, proposed a raising of the school leaving age to sixteen, earlier retirement and a shorter working week. Meanwhile a number of prominent Labour figures, such as G. D. H. Cole, Douglas Jay, Hugh Dalton and Herbert Morrison were beginning to reshape Labour policy towards an acceptance of planning and Keynesian economics, through books, pamphlets, discussion circles and the work of bodies such as the New Fabian Research Bureau, founded in 1931. Liberal improvers, progressive Conservatives and socialists found themselves sharing some common ground in this assumption that it was the duty of the State to provide a better life for its citizens and which found expression in support for comprehensive social welfare, a national health service and a more humane treatment of those in need. For Labour as for 'middle opinion' as a whole, increased State intervention and central direction went hand in hand with faith in a more rational and ordered treatment of social questions – an essentially technocratic approach – which found its most characteristic expression in the enthusiasm for 'planning'. Planning, at least in the form of extensive control of the 'reins of economic power', had traditionally occupied a central part in socialist thought, and public control of economic resources, production and allocation were part of the essential features of left-wing thought between the wars. This was reflected in admiration for the achievements of the Russian revolution and the Five Year Plans, so that during the inter-war years socialist writers such as G. D. H. Cole advocated planning in contradiction to the chaos, irrationality and waste of the capitalist system. Capitalism was indicted as a gigantic muddle, whereas socialism stood for rationality and a co-ordinated approach to economic and social questions – planning was the practical expression of socialism.[15] Thus in 1934 Barbara Wootton in *Plan or no Plan* advocated the advantages of economic planning and central, public management in promoting equality, fairness and a reduction in unemployment, while Douglas Jay in *The Socialist Case* in 1938 argued that collectivist planning was the only way to achieve a just and fair society. But while the socialist concern for planning was important, not least in view of Labour's victory at the polls in 1945, perhaps the most significant feature of the inter-war years was the acceptance by 'middle opinion' of the need for planning without the destruction of the capitalist system. Hence planning was not a uniquely left- or right-wing cause between the wars, it was a response from progressive capitalists, professional people, academics, centrist politicians and socialists who found in it a means of advance over a wide range of social and economic problems.

Up to the 1930s the word 'planning' was still associated primarily with 'town' planning and military staffwork. Indeed, the first official use of the term came in the Housing and Town and Country Planning Acts of 1909 and 1919. As late as 1933, however, the *Oxford English Dictionary* did not recognise the existence of the single word 'planning', though it was by then coming into use on the Continent as an alternative to totalitarianism, particularly in the fields of economic management and social policy. The formation of Political and Economic Planning and the publication of a 20,000 word supplement to the *Week-end Review* of 'A National Plan for Great Britain' inaugurated this use in Britain. The article criticised the 'hopeless confusion of the post-war years' which had created the risk 'that in incompetent hands this country may go drifting on either towards a sharp crisis which might have revolutionary consequences, or to dictatorship, or perhaps worse still to gradual decline . . .'. In its call for 'rigorous constructive argument' and a general reorganisation of the political, social and economic structure of the country it articulated the frustrations of a broad spectrum of opinion with existing policies.[16] Although the totalitarian overtones of 'planning' attracted some criticism and many socialists remained cool about the concept of a basically capitalist planned economy, the idea of planning had entered the mainstream of 'middle opinion' by the mid-1930s.

If by the outbreak of the Second World War there existed a substantial body of opinion which looked forward to a fresh approach to economic and social problems, this increasingly influential consensus found its moment with the coming of the war and, in particular, in the atmosphere of national emergency after the evacuation of Dunkirk and the fall of

France in 1940. A mood of collectivism and common endeavour – for a time at least – transformed the context of the debate about the conduct of economic and social policy.[17] The planning movement of the 1930s was to find its apotheosis in the conduct of the war and the plans for post-war reconstruction in almost every field from social security to new town development. PEP had set up a Post-war Aims Group even before the war began, and within a week of its outbreak had circulated a draft report on war aims. As well as devoting attention to the management of the war economy, it had by July 1942 produced a broadsheet, *Planning for Social Security*, which substantially anticipated the Beveridge report in calling for a national minimum income, universal family allowances, a national health service and a Ministry of Social Security.[18] A similar pointer to opinion was the 'volunteer army' of post-war planners who launched a series of reconstruction projects in 1940–41. Amongst the most ambitious was the Nuffield College Reconstruction Survey, proposed by G. D. H. Cole, supported by influential backers such as Arthur Greenwood and John Reith, and financed from a Treasury grant. All three main parties had reconstruction committees working on post-war plans by 1941, while professional groups such as the BMA and the Town and Country Planning Association provided their own schemes.

Interest in economic 'planning' received a tremendous boost from the sheer practicalities of the war effort. The necessities of equipping the armed forces, preserving the home population at a decent minimum level and running an efficient war economy brought government control and direction into almost every aspect of people's lives. The results were certainly dramatic in terms of the war effort. Britain was soon devoting something like half its national product to the war, a massive shift of resources, unthinkable in peacetime. The 'standing army' of over a million unemployed was mopped up during the first year of hostilities, and between 1939 and 1943 almost 3 million jobs were added to the labour market, including many jobs for women. With almost every resource in short supply, the management of the war economy required not only government control but complex and intricate planning of requirements and allocation. But these problems also had a social dimension. War production – the very continuance of the war itself – depended on civilian morale; morale determined the need to take account of the blueprints for the future which had been articulated before the war began. Once the immediate crisis of 1940 had been weathered and the country embarked upon the long haul of productive effort and austerity, groups like the '1941 Committee' pressed Britain's war aims in terms of plans for the future. The committee's first leaflet, *We Must Win*, declared: 'We must set out ideals and objectives in clear terms and we must so order our own mode of life and social system that men may know that we offer a happiness, freedom and prosperity which can never flourish under Hitler's totalitarianism.'[19] By 1942 the Labour Party Conference was also calling for a comprehensive scheme of social security, adequate cash payments to provide security whatever the contingency, a scheme of family allowances, and a national health service.

The war, then, provided opportunities, but the extent to which they were taken up depended in large degree upon the contingent circumstances of the case being argued. The influence of the Second World War on the introduction of a comprehensive system of National Insurance, the National Health Service, Family Allowances, and town and country planning can hardly be ignored. The primary mechanism suggested for this relationship of war with advances in social welfare is political: that the demands of total war forced government to make concessions to organised labour and the working classes in general which otherwise might have taken much longer to achieve. Indeed, it was Beveridge himself who claimed in the midst of the war that 'the most general effect of war is to make the common people more important'.[20] It is however, important to place the wartime advances in their appropriate pre-war context. In the case of the Second World War the point is clear. The social investigations of the inter-war years and the literature of concern about unemployment and other social problems prepared the ground for wartime legislation. The pressure groups such as Political and Economic Planning and the *Next Five Years* Group had already foreshadowed many of the policies indicated by the Beveridge report, while the BMA was already an advocate of the creation of a comprehensive health service. Hence the interwar years had seen the development of what has been called 'a consensus of social responsibility' which accepted the necessity of greater State intervention, planning and full employment as major priorities. At least as important as the arguments of the wartime planners was that their schemes emerged into a climate which was receptive to their main conclusions. Equally, it would be unwise to minimise the effects of the peculiar circumstances created by the war. There is little doubt that the national crisis of 1940–41 played a significant part in turning plans for comprehensive welfare from high-minded aspiration into practical legislation. Perhaps most important is the need to recognise that a balance of forces was usually operating at any one time: pressure groups for change, politicians, civil servants and individual personalities all had a part to play. Similarly, many different motives came into play, ranging from political manipulation to the purest altruism. Circumstances could clearly alter the balance in favour of one group rather than another and emphasise some considerations more than others. In this connection, individual policy decisions have to be taken very much in their own context by a close examination of the design and implementation of particular pieces of legislation.

Appropriately, it was the field where the term 'planning' had been first originated, town and country planning, that provided the most decisive example of the war acting as an agent of deliberate plans for the future. The Barlow Commission, which reported in January 1940, has been called the 'planners' breakthrough', with its recommendations for greater government control of industrial and urban growth, especially in the south-east of England. As it happened, the threat of bombing forced the dispersal of industry from the vulnerable south-east and demanded firm controls over the siting of factories and the utilisation of land. Moreover, the destruction wrought by the blitz turned 'rebuilding Britain' from a vaguely desirable objective into a necessity.[21] Hardly had the dust settled on the bomb damage when ambitious plans for large-scale rebuilding were pouring off the drawing boards of architects and town planners. They were encouraged by the appointment in October 1940 of Sir John Reith as the head of the new Ministry of Works, not only to supervise repairing bomb-damaged buildings but also to consult other departments and organisations about the post-war rebuilding of cities. One of Reith's first actions as Minister of Works was to appoint a panel of consultants to advise him on post-war planning. A series of objectives were drawn up which followed closely upon the views of progressive planners: they included controlled development of all areas and the utilisation of land to the best advantage, the limitation of urban expansion, redevelopment of congested areas, the correlation of transport and amenities, improved architectural treatment, and the preservation of places of historic interest, national parks and coastal areas.[22] Although Reith was dismissed in February 1942, his initiative in these areas had set in train a series of plans for comprehensive redevelopment.

One such plan was Reith's appointment of Patrick Abercrombie and the LCC architect J. H. Forshaw to draw up a scheme for the rebuilding of London. The result was *The County of London Plan*, published in 1943, and a further report, commissioned by Reith's successor,

Wyndham Portal, the *Greater London Plan* of 1944. Others were the establishment of committees under Mr Justice Uthwatt to examine the crucial question of compensation for planning development and the Scott committee on the future of the countryside.[23] Plans were also inaugurated for the reconstruction of cities and towns such as Glasgow, Exeter, Hull and Coventry. The example of Coventry perhaps best exemplifies the dovetailing of pre-war concerns with the effects of the blitz. One of the first cities to set up an Architectural Department in 1938, an exhibition in May–June 1939 illustrated plans for a redesigned civic centre, with lectures by such well known authorities on town planning as Thomas Sharp, author of *Oxford Re-planned*, and Clough Williams-Ellis, builder of the Italianate village of Portmeirion in Snowdonia. These plans remained in an abstract stage until the destruction of much of the centre of Coventry in November 1940. At their first meeting after the blitz the General Purposes Committee recommended the setting up of a City Redevelopment Committee to consider 'the steps which it will be desirable for the municipality to take to secure a worthy replanning and redevelopment of the city'. Coventry was chosen by Lord Reith as one of a handful of cities to be used as a prototype of large-scale urban planning. Although there were divisions in the local authority as to how far the plan should redesign radically the traditional city centre, it was entirely symptomatic of the mood of the time that both the City Development Committee and Lord Reith should accept the more radical scheme outlined by Donald Gibson, the city architect. Within six months of the blitz which had devastated the city centre, an exhibition of sketches and plans outlined a redesigned city centre, based on the principle of pedestrian shopping precincts, zoned development and an inner ring road.[24]

The creation of the Ministry of Town and Country Planning in 1943, followed by the Town and Country Planning Act of 1944, provided both the machinery and the powers for comprehensive redevelopment on the lines envisaged by the more ambitious advocates of planning. Subsequently the 1947 Town and Country Planning Act brought almost all development under control by making it subject to planning permission. Development plans were to be prepared for every area of the country, the powers being transferred away from the small district councils to the county and borough councils. Co-ordination of local plans was to be carried out by the Ministry of Town and Country Planning, while development rights in land were nationalised. Similarly, the New Towns Act of 1946 provided for the setting up of Development

Corporations to plan and create new towns where considered 'expedient in the national interest'. The corporations had wide powers of acquisition and management of the requisite areas 'and generally to do anything necessary or expedient for the purposes of the new town or for the purposes incidental thereto'.[25] Similarly, the war provided a receptive atmosphere for a reappraisal of the economic and recreational role of the countryside. By 1941 L. F. Easterbrook, the agricultural expert and journalist, associated with Lloyd George's plan for the land, was urging through the pages of *Picture Post* the need for a 'Land Commission' which would operate a national strategy to apportion land for agriculture, forestry, building, roads, allotments, factories, playing fields and national parks, while others supported the demand for public access to the countryside and the creation of specially designated areas as 'lungs' for the urban areas. The Scott report, published in 1942, urged the setting up of a planning system embracing the countryside as well as the town, mainly with a view to preserving the best agricultural land from urban development, but also recommending the setting up of national parks. Following the appointment of the first Minister of Town and Country Planning in 1943, the government committed itself to create National Parks. The issue of control of land use remained more contentious; a White Paper on the control of land use was shelved by the coalition government and not dealt with until the Town and Country Planning Act of 1947 under the post-war Labour administration. The proposal for National Parks, however, received further support in the Dower report, published in 1945, and that of the Hobhouse committee, which proposed setting up a National Parks Commission paid for out of public funds. These were eventually embodied in the National Parks and Access to the Countryside Act of 1949.[26]

Town and country planning were important symbols of the more far-sighted and strategic uses of planning, of necessity areas which would take years to come to full fruition. These aspirations were shared by the Beveridge committee on social insurance which was set up in 1941 at the same time as the Uthwatt committee and the Scott committee. The Beveridge report was to breathe the same spirit of optimism and confidence that long-standing problems could be tackled. Just as the slums, squalor and muddle of towns and cities could be overcome by planning, so could social evils. As Beveridge himself stated plainly:

The Plan for Social Security is put forward as part of a general programme of social policy. It is one part only of an attack upon five great evils: upon the physical Want with which it is directly concerned, upon Disease which often causes Want and brings many other troubles in its train, upon Ignorance which no democracy can afford among its citizens, upon the Squalor which arises mainly through haphazard distribution of industry and population, and upon Idleness which destroys wealth and corrupts men, whether they are well-fed or not, when they are idle.[27]

Guided by these principles, the 'Beveridge plan' assumed that the government would provide family allowances, create a comprehensive health service and maintain full employment. His plan for social insurance envisaged a single weekly flat-rate contribution which would provide a comprehensive system of social insurance 'from the cradle to the grave', including unemployment benefit, sickness benefit, disability benefit, workmen's compensation, old age, widows' and orphans' pensions and benefits, funeral grants and maternity benefit. A system of 'National Assistance' was to be maintained for all those who fell outside the other benefits to be paid for by the national exchequer. The level of contribution was to be fixed at a level within the reach of every employed person, with benefits paid at a 'national minimum income for subsistence', and the whole system co-ordinated by a new Ministry of Social Security.

Beveridge's scheme was not, as has been stressed many times, revolutionary. Through a 'deal' with Keynes at the Treasury, the financial implications of the report involved only an extra £100 million per annum from central government, far less than Beveridge himself had initially estimated. Essentially his proposals were a rationalisation of existing insurance schemes, based on the time-honoured principle of contributions from employee, employer and the State. The preservation of the principle of 'insurance' was a clear throw-back to the days of Lloyd George and, as he explained in a radio broadcast, his 'Plan for Britain' was 'based on the contributory principle of giving not free allowances to all from the State, but giving benefits as of right in virtue of contributions made by the insured persons themselves'. It provided a national minimum, not an allocation of relief on the basis of need. None the less, the tone of the report was radical, particularly in Beveridge's expressed desire to abolish the 'five giants', to give a new sense of purpose to democracy, to promote national solidarity, and define the goals of the war. As he observed in the report, if the Allies could 'plan for a better peace even while waging war, they will win together two victories which in truth are indivisible'.[28] But the Beveridge report was just that – a report, not legislation. There was a much more cautious response to the Beveridge proposals among politicians and administrators. Above all, Churchill was opposed to passing major legislation before the war was won. Parliament merely welcomed the proposals and Churchill warned of 'a dangerous optimism' and the raising of 'false hopes'.[29] None the less, the enthusiasm aroused by the report and the wide support it achieved among Labour politicians, sections of the Conservative Party and a broad spectrum of opinion led to a series of government White Papers in 1944 organised by the Minister of Reconstruction, Lord Woolton. In February *A National Health Service* proposed a free comprehensive health service covering every branch of medical and allied activity. In May a paper, *Employment Policy*, accepted the Keynesian economic argument of using public expenditure to avoid cyclical unemployment. Decaying regions were to be given aid to create new industries along the lines of the Barlow report of 1940. In September 1944 a third White Paper, *Social Insurance*, accepted most of the proposals of the Beveridge report, especially that of comprehensive coverage for all persons and types of risk, and formed the basis of Labour's Insurance Act of 1946. With the Butler Education Act of 1944 and the introduction of Family Allowances in 1945, the chief elements of the 'Welfare State' were put in place in the last years of the war.[30]

But these schemes, dramatic as they seemed, fell somewhat short of the comprehensive social planning dreamt of by some to eliminate social evils. Crucially, they awaited implementation until after the war was won, when their plans would be vulnerable to the necessities of the moment. In itself the Beveridge structure rested on a set of assumptions about employment and family allowances which could not be planned for and might easily have proved disastrously misplaced. As an example, when Family Allowances were finally accepted by the Treasury it was partly to avoid the risk of wartime inflation through wage rises and the more expensive – and some would have said more efficacious – solution of a minimum wage. As it was, the Treasury set rates lower than Beveridge thought necessary to solve family poverty.[31] Very quickly, by the early 1950s, the idea that a true 'Welfare State' had been created and that it offered an effective means of solving social inequalities was being criticised by the likes of Richard Titmuss. Titmuss, like other contemporaries, wrote in the context of an awareness that poverty and other social problems had not been eliminated. For example, it was apparent that the belief that with the establishment of a comprehensive system of National Insurance fewer and fewer people would need the 'safety net' of National Assistance was being proved false, with over a million allowances being paid out weekly in 1949. Similarly, the 'rediscovery of poverty' through studies conducted by people such as Brian Abel-Smith and Peter Townsend revealed hundreds of thousands living at or below the standard of income recommended by the National Assistance scales and a continuing increase in the numbers claiming National Assistance benefits.[32] Concern too with low pay, one-parent families, the elderly, and inadequate housing – often backed by new post-war pressure groups – implicitly cast doubt upon the magnitude and wisdom of the 'welfare revolution' achieved in the 1940s. Titmuss was one who called into question the effectiveness of the legislation achieved in the creation of the Welfare State. He called for a more critical approach, one which recognised the failures and shortcomings of what had been achieved, an accurate assessment of the intentions of policy-makers and legislators, and proper consideration of alternatives which might have been adopted.[33]

Above all, however, it was perhaps in the field of economic planning that the failure of the planning movement to fulfil its ambition is most clear. Paul Addison has argued that the character of the 'Attlee consensus' was one which fell far short of full-blooded planning of a totalitarian kind:

In general, the reform programme originated in the thought of the upper middle class of socially concerned professional people, of whom Beveridge and Keynes were the patron saints. To render capitalism more humane and efficient was the principal aim of the professional expert. In World War II the humane technocrat provided a patriotic compromise between Socialism and Conservatism which virtually satisfied the desire of the Labour Party for social amelioration, without in any way attacking the roots of exploitation and injustice.[34]

Another writer has argued that, apart from the period of financial crisis in the immediate aftermath of the war, government control amounted to little more than the application of Keynesian nostrums and wartime controls rather than the application of thoroughgoing plans for the reconstruction of industry.[35] The central feature of Labour's economic plans was nationalisation, and of a particular kind, through the public corporation, which changed ownership but neither management nor control. The nationalisation programme was soon to be regarded as failing to tackle many of the country's more fundamental economic problems, such as the still heavy reliance of the old industrial areas upon a narrow range of traditional industries – a reliance, if anything, re-emphasised by the needs of war – and the chronic problems of poor management, the commercial application of new technology, and industrial relations. 'Planning' in this context was more apparent than real. Critically, the proposal put forward by Keynes and others in the inter-war years for an 'Economic General Staff' responsible for planning policy was never implemented. Although attempts to inject a more strategic element into economic management were made in the aftermath of the fuel crisis of 1947, in practice they went little further than attempts at greater co-ordination. [36] Another generation of Labour leaders, in the 1960s, were still left to search for the Holy Grail of economic planning. Richard Crossman, for one, in 1965 lamented, 'How much more humane and imaginative our post-war reconstruction would have proved if government departments had been invigorated by an influx of experts with special knowledge, new ideas and a sympathy for the Government's domestic and foreign policies'. [37] George Brown's National Plan of 1965 represented a belated attempt to recapture the ground perceived to have been lost since the war ended.

These and even later attempts to resurrect 'planning', especially economic planning, raise the basic difficulty in seeing the Second World War as the planners' triumph. Viewed in perspective, the planning enthusiasm of the 1930s and 1940s represented the fusion of still vital forces of optimism and social idealism with the scientific and technocratic spirit of the twentieth century. Characterised by its faith in 'experts' and a certain high-mindedness, 'planning' offered an attractive vogue word for a host of widely differing objectives and impulses. As post-war critics of both social and economic policy were to indicate, strategic planning with clear long-term goals and the machinery to implement them was rarely to be found. In a post-war climate where nationalisation was the key component in the economic sphere, and reorganisation and rationalisation of what already existed the most characteristic feature of social policy, 'planning' failed to dislodge the established administrative systems or to overcome the temptation to make do with *ad hoc* measures. Both features – a faith in traditional institutions and short-term solutions to particular problems – were to remain characteristic features of public policy well into the post-war era.

Notes

1 *Picture Post*, 4 January 1941, p. 4.
2 *ibid.*
3 See P. Addison, *The Road to 1945: British Politics and the Second World War*, London, 1975, ch. X.
4 B. S. Rowntree, *The Human Needs of Labour*, London, 1918, pp. 9–10.
5 For the link between wartime housing schemes and post-war housing policy

see M. Swenarton, *Homes for Heroes: the Politics and Architecture of early State Housing in Britain*, London, 1981.

6   *P.P.*, 1919, Cmd 165, p. 3; cited in A. Marwick, *The Deluge: British Society and the First World War*, London, 1965, p. 262.

7   W. H. Beveridge, *The Public Service in War and Peace*, London, 1920, p. 5, cited in J. Harris, *William Beveridge: a Biography*, Oxford, 1977, pp. 200–1; see also pp. 258–62.

8   R. Barker, *Political Ideas in Modern Britain*, London, 1978, p. 49.

9   For a sample of the social enquiries of the interwar years see J. Stevenson (ed.), *Social Conditions in Britain between the Wars*, London, 1977.

10   M. Muggeridge, *The Thirties*, London, 1971, pp. 253–6.

11   See J. Macnicol, *The Movement for Family Allowances, 1918–45: a Study in Social Policy Development*, London, 1980, especially pp. 16–37.

12   H. Macmillan, *Reconstruction*, London, 1933, p. 18.

13   A. Calder, *The People's War: Britain, 1939–45*, London, 1969, pp. 33–4.

14   M. Nicholson, 'P.E.P. through the 1930s: growth, thinking, performance', in J. Pinder (ed.), *Fifty Years of Political and Economic Planning: Looking Forward, 1931–1981*, London, 1981, pp. 51–2.

15   For a brief statement see G. D. H. and M. I. Cole, *The Condition of Britain*, London, 1937, pp. 382–6, and more fully, G. D. H. Cole, *Principles of Economic Planning*, London, 1935.

16   See M. Nicholson, 'The Proposal for a National Plan', in Pinder (ed.), *op. cit.*, pp. 5–8.

17   See Addison, *op. cit.*, especially ch. IV.

18   M. Young, 'The Second World War', in Pinder (ed.), *op. cit.*, pp. 81–92.

19   Cited in A. Marwick, *Britain in the Century of Total War: War, Peace and Social Change, 1900–1967*, London, 1968, pp. 304–5.

20   W. H. Beveridge, *The Pillars of Security*, New York, 1943, p. 108.

21   See J. B. Cullingworth, *Town and Country Planning in England and Wales: an Introduction*, rev. edn, London, 1967, pp. 23–31.

22   Addison, *op. cit.*, pp. 175–7.

23   *Ibid.*, pp. 175–6, 178; J. B. Cullingworth, *op. cit.*, pp. 29–31.

24   K. Richardson, *Twentieth Century Coventry*, Coventry, 1972, pp. 281–90.

25   Cullingworth, *op. cit.*, p. 227.

26   *Ibid.*, pp. 30, 142–3, 157–8, 166–76.

27   *Social Insurance and Allied Services*, report by Sir William Beveridge, Cmd 6404, 1942, p. 170.

28   *Ibid.*, p. 172.

29   See Harris, *op. cit.*, pp. 244–6; Addison, *op. cit.*, pp. 213–28.

30   Marwick, *Britain in the Age of Total War*, *op. cit.*, pp. 315–23.

31   Macnicol, *op. cit.*, pp. 186–94.

32   See R. Titmuss, *Problems of Social Policy*, London, 1950, and PEP, *Planning, XIX*, 1952; P. Townsend, 'The meaning of poverty', *British Journal of Sociology*, XIII, 1962; B. Abel-Smith and P. Townsend, *The Poor and the Poorest*, London, 1965.

33   Marwick, *Britain in the Century of Total War*, *op. cit.*, pp. 433–4: R. M. Titmuss, *Essays on 'The Welfare State'*, London, 1958.

34   Addison, *op. cit.*, p. 277.

35   H. Eckstein, *The English National Health Service*, Cambridge, Mass., 1960, pp. ix-x.

36   Marwick, *Britain in the Century of Total War, op. cit.*, pp. 336–43.

37   R. Crossman, 'The lessons of 1945', in P. Anderson *et al.*, *Towards Socialism*, London, 1965, p. 155.

Rory MacLeod

The promise of full employment

Introduction

The fortunes of wartime Britain were at a low ebb in July 1941. Every one of the European allies by whose side she had fought against Nazi Germany for the previous two years was now defeated and occupied. Her latest ally, Soviet Russia, was reeling under Hitler's onslaught and it was widely expected she could not last out the year. In the Middle East, Rommel was inflicting defeat after defeat on the Eighth Army. Final victory over Germany appeared a long way off. And even if victory were achieved, what would be the state of the country after the war? In particular, what would be the job prospects for the men who would be demobilised? In the short term many had been promised their old jobs back, but there was much gloom about the longer term. Mass-Observation, the pioneering surveyors of public opinion, recorded in July that 'a large proportion [of the public] clearly feel that post-war unemployment; (a) *will* occur, (b) *is avoidable*. That is to say, they expect it but think it will be due to government and other errors'.[1]

What made people feel mass unemployment after the war was inevitable? It was very probably the memory of what had happened after the previous war. Demobilisation was muddled and the government made no attempt to help returning servicemen resume their former employment. The result was a lot of unemployment and bitterness among the ex-soldiers.[2] Economic controls were lifted as quickly as possible. There was a short restocking boom which was followed by a slump. In 1921 unemployment averaged nearly 14%, and it obstinately refused to clear up throughout the decade. When a change finally did occur in 1929 it was for the worse. Unemployment rose from a level of about 10% (which had been maintained throughout most of the '20s) to a high of 23% in 1932. The recovery was slow and by 1937 the rate was still at 9%.[3] By 1941, then, people looked back across two decades of mass unemployment to the end of the previous war, and by and large they assumed the same thing would happen again.

Yet, as Mass-Observation reported, there was a feeling that matters could be handled differently. The preparations for war had boosted employment, and there were no dole queues by July 1941. As the war went on, the feeling grew that unemployment was a preventable evil. The phrase 'full employment' became popular. It was often used simply to mean a situation better than had prevailed before the war and it had a powerful if vague appeal. In the Beveridge report an average unemployment rate of 8½% was mentioned, but as optimism grew figures as low as 3% came to be used. Although many people had no clear idea of what level of employment was 'full', none the less they felt it would not be the level of employment of the '20s or '30s. By 1944 public concern that there should be no repetition of the errors of that period resulted in a government commitment to pursue peacetime policies aimed at maintaining a high and stable level of employment.

In July 1941, however, the prevailing mood about post-war employment was pessimistic. Mass-Observation gives us a glimpse of this mood in that month of July, using a piece of reportage submitted by one of their investigators:

Investigator [to RAF service policeman in café]. You look all very well in that uniform now, but what chance will you stand after the war?'
M40C [i.e. male, forty, social class C]. Oh, he'll stand a fine chance – if he's musical. You know how it was in 1919? You're all right if you can play a musical instrument – one o' these one-string fiddles, Jew's harp, ham-bone, play the comb, or one o' these sewing-machines (gesticulates with his hands, pedals with his feet); you can stick up a board in front of you saying 'Ex-Service Man', 'Hero', put on a row of medals – an' you can go into any of these back streets and nobody'll stop you. Hundreds of soldiers doing it after the last war – and airmen. What you want to do is learn to play the organ.[4]

Thinking in Whitehall on full employment

The discussion about the service policeman's job prospects might have been more sanguine had it been known that civil servants in Whitehall were reading a provocative paper on full employment policy. The author was James Meade, a young economist working in the Cabinet Office.[5]

Before the war he had been an academic. When the war began the civil service was expanded to cope with a multitude of new tasks. In particular, economists and statisticians were needed to help formulate economic policy, not only in the departments but in the Cabinet Office as well. By January 1941 a Central Statistical Office was turning out regular reports on production figures, inflation, consumption and manpower resources. Churchill had S Branch, his own unit of economists and statisticians. But most important was the Economic Section of the War Cabinet Secretariat. It was this body to which Meade belonged.

Working for the Lord President's Committee, chaired by Sir John Anderson (which was described to Roosevelt as 'an Economic War Cabinet'), the Section was at the heart of economic policy-making.[6] It developed a close relationship with S Branch. Some of its members had moved in left-wing circles before the war and there was tension between them and the permanent civil servants.

The economists had considerable prestige inside the government, based on their success in wartime planning, particularly the counter-inflation policy. Keynes had published work during 1939–40 to show the size of the incipient wartime inflation problem. This work had two novelties. First, it used national income figures to show the size of the problem; secondly, its economic analysis was a genuinely dynamic one, showing clearly how the inflationary spiral was operating. Keynes suggested that a scheme of deferred pay, to be repaid to the workers after the war, would ease the problem. Repayment could be timed to smooth out the boom–slump cycle which was widely expected to follow the war.[7]

When Churchill became Prime Minister Keynes was invited into the Treasury, where he continued to press for some sort of deferred pay. Part of the inflationary gap was closed by the success of Bevin in getting the trade unions to follow a voluntary pay policy. Keynes and the economists in the Cabinet Office worked on estimating the size of the gap which remained to be closed, and the 1941 budget incorporated their approach. A smaller version of the deferred pay plan was adopted, but of equal importance was the use of national income statistics for the first time by any government as a guide to policy. This involved a wholly new emphasis upon the performance of the economy as a whole and an estimate of the effect of government policy upon it.[8]

By July 1941 the war economy was running smoothly and the economists turned their attention to post-war matters. In his paper Meade was concerned that the mistakes made after the last war should be avoided. He suggested that government controls on the economy be retained after the war to prevent the boom–slump pattern of the years after 1918 occurring again. He went on to argue that the key to avoiding mass unemployment was regulation of the level of effective demand for goods and services within the economy. The government should plan its own spending ahead to even out the booms and slumps of the coming peacetime years, and should also act to control the volume of private demand. This could be done in several ways – taxation policy, consumer credits, direct regulation of investment – directed to the one end of stabilising demand. If this was not enough, then the government should consider a policy of deficit finance, permanent if necessary, to increase demand and provide jobs. Meade was in fact suggesting that remedies for unemployment proposed by Keynes and others before the war should be adopted, and he drew upon the experience of running the wartime economy to suggest how these policies could be made to work.

Although there was widespread concern about employment prospects after the war, there was little domestic pressure on the government to consider this, or indeed other post-war plans, before the publication of the Beveridge report at the end of 1942. Meade's paper would not on its own have caused more than a few small ripples in the higher echelons of the civil service. The pledges about post-war economic policy which were extracted from the government before Beveridge were due to the United States and the importance it attached to statements of economic war aims, which were incorporated in the Atlantic Charter and the Mutual Aid Agreement between the two countries.

The Americans wanted a world-wide system of free trade. Roosevelt's advisers believed the collapse of international trade between the wars had made unemployment worse and encouraged the rise of Fascism. The Atlantic Charter signed by Churchill and Roosevelt in August 1941 called for action to give 'all states access, on equal terms, to the trade and to the raw materials of the world which are needed for their economic prosperity'. British public opinion welcomed the Charter but for the government it involved repudiating the policies of protection and imperial preference, adopted in the depths of the world depression.

Furthermore, the Charter implied that the two greatest trading nations of the world should take domestic action to expand their demand, for the international expansion of trade which the Americans wanted to see after the war would necessarily be the sum of many domestic expansions. The discussions over the Mutual Aid Agreement in early 1942 fully recognised the importance of full employment. The agreement noted that there must be 'agreed action . . . directed to the expansion, by appropriate international and domestic measures, of production, employment, and the exchange of goods'.[9]

Whitehall set to work on the implications of the Charter for post-war economic policy, but senior Ministers had no time to spare and the series of politicians who assumed responsibility for post-war planning had little weight in Cabinet. The work done at this time did, however, serve to educate the permanent officials in the new approach to economic policy. The Treasury in particular came to the view that the influence of the economists in the Cabinet Office on post-war planning was unhealthy.

Work had been done in the Treasury before the war on the introduction of a counter-cyclical element into public spending to help stabilise employment.[10] But it was a long step from this to Meade's contention that the government could by its adjustment of demand raise the level of employment permanently. The Treasury's official head from 1942 to 1945, Sir Richard Hopkins, was in favour of giving consideration to Meade's ideas but some of his subordinates were worried about the implications of managing demand to achieve full employment. They circulated to the officials working on post-war plans a paper designed to refute the Section's approach.[11]

It was written by Sir Hubert Henderson, an Oxford don recruited into the Treasury at the start of the war. He was pessimistic about Britain's economic prospects and felt that a free-trade policy would leave her at the mercy of economic storms like that of 1931. If full employment were to be achieved the economy would suck in imports and exports would be diverted to the domestic market. This would lead to a balance of payments crisis and devaluation, coupled with domestic inflation as wages were bid up by employers' demand for labour. He felt the major risk after the war was not unemployment but inflation caused by shortages of goods. The government should be devoting more time to considering how the wartime counter-inflation policy could be continued in peacetime.

As Keynes pointed out, the Treasury's opposition to planning for post-war full employment was a lost cause, because when post-war plans came under the political spotlight the Labour members of the government would undoubtedly press for an expansionist policy.[12] The Treasury was under a cloud from 1940 to 1943. This was partly because Sir Horace Wilson, a close adviser of Chamberlain and greatly disliked by Churchill and the Labour Party, remained its official head until 1942. In part it was due to the association of the Treasury with the economic policy of Baldwin and Chamberlain, men now discredited as appeasers. The

Treasury was consulted less about economic matters, and its place in servicing the relevant Cabinet committees was taken by the Economic Section. To some extent this was natural, for, as economic mobilisation became total, finance took a back seat to the direct controls over labour and materials.

It took some three years of war before the political spotlight began to play on employment plans. After the fall of France in June 1940 there was little time to think about the shape of the post-war world. Wartime opinion surveys showed consistently, however, that unemployment remained a matter of concern. For instance, an opinion poll taken in September 1941 indicated that 44% of the sample felt a return to mass unemployment inevitable. But from 1941 onwards there was a gradual increase in optimism. By September 1943 (when Italy surrendered) the proportion of people who felt mass unemployment was inevitable had fallen to 19%.[13]

The public's ideas for providing full employment were coloured by the success of wartime planning, but they remained largely the notions of the years before the war, as Table 1, compiled immediately following the publication of the Beveridge report in December 1942, shows: a public works programme was mentioned four times as frequently as socialism, which was less popular than solutions based on reducing the amount of work to be done by individuals, and in the number wanting work. A continuation of wartime industrial conscription was a popular choice.

Table 1 Suggested methods of dealing with unemployment (most frequently mentioned suggestion = 100)

Public works	100
Control, plan, nationalise some things	61
International solutions	46
Slow demobilisation	43
Conscription into industry	41
Shorter hours	41
New system	32
Reduce numbers employed	29
Socialism	25

Source. Mass-Observation, *Bulletin*, December 1942, p. 10.

The Beveridge report brought the topic of full employment into public prominence. The coalition had to agree in principle to the report, announcing its determination to implement the report's assumption that mass unemployment must be prevented. Beveridge argued that this assumption was necessary, for otherwise there would be no effective test of a willingness to work. Also, the social insurance scheme would cost more if there was a high level of unemployment. A member of the Section was secretary to Beveridge's committee and the Section suggested several devices to alter the volume of effective demand. For instance, a scheme (devised by Meade) to alter social insurance contributions according to the state of the economy, so they rose in a boom and fell in a slump, thus helping to stabilise purchasing power, was mentioned to Beveridge. [14]

Conservative Ministers were supported by the Treasury in arguing that no commitment should be made to implementing the Beveridge report. Churchill was initially against promising post-war reforms, but his adviser Lord Cherwell, who was in touch with the Section, persuaded him it was impracticable to reject Beveridge. In March 1943 the Prime Minister broadcast on the theme of a Four Year Plan for peace, and announced the government's intention to plan to prevent the return of mass unemployment after the war. He indicated this would be done by a public works policy which 'would have a balancing effect on development and can be turned on and off as circumstances require'. [15] Nonetheless the Conservatives' opposition to Beveridge disillusioned many people who felt they could not be trusted to implement the report, regardless of any promises they might make.

Labour Ministers were eager to press ahead with plans for the peace, and Dalton told the Commons that he looked forward to a full employment target which would be considerably below Beveridge's $8\frac{1}{2}\%$. [16] More pressure was put on the government when Beveridge, disappointed in his hopes of conducting an official enquiry into full employment, set up his own private investigation. It would have been embarrassing if Beveridge were to come out with another popular report. There was now a deadline to discussions about full employment – the government had to come forward with a policy before Beveridge.

The first step they took was to estimate figures for national income after the war, so that the scale of spending necessary to raise employment could be estimated. The Section took over this work from the Treasury (who had made some embarrassing errors in their calculation) and submitted detailed proposals for post-war full employment to a Cabinet committee chaired by Anderson in May 1943.[17]

The proposals were similar to those in Meade's paper of July 1941. They suggested a public investment programme which could be planned ahead to counteract the fall in private investment during a slump. The budget need not be balanced every year but should be balanced over the trade cycle, with surpluses in booms and deficits in slumps. The volume of consumption should be adjusted by altering taxes and social insurance contributions, raising them to dampen down a boom and cutting them at the beginning of a depression. The Section went a long step further than this, however. They suggested that if a policy of balancing a budget over the trade cycle still resulted in unacceptable high unemployment, then a permanent policy of deficit finance would be called for to provide extra jobs. In other words the State should, if necessary, permanently provide jobs and accept a continuing increase in the national debt.

Sir Kingsley Wood, the Chancellor of the Exchequer, who sat on the committee, wanted this paper shelved, but his view was rejected. The Treasury prepared a response which concentrated on the difficulty of translating economic theory into practice, and on the political implications of the economists' suggestions. For instance, what level of full employment should the government aim at, and what level of spending would be required to achieve it? What period was to be taken as the 'trade cycle' over which government spending would balance? The Treasury felt strongly that changes in taxation for purposes of stabilising employment would immediately become a political football. Governments would find it easy to cut taxes and unbalance the budget when unemployment was rising, but there would be a lot of resistance to raising taxes to create a surplus of revenue when prosperous times returned. The optimism of the Section's paper, summed up in its conclusion that 'we are finally coming to understand the governing tendencies of the economic mechanism', was rejected by the Treasury, who felt it was 'academic and dangerous'.[18]

Meanwhile Bevin, the Minister of Labour, was involved in talks with Churchill on continuing the coalition after the war. He wanted to take responsibility for employment policy. Bevin remembered the mistakes of the years after 1918 when, he felt, the returning soldiers had been cheated of the social and economic reforms they had a right to expect. He suggested that the peacetime Ministry of Labour should assume responsibility for co-ordinating the implementation of a full employment policy.[19]

The discussions encompassed the minimum programme for such a peacetime coalition. Cherwell argued to Churchill that what he termed plans for social betterment, among which was a full employment policy, were non-political and should be part of an agreed programme. In any event, Cherwell felt, it would be politically unwise to suspend work on full employment, given the public interest and the fact that Beveridge was working on his own report. Churchill agreed and decided that, regardless of the outcome of the talks about continuing the coalition into peacetime, 'any decisions which are needed for the supreme objects of FOOD and EMPLOYMENT in the years immediately after the war must be taken whether they involve legislation and whether they are controversial or not'.[20] Talks on a post-war coalition concluded indecisively, but the Prime Minister had called for progress to be made on plans for full employment.

Meanwhile work on full employment policy had been handed down by the politicians to a committee of officials. Given the divisions between Labour and Conservative and the unresolved question of which Whitehall department should have responsibility for the policy, this was a predictable response. The committee was chaired by Hopkins, the senior Treasury official most sympathetic to Keynesian ideas, and he used his power to amend, but not fundamentally to alter, the approach of the Section to achieving full employment. That battle had been fought and won over the Beveridge report.

Before Hopkins's committee could meet Wood died and was replaced as Chancellor by Anderson. This weakened the Section's influence at a crucial time and correspondingly strengthened the hand of the Treasury. Attlee took over Anderson's job but the Section had less influence under him. The Treasury now enjoyed the advantage of a strong Chancellor, respected throughout Whitehall as Wood had not been. Why did Anderson seek the Exchequer? Churchill had already earmarked Lyttleton for the job. Part of the reason may have been his desire to strengthen the Treasury's hand in discussions about economic policy, particularly given Bevin's desire to move responsibility for full employment policy to the Ministry of Labour. If so, he was successful. The renaissance of the Treasury may be dated from his appointment in September 1943.

When the committee met Hopkins resisted the Section's attempts to get a new definition of full employment of 2½% unemployed, preferring to stick to Beveridge's 8½%. He was in favour of a counter-cyclical public investment programme to even out booms and slumps and, like Keynes, he supported Meade's scheme for varying social insurance contributions, but he was wary of wider plans for altering taxation to influence demand.

Those in the Treasury who had tried to stop consideration of demand management attacked again.[21] The thrust of their argument continued to be on the political implications. They did not deny that the fundamental cure of the trade cycle was to stabilise demand, but they felt that the remedies suggested by the economists would be difficult to implement and would have undesirable side effects. Politicians would be tempted to unbalance the budget and raise public spending by borrowing money, citing Keynesian doctrine to provide intellectual justification for a populist move. The public would become used to high employment financed by permanent deficits and would object to any attempt to cut the deficit by raising taxes. Inflation would quickly result, and there would be a collapse in business confidence. This would result in a countervailing fall in private investment as public spending rose. The Treasury of 1943 was not skilled at arguing about economic theory or the details of national income statistics, but they felt that the new economic approach ignored practical problems which they, rather than the academic economists, were best qualified to judge.

The committee's report was a compromise.[22] The Treasury accepted that a five-year programme of public investment should be planned, and that if it failed to prove adequate to secure full employment, then changes in taxes to encourage private investment and consumption should be made, but the question of budget deficits remained a bone of contention and was fudged in the report. It was concluded that the net effect of all the plans outlined would be to affect employment by not more than 10%. Since unemployment had risen as high as 23% between the wars the committee did not satisfy everybody who was involved in the full employment discussions.

The question of whether inflation would result from demand management was not seriously tackled. There were two reasons. The first was that the informal wages policy arranged by Bevin had been successful in stemming wartime inflation, and it was assumed this could be continued in peacetime. The second was that the economists were complacent about the problem. Inflation would have some good effects, they felt; it would impoverish the *rentiers*, reduce the burden of the national debt (as it had done in France after World War I) and transfer purchasing power to successful new businessmen and workers. The report concluded, 'we should be very foolish to argue that the economic system would not work if prices and incomes were behaving as they have behaved during some of the most prosperous epochs; that is to say, rising slowly'.

An important proposal was that the government should have an anti-trust policy to curb monopoly power in business. The question of the monopoly power of the trade unions however, was not tackled. It was hoped that the responsibility and sense of restraint they had displayed under Bevin's guidance would continue. Location of industry policy, for which Dalton was pressing strongly, was referred to in an aside but not discussed in any detail.

The report was necessarily a compromise, given the opposition to a powerful full employment policy. The Section, whose attention was anyway moving towards international measures co-ordinated with the Americans to promote trade, rested content with the general endorsement of the demand management approach. The Treasury was prepared to accept this provided there was no commitment to immediate action. The intellectual drive which had propelled the Section's plans for demand management up to senior politicians had fallen off, and full employment policy was coming to consist more of vague intentions than of concrete measures to assure the fulfilment of the promise already made to the public. Keynes thought it resembled a Gruyère cheese – holes without the surrounding cheese![23]

While the Hopkins committee was sitting Churchill upgraded the status of post-war planning by appointing Lord Woolton as Minister of Reconstruction. The aim of the discussion on full employment policy in his Cabinet committee was to put out a statement before Beveridge, and the politicians were prepared to slide over practical difficulties in implementing the policy – all that was required was a statement of principles.

It was now spring 1944 and Beveridge was reported to have his book ready for the printers. The government was running out of time. A White Paper on employment policy, based on the Hopkins report, was considered by the War Cabinet, and published on 19 May.[24] Its foreword contained the kernel of the policy: 'The Government accept as one of their prime aims and responsibilities the maintenance of a high and stable level of employment after the war.' Keynes thought this was worth the whole of the rest of the White Paper put together. Then came the inevitable qualifications – much depended on the state of international trade and on the efficient running of industry.

The approach used analysis of national income data to quantify the regulation of demand, and when the statement turned from discussion of the transition to a peacetime economy it became a standard exposition of Keynesian policy prescriptions as interpreted by the academic economists in Whitehall. The pre-conditions of mobility of resources and price–wage stability were set out, and within this framework the effects of altering demand were explained. The main tool of policy was to be public spending, but work in Whitehall on schemes for the regulation of private investment and consumption was to continue. The most developed of these, Meade's scheme for varying social insurance contributions, was given special prominence. The public were promised that it would be introduced after the war (it never was) and if successful would be followed by tax changes and other ideas such as tax credits to regulate demand.

As in the Hopkins report, the crucial issue of deficit finance was fudged, and it was stated that none of what was proposed would involve 'deliberate planning for a deficit in the National Budget in years of sub-normal trade activity'. The implication was that balance would be achieved over the trade cycle.

The White Paper was the first the public had heard of the discussions on full employment policy since the Beveridge report. It proposed not a planned economy in which the State would direct resources but a managed one where the State would influence the use of resources through its fiscal policy. Its analysis was straightforwardly Keynesian and in that sense was revolutionary, but its actual proposals were weak, reflecting the government's desire on the one hand to pre-empt Beveridge and on the other not to commit the coalition to detailed policies.

Within a month the Allies invaded France and public attention shifted to the fighting there. In Whitehall there was a falling-off of interest in full employment. The Section became engrossed in the preparations for Bretton Woods and the founding of the IMF, and the Labour politicians who had pressed for a declaration of post-war policy were getting ready to fight the next general election. Dalton did succeed in getting a Distribution of Industry Act passed before the election, but anti-trust policy made no progress (although the anti-trust ideas in the White Paper were enacted as the Monopolies and Restrictive Practices Act of 1948).

The White Paper promised that information would be gathered to help implement demand management, but no work was done until the autumn of 1945. The Treasury assumed departmental responsibility for full employment policy when Sir Edward Bridges succeeded Hopkins in early 1945. The Section continued in being but declined in importance after the war when many of its members returned to academic life, and it was eventually absorbed into the Treasury.

Thinking outside Whitehall on full employment

The employment White Paper was published under a coalition dominated by Conservatives and Labour, but it was not the result of discussion within each party, and although leading politicians on both sides endorsed its policy it would be wrong to say that it reflected the considered view of either party.

One Conservative pressure group was interested in the subject – the Tory Reform Group. It was set up at the time of the publication of the Beveridge report by a group of young MPs who had strong links with the forces. They sensed the change in political mood and were anxious that the Conservatives should not get out of step with the public. The Tory Reformers agreed with the Keynesian analysis of trade depression. They felt that after the war the government should take powers to control the volume of investment, and the resources of the economy should be centrally assessed and allocated with the aim of reaching and staying at full employment. Interests which might stand in the way of this programme, such as the Bank of England, would be nationalised. Their policy would involve vigorous anti-trust action.[25] However, they had little effect on the mainstream of Conservative thinking.

The party was looking at full employment and a committee reported on the question in January 1944. It accepted that public spending should be used counter-cyclically after the war, but private firms were merely to be exhorted to plan their spending to iron out booms and slumps, and there was no mention of the thorny question of anti-trust policy. Controls should be lifted as soon as possible after the war. The document left many questions unanswered and when it was not endorsed by any major party figure it slid into oblivion.

The party conference of March 1945 endorsed the policies outlined in the White Paper and called for the abandonment by industry and unions of restrictive practices. However, the electorate did not trust the Conservatives on full employment policy, and this feeling was confirmed by the aggressive anti-socialist tenor of the election campaign, when the rallying cry was for decontrol as quickly as possible.[26]

Just as many Conservatives were suspicious of the middle ground in domestic politics occupied by the coalition, so were many Labour Party activists. The Labour Ministers were educated in the language and concepts of Keynesian economics by the academic economists in the government. It seemed plausible that demand management could be continued in the longer term in peacetime, and it fitted in with many of Labour's goals. For instance, demand management might require that government spending should be held at a high level to keep the economy at full pressure, while Labour's plans also called for a high level of State spending. If, as seemed likely, one cause of unemployment was an excess of savings over investment, the equalisation of decisions to save and decisions to invest could be brought about by Labour's plans for progressive taxation which would redistribute income to the poorer sections of society. These would spend a larger proportion of their incomes and so net savings would be reduced. The need for a stable rate of investment to aid the planning of demand could be used to advocate the take-over of sections of the economy and the regulation of their spending. Finally, the Keynesian approach provided arguments for the Beveridge plan, which would among other things increase the worker's purchasing power in a depression.

However, the implications of the Keynesian approach to the economy were far-reaching. Labour advocated measures such as nationalisation to help run the economy more efficiently and provide full employment with prosperity. If the Keynesian approach were correct and demand management (and associated changes in public spending and tax policy) could equally well produce full employment and prosperity, then some of Labour's policies would become unnecessary on strictly economic grounds. For instance, nationalisation of basic industries could be advocated both from a Keynesian and a socialist viewpoint, but for a Keynesian it was not an initial step preparatory to full common ownership of the means of production, distribution and exchange, but a pragmatic move to enable the economy to be run more efficiently. There was here a latent tension, perhaps most fully apparent in the contrast between socialist demands for State corporations and the Keynesians' call for an anti-trust policy to oppose monopoly power.

Dalton interwove the two viewpoints in Labour's June 1944 statement on full employment (which he described as largely Keynesian with some socialist additions)[27] and Labour's 1945 election manifesto was more convincing on full employment than anything put out by the Conservatives. In the long run full employment was to be achieved through the overall control of purchasing power, and monopolies and cartels would be subject to State supervision to promote efficiency and an expansionist economic policy. The tension between Keynesian and socialist viewpoints remained latent.

The White Paper stated, '. . . employment cannot be created by Act of Parliament or Government action alone'. The government hoped that industry and the trade unions would co-operate in measures to achieve full employment in the context of an efficient and internationally competitive economy, but the response was not very encouraging. There was a consensus of sorts among businessmen and trade unionists, but it was a consensus for protection of the home market and statutory cartels to control output and prices.

There were businessmen who welcomed Keynesian ideas and accepted the popular wartime view that industry had strong social obligations. Samuel Courtauld, the textile industrialist, and his supporters warned that industrialists must come to terms with the new mood in favour of government intervention. The government had the right to control private investment in the interests of society, and Courtauld agreed with Beveridge that to surrender this freedom would not necessarily lead to the erosion of others.[28]

However, most businessmen looked forward to a speedy lifting of wartime controls. The post-war economic policy which they preferred was articulated by the Federation of British Industry (the predecessor of the CBI) in 1944.[29] It called for a strengthening of trade associations after the war, with statutory power to fix prices and output levels. These cartels would protect industry against any post-war slump, and in return industry would co-operate with government economic policy, though not to the point of accepting restrictions on profits or investment. Imperial preference and taxes to discourage imported goods should be maintained.

In fact businessmen wanted State assistance but they were not prepared to offer any real *quid pro quo* in the shape of control over their activities. Nationalisation and anti-trust policies were both rejected. Full employment was a desirable goal, but if the price of full employment was State restriction on the freedom of businessmen to order their own affairs, then that freedom must take priority even if mass unemployment was the result. They feared a post-war depression but wanted a return to pre-war policies.

This fear was shared by trade union leaders, who saw such things as restrictive practices (condemned in the White Paper) as a protection against unemployment. They feared that if there was another depression the unions would be left defenceless if they abandoned traditional practices which preserved jobs in the short term.

The TUC's plans for the part of the economy which it did not want to nationalise were far removed from the anti-trust policy which the coalition was considering. It too wanted statutory producer groups to protect jobs and profits. There were elements in its thinking, however, which were akin to the Keynesians' views. A national investment board should decide on the overall level of investment to preserve full employment, and deficit spending was advocated if it were necessary to prevent unemployment.

The TUC was not prepared to abandon its sectional interest if measures to secure full employment were thought to be contrary to the interests of the unions. It went to the extent of stating, '. . . the TUC could not at any stage commit itself in advance to approve or acquiesce in the methods to be adopted to reach full employment simply because those methods can be shown to be well fitted and even necessary to the achievement of that objective . . .'.[30] The unions and employers both wanted full employment, but on their own terms.

The conclusion must be that neither side of industry was prepared to give up the old ways of doing things to achieve full employment. Even the government's limited plans for post-war intervention aroused their opposition and they were far more opposed to the far-reaching controls advocated by Beveridge.

The popular success of his report had made Beveridge's a household name. Assumption C, 'the maintenance of employment and the prevention of mass unemployment', was the third of the Assumptions in his report. A low level of unemployment would certainly make the finance of the social security scheme less perilous but there had been no organised lobbying for a full employment policy. Beveridge had some contact with the Section, but it was not the Keynesians who changed Beveridge's mind about the practicability of providing full employment in time of peace.

It was the war itself which convinced him that economic planning by the State was necessary to prevent a return to mass unemployment. His views on the kind of action which would be needed changed as he was educated in Keynesian economics after 1942. His initial prescription was a cure based on State control of production and on detailed planning of labour. Later he placed more emphasis on the indirect regulation of demand by State spending and tax policy, although his ideas still incorporated a detailed interventionist role for the State.[31]

In autumn 1943 he presented a paper at one of the Nuffield conferences organised by G. D. H. Cole to discuss post-war prospects.[32] He was convinced that full employment could be achieved without requiring all the measures of State intervention which a year before (at a previous conference) he had argued were essential. The economists advising Beveridge had converted him to their own views, which Beveridge described as 'the socialisation of demand'. The State should continue the control of interest rates, and to this should be added alterations in taxation, and policies to redistribute income in order to raise purchasing power and cut savings. Private investment should be supplemented by State spending to ensure full employment of resources. Nationalisation plans were tentative and not in the forefront of his measures to keep full employment.

The main influence on Beveridge's thinking on full employment policy came from Kaldor and his exposition of alternative fiscal policies.[33] He set out several routes by which the government could raise employment. Some would involve deficit finance and an unbalanced budget; some would not. Some routes would mean that the State's share of total expenditure would rise; some would not.

Using the information provided by the White Papers on National Income and Expenditure begun in 1941, Kaldor showed how each route to full employment would have worked before the war. He demonstrated that a rise in State spending unaccompanied by an increase in taxes would have stimulated the economy towards full employment with the smallest change. The fact that he could provide a series of alternative policies to achieve full employment led Beveridge to claim that he had avoided the controversy between socialism and capitalism as the only ways of operating a modern economy. The desired levels of consumption and public and private investment would be achieved by taxation, increased State spending and the licensing of all private investment projects. Unlike the employment White Paper, which concentrated on varying public investment to counterbalance changes in private investment and consumption, Beveridge wanted to regulate all three.

Beveridge became more sanguine about the level of full employment which could be achieved at the same time as he proposed less control by the government over the economy. In December 1942 the Beveridge report considered that if not more than 8½% of workers could not obtain jobs, this might be an acceptable level of post-war employment. In the same month he told a Nuffield conference that his proposals should ensure that only 6% of the workforce were unemployed. In his book he played with various figures – unemployment equal to vacancies, vacancies greater than the number of unemployed – and settled for 3%

unemployment (1% frictional, 1% seasonal and 1% for the unavoidable variations in foreign demand for British goods). [34]

As we have seen, Beveridge claimed that 'the socialisation of demand' approach to full employment by-passed the controversy about socialism versus capitalism. This was disingenuous, for the policy in practice would involve greater State intervention, and Beveridge certainly thought that the share of resources taken by the State would rise markedly. His team went further in hoping that only a quarter of total investment would remain in private hands. The programme Beveridge put forward in his book was in fact fundamentally radical. It was published at the end of 1944 and had far less political impact than his report. The government had published the employment White Paper, and the war was drawing to a close.

Conclusion

The conventional explanation of the coalition's commitment to provide 'a high and stable level of employment after the war' is that men in positions of power were convinced the aim could be achieved by a policy of managing effective demand, as advocated by Keynes and his supporters. The publication of the General Theory before the war was part of Keynes's campaign to persuade his fellow economists that his proposition – that the trade cycle could be ironed out by the government adjusting the volume of demand in the economy – was correct. When economists took up positions in government during the war, the theory goes, they acted as missionaries, converting politicians and civil servants alike to Keynesianism. [35]

This view, which asserts the seminal role of ideas in history, derives from Keynes himself. It is clearly attractive to those whose sense of professional worth is linked to a belief that ideas are important in determining events. And in this case there is some evidence to support it. Economists were recruited into Whitehall in large numbers. They did exercise great influence. Some of their ideas were shown to work; the counter-inflation programme (or at least that part of it which closed the inflationary gap from the fiscal end) was worked out by them and was a successful contrast to the experience of World War I. Yet by itself the explanation is inadequate. Other ideas which circulated before the war, and which were adopted as policies during the war, did not gain acceptance as post-war aims – a national food and dietary policy for instance, or the State production of cheap, well made, utility goods.

Equally important in explaining the full employment promise is the public mood of economic and social radicalism which characterised Britain during the war years. Every commentator of the period remarked upon it and many explanations were offered – the rationing of goods, which involved equality of sacrifice; the evacuation of the towns, which showed the middle class the relative deprivation of youngsters in the working-class urban areas; and so forth. The war changed national life and individual ways of living, and so in a general sense it struck at the very roots of conservatism. However, this explanation cannot be directly linked with the popular pressure for a post-war full employment policy. There were two crucial links in the process.

The first was the experience of what had happened after World War I. The government's retreat from many areas of economic life had been followed by a prolonged depression. There is nothing like the existence of a disastrous parallel for concentrating attention on alternative courses of action. The ending of wartime controls over the economy when peace came was not a popular cry, whatever the Conservative Party and business interests may have thought.

The second was the rhythm of the war itself, which gave time for the detailed discussion of post-war policy. The importance of the pattern of military events cannot be underestimated. World War I had been a desperate see-saw battle up till its closing days. World War II was very different. After the battles of Midway, El Alamein and Stalingrad it was apparent that, to paraphrase Churchill, the ring was closing round the Axis and there could be only one outcome. Britain's armed forces were not fully committed to the struggle until after D Day, and it is this gap in time between the turn of fortune and the invasion of Europe that saw the most intense interest in post-war planning and, in particular, full employment policy. After June 1944 public interest was concentrated on the battlefront in France. Hence in part at least the lack of interest in Beveridge's plans for full employment, which were published at the end of 1944.

It is therefore incorrect to attribute all the credit for the promise of full employment to the conversion of men of power and influence to Keynesian ideas. Equally it is inadequate to say the promise was given solely as a response to the political pressure of wartime radicalism. Full employment would never have occupied the attention of the government to the extent it did had there not been pressure to give both a commitment and some explanation of how it would be honoured. On the other hand the unequivocal wording of the promise and the particular path of demand management which was to be followed were indeed due to a growing intellectual conviction at the centre of the government machine that full employment need not involve root-and-branch change in the economy and society.

The role of Churchill in the development of full employment policy is greater than has generally been supposed. It is true to say that he was almost exclusively concerned with military operations, and he spent much of his time in the latter stages of the war at a series of international conferences. The evidence is strong, however, that he put his weight behind a full employment policy. His advisers in S Branch provided an alternative source of economic advice to the permanent civil servants, and they were strong supporters of the Section's approach. Churchill's decision to set up S Branch and his support for the economists within the Cabinet Office stemmed from an enduring distrust of official advice on economic policy which can be dated back to his unhappy time at the Treasury in 1924–29, particularly his much criticised decision, taken on official advice, to return to the gold standard in 1925.

The concept of altering demand to remain at full employment was one he did not find it difficult to grasp. Several stories illustrate this. A typical example is his remarks at the Cabinet meeting which approved the employment White Paper, when he suggested that at the beginning of a slump the Cabinet should declare a 'Salute the stomach' week along the lines of the wartime 'Salute the soldier' weeks, but with the emphasis on spending rather than saving. He would hold a series of great banquets at No. 10 as an example to the nation to spend its way out of depression.[36]

At crucial moments Churchill swung his weight behind the Keynesian approach. Initially reluctant to tackle the area of post-war policy (doubtless with thoughts of Lloyd George's empty words of a quarter-century previously), when he did so he insisted on a full-blooded promise over the opposition of many in his party and administration.

Since the coalition broke up after the defeat of Germany there is no way of knowing how the policy outlined in the full employment promise of May 1944 might have been implemented without the profound changes in the role of the State in peacetime economic life introduced by the post-war Labour government. There is no knowing either whether the measures to prevent a depression would have worked in the years after the war, because the problems were inflation and a balance of payments deficit, just as the anti-Keynesians at the Treasury had predicted. The full employment promise was never tested in those years. It was given at a time of full employment and full employment persisted into the post-war world.

Another generation found the promise tested, and found it wanting. Between 1974 and 1976 the Labour government tried to operate a counter-cyclical policy to keep full employment in the face of the first world depression for forty years. That policy collapsed in the face of determined financial opposition to the growth of public-sector borrowing and a precipitous decline in the exchange rate. Both those obstacles had been foreseen by the anti-Keynesians at the Treasury thirty years before. The sterling crisis was a natural consequence of trying to maintain domestic demand without import controls; the investors' strike was due to unease about the social changes, including the effects of rapid inflation, which it was feared would result from the government's restoration of full employment.

The consensus on full employment lasted as long as measures to achieve full employment involved only marginal changes to society. When the necessary changes became radical the consensus disappeared. In this sense the wartime consensus was an illusion based on the extrapolation of wartime solidarity into peacetime and on the fact that all that was required was the maintenance of full employment, not its creation anew.[37]

Since that period government has retreated from the promise of full employment. Did the belief in the effectiveness of that promise affect Britain during the era of full employment? It is arguable that it did. The demand management policies by which it was to be achieved seemed to offer a progressive alternative to socialism by providing the economic background which would allow measures of social betterment to be carried out without socialist control of the economy. Thus it provided an underpinning for the social democratic viewpoint in political life. Next, the implication that full employment could be achieved by budget deficits encouraged the separation of decisions to spend from decisions to tax, and there has been a tendency for the former to grow faster than the latter. The notion that spending and taxation would be balanced over some notional trade cycle was never realistic politics.

The most interesting question of all can never be effectively answered. Was the uninterrupted growth and full employment of the '50s and '60s partly due to a belief (which can be traced back to World War II) that demand management would prevent mass unemployment if it ever showed signs of recurring? In retrospect it seems remarkable that economic policy should have paid lip service for so long to an untested hypothesis.

Notes

1 Mass-Observation Archive (University of Sussex), Work, employment, etc., topic collection, box 2.A. Mass-Observation Archive material is quoted with permission of the Trustees of the Mass-Observation Archive, University of Sussex.

2 A. Marwick, *The Deluge*, London, 1965, pp. 266–70.

3 H. W. Richardson, *Economic Recovery in Britain, 1932–39*, London, 1962, p. 86.

4 Mass-Observation Archive, box 2.A.

5 PRO, Cab. 87/54, IEP(41)3.

6 PRO, Prem. 4/94/5, 30 December 1940.

7 J. M. Keynes, *How to Pay for the War*, London, 1940.

8 D. N. Chester (ed.), *Lessons of the British War Economy*, Cambridge, 1951, pp. 83–101.

9 R. N. Gardner, *Sterling–Dollar Diplomacy*, Oxford, 1956, pp. 40–68.

10 G. C. Peden, *British Rearmament and the Treasury: 1932–1939*, Edinburgh, 1979, p. 90.

11 PRO, Cab. 87/54, IEP(42)21.

12 Henderson papers (Nuffield College, Oxford), Keynes–Henderson, 8 April, 15 April 1942.

13 Mass-Observation, *The Journey Home*, London, 1944, p. 44.

14 J. Harris, *William Beveridge*, Oxford, 1977, pp. 370–418.

15 P. Addison, *The Road to 1945*, London, 1975, pp. 223–8.

16 *Hansard*, 5th Ser., Commons Debates, 386/917–95.

17 PRO, Cab. 87/12, PR(43)26.

18 PRO, Cab. 87/12, PR(43)28; T161/S. 52098 Hopkins–Wood, 26 May 1943.

19 A. Bullock, *The Life and Times of Ernest Bevin*, II, London, 1967, p. 311; PRO, Cab. 123/229, Bevin–Anderson, 22 May 1943.

20 Cherwell papers (Nuffield College, Oxford), box 33, Cherwell–Churchill, 24 November 1943; PRO, Cab. 66/42, WP(43)465.

21 PRO, Cab. 87/63, EC(43)6.

22 PRO, Cab. 87/7, R(44)6.

23 PRO, T161/S. 52099, Eady–Brook, 22 April 1944.

24 HMSO, Cmd 6527, *Employment Policy*.

25 Tory Reform Group, *Full Employment and the Budget*, London, 1944.

26 Addison, *Road to 1945*, pp. 258–69.

27 H. Dalton, *The Fateful Years*, London, 1957, pp. 422–3.

28 S. Courtauld, *Ideals and Industry*, Cambridge, 1949, p. 3; Unilever, *The Problem of Unemployment*, London, 1943.

29 FBI, *The Organisation of British Industry*, London, 1944.

30 TUC, *Interim Report on Post-war Reconstruction*, London, 1944, pp. 29–30.

31 Harris, *Beveridge*, pp. 414–17.

32 Nuffield Conference Papers (Nuffield College, Oxford), 6th, 9th, 16th Conferences.

33 W. Beveridge, *Full Employment in a Free Society*, London, 1944, appendix C.

34 Beveridge, *Full Employment*, pp. 18–21.

35 This view underlies, for instance, D. Winch, *Economics and Policy*, London, 1972.

36 PRO, Cab. 65/42 WM(44), 60th meeting.

37 As pointed out in J. Tomlinson, *Problems of British Economic Policy, 1870–1945*, London, 1981, pp. 121–2.

Deborah Thom

The 1944 Education Act:
the 'art of the possible'?

R. A. Butler believed the Education Act that was introduced and passed during his tenure as President of the Board of Education was a major change, in the direction of making Britain educationally 'one nation, not two'.[1] In 1945 his leading civil servant, Sir Maurice Holmes, took a much less dramatic (and optimistic) view.

I take it that it was the clear intention of Parliament (certainly it's in line with my own inclination) that the net of secondary education should be cast more widely into the lower income scales; that class-distinction should be tempered and blurred throughout the educational field, and that merit – whatever that may be – should be the test, rather than money or social background, of a person's fitness to receive an expensive secondary education. It was not the intention, of course, that all of this should come to pass at one stroke, nor is it clear that it can ever wholly come to pass. Nevertheless, the goal is further 'democratisation' (is there a decent word for this?); whether the goal is a worthy one or not – this is of course arguable – we are bound to proceed towards it.[2]

How was it that secondary education for all, the organising impulse behind the 1944 Act, should have been interpreted in so restricted a way? Why did the manner of its interpretation mirror the existing grammar school education of 20% of twelve-year-olds rather than the needs of the rest, the majority? How much was changed by the Act? Arthur Marwick has argued that 'vested interests prepared to frustrate other social reforms accepted the need for educational reform'.[3] I want to argue that Holmes was right – that the Act created little that was new; it refined an existing, highly meritocratic system. Vested interests shaped the reform. This system was already elaborated in pre-war policy documents and substantially accepted by policy-makers.[4] The first years of war extended the pre-war system as constraints on expenditure were removed. They also ensured that local authorities would not, and could not, create new administrative systems for education in the post-war period. Wallace summarises the Act as:

no more than the embodiment of administrative arrangements which would give order to a confused system and some of which had been recommended and accepted as desirable during the previous two decades.[5]

In order to demonstrate this thesis I shall look at the changes in the examination filter that separated children at the age of eleven into different types of secondary education – the 'eleven-plus'. This, if anything, was an explicit embodiment of the notion of merit and that notion of educational distinction which Butler saw replacing class distinction. It was at the local level – where educational policy was put into organisational shape – that change actually took place. The change that occurred was mostly before the Act, either despite the war or hindered by war conditions. The educational aspects of social change can be assessed only by looking at the local education authorities. They administered education in conformity with the law and the controls on grants for special places but they had considerable autonomy within those constraints.

The pre-war situation

In 1938, when the Spens report elaborated the demands for reform which had been expressed throughout the interwar years, the educational system was clearly having undesirable social effects. Secondary education, mainly in schools now known as grammar schools, was available nationally for 20% of children over the age of eleven, with pronounced regional variations. In some areas technical and central schools also provided for children who stayed on beyond the leaving age of fourteen. The rest were educated from five until fourteen in elementary schools. Elementary schools were free and governed under one set of regulations. Secondary schools charged fees and were governed by another. Teachers in elementary schools were trained specifically to teach in them, secondary school teachers were mostly graduates and their wages and social standing were much higher than their elementary colleagues'. During the 1930s more and more areas allocated children to secondary education entirely by examination in which the places in secondary schools were 100% 'special places', in an attempt to widen the social range of secondary schooling. Fees were assessed by a means-tested scale, approved by central government, which meant that children of large, poor families paid none.

To win a special place a child had to demonstrate 'ability to profit' from secondary education.[6] Profit was measured broadly by success in the matriculation examination, the school certificate. Parents of children who qualified for secondary education signed an undertaking that the child would complete the course, and they could be fined if they failed to keep their word. Profit was also demonstrated by worldly success after school, since an elementary education was a major barrier if a young person wanted any job of middle-class status or rewards. The separation of children at eleven was a classification system that perpetuated social class division; it was also an educational typology. However poor, a child who passed the hurdle of the special place examination would get an education which would open up university or further training and, if not that, a white-collar, clean, respectable job – and in many cases an allowance to help with his or her maintenance. So the theory went, and the ideology of an education available to talent was sustained by new developments in psychometry which made the notion of ability one much easier to substantiate. The ideology of merit as the criterion of access to secondary education and its subsequent social and economic rewards was well entrenched by the time of the outbreak of war, as were the mechanics of separation into two distinct types of education.[7] Dr Gillian Sutherland's book *Ability, Merit and Measurement* has shown how testing in some ways preceded theoretical elaborations of the intelligence quotient – and how this was established by the time of the Spens report of 1938.

The ideology of merit in the inter-war years

The ideology of the educational system which had gained most ground by 1944 was the notion of merit. Godfrey Thomson, who had most effectively established intelligence tests as a means of identifying children with potential for a grammar school education through Moray House tests, saw his life's work as establishing equality of access to further education for all children. He had been most concerned with the inequality of provision between rural and urban areas which made tests of attainment a massive handicap for rural or impoverished urban children.[8] Tawney perceived the same problem throughout his career of commentary on the education system. His attempts to reform it were guided by the insights of close collaborators from within the educational system, in particular William Brockington, Chief Education Officer of Leicestershire, and Lady Simon, of the Manchester Education

Committee. Both had been involved in the discussion of policy of the Hadow report *On the Education of the Adolescent* of 1926 and the Spens report of 1938.[9] Both documents shared the same basic principles: education should divide at eleven; it should be free in both primary and secondary stages; and that the secondary stage should reflect the variety of abilities and aptitudes of the adolescent in institutional form. Tawney can be said to have both formulated Labour Party education policy by writing in 1922 the key document, *Secondary Education for All*, and to have reflected the demands of successive conferences for educational reform – particularly for the secondary age group. His writing both expressed and shaped the 'secondary education' that was demanded. Most 'educationists' subscribed to the same principle, although a few teachers in the National Association of Labour Teachers and the TUC had begun to look beyond 'equality of opportunity' to equality of provision.[10] There was a tension in Tawney's thought between the demands of the *exceptional*, the wasted talents of children denied access to secondary education by poverty and lack of provision, and the demands and needs of the *average*, who had no secondary education at all, but subsisted on the same educational diet throughout their school career. By the late 1930s the argument had swung emphatically towards the first of these two aspects of the idea.

Unless a society is to utilise only a fraction of the intelligence at its disposal it must obviously in one way or another make sufficient provision for vertical mobility to ensure that capacity passes, unimpeded by vulgar irrelevancies of class or income to the type of education fitted to develop it.[11]

Tawney wrote of the great waste of 'exceptional talent, which is sterilised for want of educational opportunities'. The biologised vocabulary of this description is part of the explanation for increased concern over wastage of talent.

Others shared this concern and used similar terms in the late 1930s. The work of the Social Biology Unit under Lancelot Hogben at the LSE (published mainly in *Political Arithmetic*) sustained a powerful, bleak argument based on both the presumed inexorable decline of population in Britain and the associated decline and waste of national intelligence.[12] Grace Leybourne buttressed such arguments in *Education and the Birth Rate* by demonstrating that the middle classes and the intelligent were paying for the high costs of education by family limitation at the dysgenic expense of the national interest.[13] Olive Maguiness argued that the scholarship system itself was dysgenic because of its effects on social mobility; she wrote that the bright members of the working class were removed from their environment, which encouraged fertility, and encouraged to defer child-bearing in favour of career.[14]

The effect of such formulations on those who enacted education policy is difficult to estimate. Individual authors could write on the decline of national intelligence but public debate did not necessarily lead to action. Pressure groups also raised the issue. The Eugenics Society, with about 800 fellows and members in 1938–39, was deeply concerned, and had moved to the left on the issue of educational reform as a result. J. B. S. Haldane argued in 1938, 'We may, I think, if the existing differences in fertility of social class continue, expect a slow decline of perhaps 1 or 2 per cent per generation in the mean intelligence quotient of the country'.[15] He was doing so in a book which, in the main, attacked eugenics.

The Titmusses quoted this gloomy conclusion in *Parents Revolt*. They argued that the dysgenic effects were not as great as this figure, since the difference in intelligence between social classes was not that great, but they accepted the logic of an argument based on differential fertility by social class.[16] Titmuss was funded by the Eugenics Society as Secretary of the Population Investigation Committee and was himself a leading member of the society. He can be seen as representative of the pre-war analysis of social problem in biological, hereditarian terms although he was firmly on the dominant environmentalist wing of the Eugenics Society itself.[17]

Local education officers and civil servants rarely used the biologised terms of debate common within the Eugenics Society or the wider, scientific community. They did, however, cite the arguments of those who did. The Labour Party and the Fabian Society both published pamphlets on educational reform which acknowledged this strand of thought while not totally accepting it. They referred to 'equality of opportunity' *tout court* or of the waste of talent.

The professional press, on the other hand, *was* specifically concerned with the question. The *British Journal of Educational Psychology* published an article on the negative correlation between fertility and intelligence by Gerald O'Hanlon in 1940 and an attack by Charlotte Fleming on the assumption that socio-economic level and intelligence were highly related in 1943.[18] *The Times Educational Supplement* reviewed Maguiness's book *Environment and Heredity* without querying the causal assumption that intelligence was mainly inherited.[19] Cyril Burt published in 1943 and 1944 his two most fraudulent pieces demonstrating a link between heredity and social class with intelligence as the major factor in the link. These pieces did not go unchallenged. The challenge was against the conclusion he drew – not against his hereditarian assumptions or his statistical expertise. Both appeared in the technical educational psychology press, which was read by some teachers; both were cited in the journals which were read by most teachers – the *TES* and the journal of the Association of Education Committees, *Education.* [20]

Such evidence is negative. Absence of comment does not equal approval. I would argue though that publication of such material when other writers could not get published is an indication of the bounds of the acceptable in public debate. [21] The question of the birth rate was to be more crucial in the years after the Education Act, in the debates around the Royal Commission on Population, which reported in 1948–49, but the existence of the commission itself from 1943 demonstrates public and official concern with such ideas in the first few years of the war. [22] The discussion of national intelligence and the psychologists' debates over it did not initiate the idea of a system of education specifically designed to foster talent, to prevent waste of intelligence as a national resource. That system had been intended for some time. But the discussion did give added weight to the demand for reform at a time when concepts of national interest were more frequently deployed – wartime.

Reform of 'special places' and equality of opportunity

Contemporaries all agreed that there must be radical change in the 'special place' examination. Tawney called it 'a barbarity', 'an abomination' and insisted that it should go. [23] Professor C. W. Valentine of Birmingham, when reviewing a study of the system in the West Riding of Yorkshire, talked of the undesirable backwash effect of the examination, and recommended an intelligence test instead because of its 'reliability and speed of marking'. [24] *The Times Educational Supplement* applauded the increased use of intelligence tests and deplored the existing exams: 'Some day our successors may come to marvel at the degree of assurance which leads us to think that ability to profit can be predicted thus.' [25] There was little public knowledge of the extent to which intelligence tests had already become part of the machinery of secondary selection by 1940, nor how far their use was tied in with that of standardised tests of attainment in English and arithmetic, which were provided, marked and correlated by the same person or organisation. English pragmatism had made it possible for many educational administrators to use an intelligence test in addition to examinations of attainment, as a refinement of their selection process. This proceeding ignored the current theory that intelligence was independent of social background. By 1940 at least sixty-eight local authorities were already using some sort of intelligence test; about half these also used standardised attainment tests. Some forty local authorities in England had used tests from Moray House, which was the main agency for group tests. It was headed by Professor Godfrey Thomson and already produced tests which correlated very highly with secondary school success. Moray House advocated using tests for selection, testing *all* children at eleven, and making adjustments for age and sex to achieve even-handed distribution of secondary school places.[26] The notion of a career freely open to all talents was thus considerably stimulated by the provision of a fair, visibly fair, method of allocation.

The demand to separate out tests of intelligence from tests of attainment was one based on a simple belief – that, in the words of Cyril Burt, 'By intelligence is meant inborn, general intellectual ability'.[27] The Mass-Observation reports of 1942 and 1944 indicate one group of well informed people who accepted this notion of intelligence. The panel of observers were asked their desires for educational reform. Their answers showed an 'unprecedented unanimity'.[28] Seventy-one per cent of respondents wrote and said that the change they would most like to see was 'equality of opportunity'. This was interpreted variously but making secondary education free, providing better facilities and raising the school leaving age were seen as the most obvious means to that end. They also saw the best means of placing children in secondary education as tests of ability, usually described as intelligence tests.[29] This belief in the capacity of intelligence tests to measure the entire child population was echoed by the rarer suggestion that educational psychologists should play a greater part in the allocation process.[30] Many quoted approvingly the popular metonymic slogan that 'the sons of duke and dustman should sit side by side',[31] demonstrating a romanticism about class relations very common in Reconstruction rhetoric. The intelligence test was seen as the direct means of overcoming class difference in access to schooling – although this remained a means of social reform, not reform itself.

The work of educational psychologists helped to ratify the use of tests, the technical solution, as a key component in educational reform, by altering the special place exam. In 1942 the Scottish Council for Research in Education published the conclusions of McClelland's study of selection procedures for secondary education. This survey demonstrated that the best single predictor was an intelligence test, but the best compound one was a battery of tests (the 'best' meaning, in this context, the method that correlated most directly with success in secondary school certificate exams). The survey was widely reviewed and accepted as authoritative. [32] It allayed doubts about the technique and its freedom from cultural determinants that were already being expressed. One correspondent to the *TES* wrote that what was being measured was too simple to determine a child's future. [33] The four NUT representatives who spoke to the Norwood committee in 1943 denounced tests; their executive committee demanded that their use 'should not result in children with the highest intelligence being allocated to any one type of secondary school'. [34] A few observers had already commented on the effectiveness of coaching for tests, a factor which was to lead to the first serious public disquiet over tests as measurement of innate, unalterable and asocial ability – although such comments were not yet thoroughly substantiated. [35] These technical, professional discussions had already shaped the direction of change before the Act was drafted, in and out of war. War conditions added to the general impetus for change but at the same time they also inhibited change.

War and evacuation, 1939–42

The immediate impact of war on the educational system was to expose the disparities of secondary provision between local authorities. Several London children who had been allocated to secondary education in a grammar or central school found, after they were evacuated, that they were denied it by the absence of such provision in their reception area. (The children of foreigners, particularly from 'enemy' countries, got a nasty response from some local authorities.) [36] Another disparity was the different levels of income used in means tests for 'special places'; parents could move house (as they were more likely to in war) and suddenly find themselves liable for greatly increased fees. Rising levels of income meant that some ungenerous authorities were taking fees from almost all parents of secondary school children. Surrey, for example, was described as 'not sufficiently generous' when it raised the income scale to allow for the rise in wages to match the cost of living. The official of the Board concerned, G. G. Williams, sounded almost regretful when he said, 'It is not our practice to interfere with an Authority's discretion when the scales are not over-generous in our opinion'. [37] It remained the case that the Board would not *encourage* more spending.

War also had a clear effect on the perceptions of the child population by professionals. In theory evacuation turned the child population over to the State – although, in practice, however much the *TES* called for it, government did not make evacuation compulsory. Evacuation, Cyril Burt argued, presented an 'opportunity for the teacher . . . A vast amount of information could be collected about the instinctive and emotional development of the normal child and its relation to his intellectual growth and interests'. [38]

In a sense the normal child was turned into a problem by the process of evacuation. Child society was thrown open to public scrutiny by the detachment of so many children from their family of birth. The effects of evacuation were perceived in terms of social pathology, so that although evacuation was pronounced less harmful than had been feared the effect of the analysis was to see the normal development of children as problematic, and to *emphasise* the compensatory role of agencies outside the family – school and its directing bodies in particular. [39] Paradoxically, though, schools themselves were not always treated carefully. The most extreme case was the school in Norfolk which was divided into twenty-three parts. Schools also found themselves expropriated by the ARP or other military or civil defence organisations. [40] Changes in the function of the school and the home encouraged the expansion of child guidance and thence the educational psychology profession. 'War put child guidance on the map', wrote Doris Wills – but it also put educational psychologists on the map, accentuated their claim to a permanent place in the education system as mediators between society and the educators. [41] At the same time war focused attention on schooling.

Changes occurred as a by-product of war emergency which greatly affected people's view of the secondary selection system. The first change was in the means test itself. Income levels rose, as did prices. Fixed scales for the rate at which fees would be paid excluded hardly anyone; as a result parents who were comparatively poor suddenly found themselves liable for fees. The local authorities tended to be more generous in their revision than the Board desired but most of the arrangements agreed showed that the authority usually got its way. [42] If it did not, it could always argue that many more children would be withdrawn from school altogether. Many authorities were making a conscious effort to expand the social group from which their secondary pupils were drawn. There continued, then, to be systematic efforts to standardise examination procedure, to apply it to the whole age group, and to make it more equitable.

The role of the inspectorate

The inspectorate, who came into most frequent contact with the diversities of local procedures, were consistently interested in 'modernising' the selection system, and in some ways they were the single group most responsible for altering local authority activities. Some of them obviously exceeded their duties in their zeal for examination improvement, as a memo of December 1942 makes clear:

These examinations are to be regarded as a domestic affair of the Local Education Authorities for the conduct of which no responsibility must rest upon Inspectors . . .

If an inspector was consulted

on the value of intelligence tests or of the reliability of certain statistical devices used in these examinations, there is no reason why he should not give his views, but he will no doubt make it clear how far the views are personal to himself. [43]

And, the memo went on, it was his duty to make representations about the conduct of the exam 'where that leaves something to be desired'. An example of such pressure involving an attempt to change an inequitable system that appears to bear no relation to wartime was on the Isle of Ely. Here its own Examination Board had recommended dropping dictation in the exam but the Education Committee 'missed the point' and persisted in keeping it. By 1941 the arguments of some of its own members and the increasingly acerbic comments of the inspectorate succeeded, and the committee abandoned dictation. It then accepted a new structure in which a minimum standard of English and arithmetic qualified a child to go on to an intelligence test to measure its 'capacity'. [44] The inspectors could encourage change but not enforce it – central bodies had no direct power over secondary selection.

Local authority initiatives

In the three years 1940–43 twenty-four local authorities are recorded in the press as altering their examination procedures. [45] Several more did so without informing the press, as their minutes show. Such alterations ranged from the introduction of record cards with 'unique' assessment of character in Sheffield to the attempt to reduce the age-range of candidates in Caernarvonshire to those between the ages of ten and thirteen. [46] Such changes were frequently described as implementing Hadow. In so far as they established the break at eleven years of age and encouraged a different curriculum from that of the elementary school the description was apt, but these changes also refined the older system of sponsored mobility for a few. Several authorities raised the number of special places (accessible by open competition) and thus reduced the number of fee-payers. They raised them to 100% so that all secondary education was to be carried out on selection by merit. [47]

Several authorities increased their maintenance allowances, paid to the children of very poor families to stay on at secondary school, [48] to compensate for the failure to raise the school leaving age to fifteen, scheduled to take place in 1939, but held back by the war. The result was to move towards increasing the secondary school population, especially from the poor but intelligent children kept out by existing provision.

There were other ways in which the years 1938–43 can be seen as a continuum in which reforming hopes of the interwar years no longer had to be deferred. For example, ten new schools were opened by various local authorities in 1938–39 as barriers against substantial expenditure were lifted. [49] In the localities innovation often preceded the 1944 Act, because it was innovation created by the conclusions of the Hadow committee of 1926 rather than a novel revision of the system. Change also occurred because of temporary exigencies of wartime administration. Homogeneity increased. Hertfordshire, for example, wished to examine all eleven-year-olds in its area. They 'borrowed' Essex's exam on payment of a small fee. [50] The number of authorities using Moray House tests rose dramatically in 1941 and 1942. They were already validated and could be bought as a package. This was probably cheaper than setting or marking exams locally or than employing an individual solely for the purpose. [51]

Nationally the major figures in educational policy were not much inclined to innovate. They had been sitting together at the top of their organisations throughout the years of cut-backs. The 'friendly and conspiratorial triumvirate' of Sir Maurice Holmes, Sir Percival Sharp and Sir Fred Mander had held their respective positions at the Board of Education, the AEC and the NUT since 1936, 1925 and 1931. [52] Sharp fulminated against any notion of equality of opportunity while the financial disparities between authorities remained, but his writing on the subject leads one to suspect that he viewed it as a 'shibboleth' in more ways than financial ones.[53]

It was in the localities that the war stimulated innovation in classroom practice, but such innovation was usually makeshift, not prefigurative, and much of it was for the duration only. Nationally the war did lead to one innovation when the government created an imaginative attempt to cope with teacher shortage in the Emergency Training Service, which trained teachers without academic qualifications after national service. This did not get under way until 1943, took in the first students in 1944 and produced its first teachers in 1946.[54] Little was done, or could have been done under the imperatives of war needs as interpreted at the time, to close down the schools on the Black List, long overdue for closure and replacement, or to rebuild inner-city schools. Problems such as overcrowded classrooms became newly visible both in debates over reconstruction and evacuation and in the concern with 'the state of the nation' as expressed in fears for 'the visible embodiments of posterity', the nation's children.[55]

The construction of the Act

As *The Times Educational Supplement* argued in suggesting the outlines of educational reform:

The basis of that conception must be that citizenship begins at twenty-one; that up to that age all boys and girls are wards of the State and are to be regarded as in a state of tutelage; and that during these twenty-one years no effort must be spared to give each one according to his capacities, and limited by no other considerations, the fullest opportunity to develop every innate power. Only thus can we hope to produce a noble race.

Earlier in the same piece the editor had pointed out that the education system had been 'The most effective safeguard of the social stratification we all in our heart of hearts bow down and worship'.[56] The plans for reform in the Board of Education Green Book, the White Paper and the Bill as eventually published showed increasingly less sign of any such holistic enterprise – and ensured that social stratification remained safe within the educational system. Built into it were the notions of merit as a guiding principle, *and*, despite all the aspirations of reformers, examinations and their effects continued to shape the structure of English education.

It was the beginnings of change in some local authorities and the pressure from the left that created the move to reform within the Board of Education. The Board began to discuss changes during Herwald Ramsbotham's tenure as president; the intention was explicitly to pre-empt more radical change. Holmes said, 'I think this is a matter on which we should lead rather than follow'.[57] R. S. Wood argued that 'Mean and meagre planning will be disregarded and officials' views discounted, and others will be asked to design the New Jerusalem'. He acknowledged that 'the war is now moving us more and more in the direction of Labour's ideas and "ideals" '.[58] Several of the Board's leading civil servants had been pressing for more equality in provision. Cleary argued forcefully for his view of war as an agent of democratisation:

Modern large-scale war, and particularly a 'total' war of democracy against dictatorship, emphasises the essential unity of the nation, the common interests of all its members and the need for making a reality of the democratic system which we profess to be defending.[59]

The civil servants who drafted the first version of the Bill, the Green Book, were not united on any issue but the simple one that there needed to be reform at all. In particular they battled over the key question for secondary education – the age of transfer and the nature of secondary school organisation. Both Wallace and Gosden have shown how the interests of existing secondary education were maintained at the Board, 'in the national interest', against the demand for multilateral schooling, which came from those most concerned with the education of the majority of eleven-to-fourteen-year-olds in the elementary and technical sections, as they were then called.[60]

The existing age of transfer was to be kept at eleven to keep the time in grammar school to at least four years, since the 'new' school leaving age was to be fifteen. R. A. Butler, who took over at the Board in 1941, warned about this major point. He minuted in October 1942:

I have for long been concerned to provide an opportunity for children to revise their choice of school between the ages of 11 and 13. That is to say I am not satisfied that the age of 11 is the one and ideal age at which children should decide upon their future lives.[61]

When he was told that transfer between schools would be possible, and that schools would be encouraged to have a common but diverse curriculum for all eleven-to-thirteen-year-olds, Butler said that he felt 'much comforted'.[62]

The process of designing the Act took nearly two years; Butler took a further year to steer it through Parliament. R. G. Wallace and Kevin Jeffereys have disagreed about the relative responsibilities of politicians

– R. A. Butler and J. Chuter Ede – and their civil servants for the reforming intentions of the Act.[63] My argument here is not on that issue, since the focus of their attention was on Parliament and parliamentary procedure and I want to introduce the other side of reform into the debate – where it has received insufficient attention. But it does seem to be the case that contemporary interest and the comments of historians have been concentrated in this way partly because of the shortage of public comment in the war on such issues. War has had a searchlight effect on historians as well as contemporaries, rendering the area outside the beam yet more obscure. Of course the debate in government and Parliament was crucial but it was not the only way in which the educational reform was tested at the time nor the only way to assess it later. In the country at large there *was* some pronounced hostility but it came mainly from one quarter and on one issue – churchmen and the religious settlement. This was largely unexpected by civil servants at the Board, though not by Churchill, but it meant that the educational problems of an extension and perpetuation of the existing system were minimised.

The White Paper

Tawney described the White Paper of 1943, *On Educational Reconstruction*, as:

a programme of reconstruction which if applied in practice would create an educational edifice not unworthy of the British people . . . That programme is a synthesis. Of the items contained in it, few are novel and some will be criticised . . . The nation will not easily forgive any group or party which deprives the rising generation of the brighter future promised by the measure outlined by Mr Butler.[64]

He felt it necessary to sound the warning bell against sectionalism to preserve the reform at all. Contemporaries feared a repetition of 1918, when post-war educational reform (the Fisher Act) had been stopped by depression and government limits on spending.[65] They feared the abandoning of the complete package for the sake of religious interests. So the plan was discussed and accepted *as a whole*; its weaknesses as innovative legislation thus went unchallenged.

The other group worried by the White Paper was the local authorities. They were to be cut. All Part III authorities (who dealt only with elementary education) were to go. The Association of Education Committees would lose, at a stroke, half its members and most of its political clout, since the remaining authorities – the municipal boroughs and the counties – already had associations which dealt with education. They were also to be subject to greater control by central government, since the Minister, as the President of the Board was to become, could intervene if an authority was not providing an education 'appropriate to the age, ability and aptitude of the child'. Parental wishes were also to be taken into account, though what that meant was unclear. Sir Percival Sharp fought for the AEC mainly on the first issue – but could find no support – so that the second, the potential extension of the power of central government, went largely unchallenged. Sharp commented frequently, with hostility, on government's novel espousal of 'equality of opportunity' in the absence of any equality of treatment of local authorities. [66]

The religious issue was solved after difficult negotiations. Butler won over his own party and a majority of Labour and Liberal MPs by shrewd use of Archbishop Temple's support for the 'agreed' syllabus. This meant that the Churches could allow some of their schools to become nondenominational in exchange for financial support of the rest and an agreed minimum of Christian instruction in all schools. The main opposition came from Roman Catholics, who organised substantial vocal heckling groups at public meetings, and several MPs who battled over the issue inside Parliament. Political controversy on this issue meant advocates of radical reform of internal school organisation were marginalised by the public discussion. Chuter-Ede advocated 'no rocking the boat'; as deputy to the President at the Board of Education he was heeded by Labour colleagues who wanted a systematic change. [67]

The Act in practice

The Bill passed into law in 1944. The immediate effect was to make local authorities examine their existing provision. All had to prepare a Development Plan describing five years' improvement to bring about secondary education for all. At the same time existing children of eleven to fourteen had to be assessed for their placing in secondary education. The instruments already used for the special place exam were the easiest to adopt, and existing eleven-to-fourteen-year-olds took the exam for reallocation. There were few transfers as a result, since the exam used had already segregated them. As later research was to show, the quality of schooling between eleven and fourteen had a pronounced effect on all measures, including the intelligence quotient. The one factor which might have altered this made little difference. In an attempt to make good the teacher shortage schoolchildren were encouraged to stay on at school to do teacher training by circular No. 1654 in 1947.[68] LEAs were allowed to open special classes or put these children into grammar schools. The result was that the existing grammar–secondary modern division was further embedded. Short-term emergency measures perpetuated a division along social grounds that inhibited long-term change. In very few education committees did the passing of the Act cause any change in the selection process at all; in many the change was cosmetic. Yet this change did not require much expenditure or creative thought – allocation as a concept could have been deployed, rather than selection. The novel techniques that had appeared represented a refinement of existing procedures, in particular the development of school record cards.[69] The new Foundation for Educational Research (later the National Foundation, NFER) saw the development of record cards as one of their first tasks. Kent already used one and it improved this, which in turn was used as the model by the NFER. In fact the extension of record cards did not make an alternative, an allocation system, but a more accurate selection system. They were mostly used to discriminate between doubtful grammar school entrants.

Lord Alexander says now that the Development Plans were never taken seriously, that it was then thought 'a nonsense' to try to project five years ahead.[70] They were variously dealt with. The form used was complicated but could not compensate for the deficiencies of information about a population that was still highly mobile and still undergoing the stresses of war.[71] Projections of secondary school population, let alone the entire existing school population, were often arbitrary. Some authorities wanted to develop new forms of secondary education. Middlesex was not allowed to build or even organise multilateral schools because they would be too large if 'appropriate' education was provided. Anglesey on the other hand could, since comprehensive schools were the easiest solution to rural isolation and the lack of any funding for new buildings. Authorities were refused the chance a few wanted to take – to interpret 'education appropriate to age, ability and aptitude' as meaning comprehensive, or multilateral, education in which all children attended the same school from eleven onwards. LEAs could do this only if they had dispersed populations. Government's new power was limited to restraint upon LEA innovation. It did not enforce innovation at all. The tripartite model of grammar, technical and modern education was more explicit in the circular which interpreted the Act – circular No.

144. Development plans which did not follow this model were rejected. [72]
Some authorities already provided technical education. More did not
– but included provision for it in the other types of school.

Local authorities had almost completely ignored the Norwood report
of 1943. This had argued, dogmatically and with no scientific evidence,
that there were three types of child mind – the academic, the practical,
and the non-verbal – which was, as contemporaries pointed out, happily
coincident with existing types of school. The majority of LEΛs did not
accept that a clearly defined technical ability could be clearly identified
at the age of eleven. Only W. P. Alexander, no longer practising as a
psychologist in 1945, believed tests could identify it. [73] Even those who
thought that spatial perception would stand in for technical ability at
age thirteen felt that the match between the specific ability and general
intelligence was too close to allow it to generate a specialised educational
form. The result was that the social results of different forms of education
perpetuated the hierarchy of demand – grammar schools first, technical
second and secondary modern for the rest. The belief of the NUT that
intelligence tests would be used to grade pupils on one scale rather than
place them on a set of scales was amply vindicated. Selection for technical
education continued to take place, generally at thirteen, but it tended
to reflect existing patterns set by two years of secondary schooling so
that grammar school successes were unlikely to change in mid-stream. [74]

Selection in the localities

In 1947 the NUT conducted a survey of local authorities' selection
procedures. The results were published in 1949 and showed an increasing
homogeneity of practice. Of the 106 authorities who responded and could
be used for analysis, seventy-eight were described as using some form
of standardised intelligence test and nearly all were using examination
procedures to measure attainment in English and arithmetic, though the
variety of standard, 'tried out' and internal tests was wider. [75] Thirteen
were recorded as *not* using an intelligence test as a determinant, though
some of these used one in a few individual cases or as a qualifier. There
was as yet no uniformity of practice among local authorities, who
continued to rely on a wide variety of examining methods, though more
had turned to external test agencies – organisations or examiners – than
in the past. This survey also showed an intention to change which
reflected the intensity of public scrutiny in the period after the Act.

The other innovation of the early 1940s had not been generally adopted. School records or reports were in use in thirty-two authorities, with thirty-nine more hoping to introduce them soon. Yet what this meant in practice varied greatly. Some used complicated test systems. Head teachers often filled them in and were asked to estimate intelligence, attainment or special abilities using tests or their own judgement. They were also asked to assess 'home environment and attitude' in thirty-one authorities, 'sociability' and 'conduct and moral character' in twelve, co-operation in eleven, and in one each imagination, personal habits and personal appearance.[76] What it meant to move towards school records could be to increase the subjective, teacher-controlled element in selection or to diminish the relative effects of differences between teachers or schools – it was never an unambiguous change.[77] As intelligence tests had not superseded the older attainments tests, so school records did not supersede the test battery. The 'eleven-plus' of the period after the 1944 Act was the 'special places examination' of advanced LEAs before the war, used by more authorities.

It is not clear why the motives of the White Paper of 1943, the intentions of the inspectorate and the hopes of educational reformers were so little heeded in the specific detail of selection. The section of the White Paper which specified 'school records, supplemented if necessary by intelligence tests'[78] was dropped from the Bill without any discussion. The obvious explanation is that the finer points of selection were to be left to the LEAs as compensation for loss of power, because central direction was unnecessary. The movement towards meritocracy was not complete. The rhetoric of equal opportunity could not finally win over the entrenched interests in a broad-meshed filter, a crude sieve for the child population. The single most important move of the 1938–50 period was the extension of selection to the entire age group, and the 1944 Act actually made this more commonplace, but it did not create the move – only forty-three LEAs, less than half, considered the whole group throughout the selection process, another forty LEAs qualified children by excluding those who did badly in a first exam as part of the selection procedure.[79] The pattern was clearly set by which the extension of secondary education, because it was *free*, would increase the pressure effect of the exam whatever form it took. Lessons in 'intelligence' were added in many junior schools to the existing basics of English and arithmetic. In 1947, when the school leaving age rose to fifteen after a battle in Cabinet, the pressures on the junior school rose further, since the difference between grammar schools and others was diminished, as there was only one year between them, not two. Many local authorities used the 'direct grant' schools (which took in at least 25% of their children by merit from maintained primary schools and had fee-payers as well) as the top rung of their local educational ladder. These schools now provided a free alternative to expensive private education – so that the number of middle-class children in them rose. The number of working-class children also rose, but the relative proportions remained approximately the same.

Halsey, Heath and Ridge have argued persuasively that the post-war education system's achievements never did match up to the meritocratic ideals of its creators. [80] In so far as progress towards meritocracy was slow – involving a gentle democratisation, as Holmes had argued – this was correct, but another factor must lie in the unmeritocratic aspirations of the local authorities, who administered the educational change. Local authorities' ideology of education varied, and was not always consistent within the LEA. Some leading figures were anti-meritocratic, like Alderman Walter Hyman, chairman of the West Riding Education Committee, and his education officer, Alexander Clegg. Clegg consulted four psychologists on the feasibility of selection for technical education at eleven (G. B. Jeffrey, Charlotte Fleming, Godfrey Thomson and Cyril Burt), and their advice was so clearly in support of his belief that it was *not* possible that he refused to select for it at all. Instead he moved slowly towards a system which allocated by ranking children by school record, then ranking schools rather than subjecting pupils to a once-and-for-all examination, eventually towards non-selective education altogether. [81] Middlesex, Southend on Sea and London all intended comprehensive schooling – London eventually acquired a modified version of it. [82]

Some were extremely meritocratic. In Sheffield there had been an attempt to rank grammar schools, and W. P. Alexander, the education officer, had argued then, and after 1945 as secretary of the AEC, for selection of 5% at the top, not 20%. [83] In practice, local authorities were constrained in the crucial years 1944–50 by existing buildings, shortage of funds for new ones and by existing teaching staff from making substantial innovations in their arrangements at all. Classrooms remained obstinately limited by size and equipment to specific purposes. Government grants were available at 55% of expenditure for capital projects but austerity measures after 1946 under successive Labour Ministers ensured that those were limited. LEAs were explicitly forbidden to use them to reorganise schools. [84] Lack of funds is only part of the answer in explaining the *ad hoc* nature of change and the limited extent of it. If people genuinely wanted social change from the educational system (and they did), they generally wanted it in familiar guise. For a few years the child population remained at pre-war size and existing facilities could match demand. By the time post-war expansion affected secondary schooling the adjustments necessary to meet the demands of central and local government had been made.

Demographic pressures were signally important in producing change in the educational system. There appears to be a crude fit between districts of expanding population and prosperity and egalitarian educational aspirations. It did not work directly, but since the end of the war did coincide with a change in personnel at local level it was quite often the case that local authorities had new education officers at a time when they were eager to innovate. The post-war generation of education officers were mainly university-educated, often had substantial educational research experience (often self-motivated and directed) and frequently had qualifications in educational psychology or law. In Hertfordshire, Wiltshire and Norfolk, for example, a young staff found themselves given a free hand to alter the educational system. In the two latter districts rural education, rather than academic excellence, was seen as a primary purpose of the local system; in such areas technical education took on a specialised meaning. [85] Local hierarchy did *not* always read off academic excellence as the desired end of local practice, so that there was less concern in these rural areas for the fate of the top few than for that of the majority. On the other hand, meritocracy could be used to argue *for* comprehensives, as in Coventry or Middlesex, as well as grammar schools as in Birmingham or Leeds. [86]

Psychologists' debates

There were also developments within educational psychology in the late 1940s which ensured that simple notions of merit did not go unchallenged. Teacher trainers in Liverpool, at the London Institute of Education, and elsewhere, argued against the prevailing orthodoxy on intelligence tests. [87] Alice Heim was beginning her work on creativity in which she claimed that verbal reasoning tests ignored vital aspects of child potential. [88] Philip Vernon was beginning to question the efficiency of tests by querying whether they measured accurately. [89] Most of these, if asked, would have been unwilling to support any increase in attainment testing or in subjective assessment of character, but their expressed unease about testing could help to feed that of others, who would then fall back on what had 'worked' in the past. A part of the ideology of 'muddling through' was an acceptance of pragmatism in social policy, even a glorying in it, which helped to sustain a distrust of too much expertise, particularly in a scientific field.

Some educational psychologists were turning away from psychometry. The child guidance movement had created a multiplying number of clinics already, particularly acceptable in wartime, and this multiplication continued when war was over. The insights of psychoanalysis fed into a science of the child mind which rooted behaviour, particularly aberrant behaviour, firmly in family relations. Susan Isaacs, Melanie Klein, D. W. Winnicott and C. W. Valentine all presented child 'maladjustment' as a pathology created by social surroundings in addition to family behaviour. These matters spilled over into the British Psychological Society and eventually in 1951–52 led to a major row on the benefits of psychoanalysis, which meant that the relationship between scientific developments and educational practice became further confused. [90] If the public acceptance of psychoanalysis meant anything for secondary selection it did mean that the scientificity of any description of the mind became more suspect – its subjectivity more evident.

Testing technique

Technically, post-war testing became more and more rigorous. Successive NFER analysis demonstrated that the most effective selection process could select only 90% of children adequately – 10% would be misplaced. So long as selection policies did not come under scrutiny this was acceptable. Once, however, the child population began to rise, a new population question arose. Free secondary education increased the pressure on space. The ideology of merit had elevated the grammar school above technical schools, technical schools above secondary moderns. The equal opportunity for social mobility was a commonplace in the public mind but pressure of numbers began to render that equality suspect, since it seemed unequal in fact. [91]

Other policies had tended to limit equality or parity between schools at the same time. The secondary teachers' unions, particularly the Joint Four, had made a great outcry about the exodus of the grammar school teachers from the profession. This was a result of the new Burnham system of teacher payment, which signally raised the pay of junior school teachers but also abolished some of the differential between them and secondary school teachers, and, in some cases, actually cut the latter group's pay. The outcry was, to a certain extent, factitious. Schools did lose staff but it seems more likely to have been a reflection of the generally low level of teachers' pay at a time of full employment.[92] It was not the highly qualified classics, history or English teachers who left, but those who could use their degrees in industry or the civil service. However, local authorities dealt with teacher shortage by using the incentive payments under Burnham (for posts of special responsibility) to 'top up' grammar school salaries.[93] Hence parity between teachers in schools was undermined. There also lay embedded in the system the inequality of paying not for the job but for the qualifications: degrees received a year's extra increment and as a result earnings differentials rose. Women, who predominated in the junior schools, did not get equal pay in principle until 1955 (or in reality until 1962), despite a vigorous campaign throughout the 1940s, so yet further inequality was built in between groups of teachers.[94]

A second factor undermining the parity between schools was the absence of new premises. Many of the schools opened immediately after the war did not result from the Education Act. They had been built just before the war and were only now being used for their intended purpose. New buildings did not appear in any numbers until the 1950s. Until then premises were provided through the effective makeshift of the HORSA programme, the main achievement of George Tomlinson, the Minister of Works.[95] This scheme housed children in large numbers in temporary prefabricated huts. The bulk of the 'new' child population was in secondary modern schools; most of these were in huts. Grammar schools already had adequate facilities or could build them from scratch. They formed a proportion of new schools greater than the proportion of children they served (though this may have been because they were more likely to have suffered from bombing in city centres). There were local variations. Many *rural* authorities followed the example of Cambridgeshire village colleges inspired by Henry Morris, the chief education officer, so that Devon, Somerset and Leicestershire all wrote the notion into their development plans and did actually build some,[96] which would support the argument that the major move towards equality that *was* achieved by the 1944 Education Act was the diminution of the gap between rural and urban children – this was not Butler's two nations becoming one but it was a step towards it.[97]

Why had innovation been perceived? Firstly because some did take place. The provision of free secondary education did make it possible for many children to get more easily the education they desired. Secondly, the raising of the school leaving age in 1947 meant that the difference between types of secondary schooling was not so marked as it had been. This was a result *not* of the Bill or of the war but of a 1938 decision whose effect was *delayed* by the outbreak of war. It coincided with the Act, though, and thus could be perceived as more integrally related. The rhetoric of reconstruction provides another part of the answer. The Education Act provided a convenient peg upon which to hang 'statist' notions of reform – from those of all political parties who advocated reform from above through increased power to central government.[98] It was the only measure of its kind achieved in wartime; and it was achieved by agreement, despite the hiccoughs in its parliamentary progress. The effect of the development plan programme was to lay existing procedures bare, to make them explicit and visible to every citizen, not just the interested parties, parents and teachers. There was some impression of novelty simply because the subject was newly looked into. Innovation had to take place cheaply, since central government could not fund much in the way of capital projects. It was at the pivot of the secondary system – the process of selection – that innovation *apparently* took place. Most commercially available tests were produced by Moray House or, to a lesser extent, until the 1960s, by the NFER. Both were charitable bodies, of high professional standards, whose main activity was the production, validation and marking of statistically appropriate selection procedures. Their tests were cheaper and apparently fairer than local 'home-made' ones and they conveniently transferred the odium that selection incurred on to a distant, impartial public body. Increased attention to secondary education meant that justice had to be seen to be done.

However, despite some change in secondary selection, it remains the case, most remarkably, that though wartime and free education made the arguments of economy, fairness and impartiality more applicable they did not make them universally acceptable. The force working most clearly for uniformity was the growth in the child population, and since that was itself not uniform it was uneven in its effects. By 1952 almost all English education authorities had adopted an intelligence test in their selection process; psychologists debated the effects of social agencies – coaching and practice – on IQ scores; but Hertfordshire gave up the eleven-plus exam altogether, after having had one for at least fifteen years.[99]

Conclusion

The Act did tend to homogeneity, to the exploitation of meritocratic notions in pursuit of pragmatic ends, but it created little in the way of innovation or social levelling. It is ironic that Holmes's acceptance of the meritocratic possibilities of democratisation should have led to an Act which allowed for the creation of the comprehensive school – but in fact the ideology he shared with other administrators was one that could embrace the comprehensive, which was, at times, argued in the context of a more successful way of providing a selective education. It is not surprising, though. R. A. Butler, Sir Maurice Holmes, G. Thomson, R. H. Tawney, W. P. Alexander, W. Brockington – all shared a strong commitment to something each called equality of opportunity. They were all in a position to publicise their beliefs, to embody them in legislation or in local authority practice. The war made their beliefs seem realisable by adding to State authority a moral authority that it had lacked, but dependence upon State action was not a novel perception or created by war. What is perhaps most startling is that so many agents of educational change – local education officers and education committees – remained so untouched by the principles. In practice direct grant schools, the perpetuation of the public school system and the vested interests of sections of teachers as well as that complex animal, parental wishes, worked to maintain the *status quo ante bellum* to a much greater extent than even the most lukewarm of reformers could have wished. It is at the local level that change needs to be assessed and at which the variety of political forces at work was best displayed. It remained the case that, as A. J. P. Taylor remarked, there was, after the 1944 Act, a class distinction between those who went to grammar school and those who did not.[100] What is more arguable is how new it was, and how very much it departed from the old.

Notes

1 R. A. Butler, *The Art of the Possible*, 1971, p. 96.

2 Sir M. Holmes, Minute on the Bedfordshire Direct Grant Schools, ED 53/151, 9 June 1945.

3 A. Marwick, *Britain in the Century of Total War*, 1970, p. 318.

4 B. Simon, *The Politics of Educational Reform, 1920–1940*, 1974. R. Barker, *Education and Politics, 1900–1951*, Oxford, 1972.

5 R. G. Wallace, 'Labour, the Board of Education and the Preparation of the 1944 Education Act', unpub. PhD thesis, King's College, London, 1979.

6 The Report of the Consultative Committee on Secondary Education with special reference to Grammar Schools and Technical High Schools (the Spens report), 1938. P. Addison, *The Road to 1945*, 1975.

7 K. Hope, 'The Ideology of Merit', unpub. ms., 1976. I am very grateful to the author for the opportunity to read this.

8 G. Thomson, *The Education of an Englishman*, Edinburgh, 1969, p. 101.

9 G. Sutherland, *Ability, Merit and Measurement*, Oxford, 1983.

10 The Labour Party, *Secondary Education for All*, 1922. NALT, *Education – a Policy*, 1930. M. Morris, *The People's Schools*, 1939. WEA, *The Future of Secondary Education*, no date, but possibly 1938–39. Simon, *op. cit.*, p. 266. This lumping together of various leftish reform demands may seem reductive but it is the case that they share far more than divides them and it is the consensus that it is instructive as a motive force for reform.

11 R. H. Tawney, *Some Thoughts on the Economics of Public Education*, Oxford, 1938, p. 9 (*cit.* Barker, *op. cit.*, p. 76). The L. T. Hobhouse memorial lecture.

12 L. Hogben, *Political Arithmetic*, 1938.

13 G. Leybourne and K. White, *Education and the Birth Rate*, 1940. G. Leybourne, *Eugenics Review*, 1939 (based on the same research).

14 O. Maguiness, *Environment and Heredity*, 1940.

15 J. S. B. Haldane, *Heredity and Politics*, 1938, p. 117.

16 R. and K. Titmuss, *Parents Revolt*, 1942, p. 87.

17 R. Titmuss file, C333, Eugenics Society collection at the Wellcome Institute, London.

18 *British Journal of Educational Psychology* (*BJEP*), November 1940, June 1943.

19 *The Times Educational Supplement* (*TES*), review, 9 March 1940.

20 C. Burt, 'Ability and income', *BJEP*, 13 June 1943. 'Intelligence and Fertility', Eugenics Society Occasional Papers, No. 2 (the Galton lecture for 1945).

21 C. Bibby, letter to author, 1983. Bibby collection, Cambridge University Library, box 7.

22 P.P. 1950, V, Report of the Royal Commission on Population.

23 *Manchester Guardian*, 7 April, 17 July 1943. Bibliography of R. H. Tawney compiled by J. Winter, *Economic History Review*, February 1972.

24 *BJEP*, November 1940, p. 225.

25 *TES* leader, 6 January 1940, p. 5.

26 Annual report to the SSRC, 1983, for project HR 7950/1, 'Mental testing and education in England and Wales, 1940–1970' (SSRC report).

27 In 'Intelligence and Fertility', p. 5, though the definition could be found in works ranging throughout his career, even if the proportion allocated to heredity changed.

28 Mass-Observation (MO) File Report (FR) A 1269, 21 May 1942.

29 For example, from the women's box, DR44, responses of 1066, 1075, 1064, 1052, 2182, 2274, 2470, 2486, 2860, 2975, 3002, 3120.

30 DR44, 3004, 2884, 3108.

31 Recorded twelve times in 100 responses.

32 W. McClelland, *Selection for Secondary Education*, Edinburgh, 1942.

33 *TES*, 17 January 1942, p. 27, 'Education planning'; 14 February 1942,

letter from G. Bason.

34   *Cit.* Wallace, *op. cit.*, p. 109.

35   *BJEP*, Hugh McRae, February 1942, 'On the inconsistency of group test intelligence quotients'; Douglas MacIntyre, February 1944, 'On the offer of practice and intelligence test results'; report of BPS, June 1944. *TES*, 'From our Welsh correspondent', 9 August 1941, p. 376.

36   ED 110, 27/LCC and 28/Middlesex, minute 3 October 1942.

37   ED 110, 41/Surrey, 25 November 1942.

38   *BJEP*, April 1940, p. 4.

39   *Cf.* M. Cole and R. Padley, *Evacuation Survey*, 1940.

40   P. H. J. H. Gosden, *Education in the Second World War*, 1976, p. 16.

41   ED 110 lists the negotiations authority by authority over change in the scale.

42   ED 135, NS 113, The Special Place Examination, 2 December 1942.

43   D. Wills, 'Fifty years of child guidance', *Journal of Child Psychotherapy*, 1978.

44   ED 110, 18/Isle of Ely.

45   *TES*, 7 December 1942, p. 490. Interview, Lord Alexander, 1982.

46   *TES* 29 November 1941, p. 570.

47   SSRC report. Authorities who changed were as follows. From Moray House records: Brighton, 1939; York, Cheshire, Reading, 1940; Oldham, 1941; Derbyshire, Derby Borough, 1942; Middlesbrough, Cambridge Borough, Blackpool, Gloucester, 1943. From *The Times Educational Supplement* and *Education*: Durham, Leeds, Wolverhampton, Stretford, Manchester, Coventry, Denbighshire, 1940; Brighton, Surrey, Hertfordshire, 1941; Wakefield, Isle of Man, Wiltshire, Caernarvonshire, Carmarthenshire, Norwich, 1942; Cheshire and Leicester again, Sheffield, Swindon, Somerset, Hastings, Westmorland, 1943. London, Essex, Middlesex and Kent as well as Surrey and Hertfordshire collaborated from 1940 to 1945 in the evacuating authorities' examination, which evacuees took in other authorities. One that changed (from local records) was Leicestershire, where tests were dropped after 1940, to be resumed in 1942 – so the decision to test was not the only 'progressive possibility'.

48   ED 110, 12/Essex, 15/Hertfordshire, 42/East Sussex, 51/Barnsley, 87/Ipswich, 103/Preston, 106/Rotherham, 114/South Shields, 124/West Ham, 146/Rhondda. (Some authorities already paid sufficiently generous allowances so do not appear on this list.)

49   *Education*, Construction report bound in at back of each annual volume.

50   *Education*, 20 March 1942, p. 257.

51   Godfrey Thomson archive, University of Edinburgh, Vol. 3.14b.

52   A. Tropp, *The Schoolteachers*, 1957, p. 215.

53   *Education*, 9 January 1942, p. 20; 24 September 1943, p. 345.

54   Gosden, *op. cit.*, p. 124 ff.

55   The phrase is C. P. Blacker's in *Eugenics Review*, 38.3, October 1946, p. 126.

56   *TES*, 28 June 1943, p. 303.

57   *Cit.* Gosden, *op. cit.*, p. 238, Wallace, *op. cit.*, p. 46.

58   Gosden, *op. cit.*, p. 248.

59   ED 136 Post-war Social Development and its Effect on Schools, 13 January

1942.

60   Particularly Wallace, 'The origins and authorship of the 1944 Education Act', *History of Education*, X, 1981, p. 4.

61   ED 136/279, 20 October 1943, *cit.* Wallace, 1981, pp. 277–8.

62   ED 136/300, 12 March 1943, *cit.* Wallace, 1981, pp. 277–8.

63   K. Jeffereys, 'R. A. Butler, the Board of Education and the 1944 Education Act', *History*, October 1984, p. 227. Wallace, 1979, *op. cit.* Wallace, 1981, p. 290.

64   *Manchester Guardian*, 17 July 1943.

65   E.g. *TES* review of Fisher autobiography, 11 January 1941, as precedent reform and Lord Butler in *The Art of the Possible*, 1971.

66   See f. 52.

67   *Education*, 19 May 1944, p. 608. Wallace, 1979, p. 70.

68   Minutes of Education Committees which cited two specifically included Cambridgeshire, Wiltshire, Leeds, the London County Council.

69   A. Yates, *The First Twenty-five Years*, A History of the NFER, Slough, 1971, p. 6. Godfrey Thomson collection, University of Edinburgh, response of Kent to question on open tests, 1954.

70   Interview, 2 February 1983.

71   ED 135/5, 267, ED 147/415, C762. LEAs had to submit thirty copies, using coloured inks.

72   Circular 144, 'The organisation of secondary education', 16 June 1947. *Education*, 23 August 1946 (Middlesex).

73   Robin Davis, *The Grammar School*, 1967, p. 71–2 (Anglesey). HMSO, Curriculum and Examinations in Secondary Schools, 1943, p. 15. W. P. Alexander, *Intelligence, Concrete and Abstract*, 1940. (I have not seen any authority citing Norwood as a motivating force for change; in one, Wiltshire, it is used to demonstrate that existing procedures are justified.)

74   A. F. Watts and P. Slater, *The Allocation of Primary School Leavers to Courses of Secondary Education*, 1950.

75   NUT, *Transfer from Primary to Secondary Schools*, 1949, p. 93.

76   NUT, *op. cit.*, pp. 102–3.

77   *Ibid.*, p. 90–1.

78   HMSO, White Paper on Educational Reconstruction, Cmd 6458, 1943, p. 9.

79   B. Vernon, *Ellen Wilkinson*, 1981. F. Blackburn, *George Tomlinson*, 1954.

80   A. H. Halsey, A. F. Heath and J. M. Ridge, *Origin and Destinations*, Oxford, 1980.

81   P. H. J. H. Gosden and P. R. Sharp, *The Development of an Education Service: the West Riding, 1889–1974*, Oxford, 1980, pp. 158–66.

82   B. Simon and C. Benn, *Halfway There: Report on the British Comprehensive School Reform*, 1976, p. 44. *TES*, 13 January 1945, 8 December 1945 (Southend on Sea). *Education*, 28 July 1944 (London). *Education*, 23 August 1946 (Middlesex).

83   *Education*, 10 November 1944.

84   Circular.

85   Minutes of the Secondary committee, Wiltshire and Norfolk.

86   In Middlesex the Act was used to argue for an increase in technical education: interview, Max Morris (then head of a technical school), 1984.

87　D. Harding at Liverpool and in the pages of *Scrutiny* (I am grateful to Dr Leo Salinger for this reference); Dr Charlotte Fleming at the Institute of Education, London.

88　*NFER Bulletin*, 1948.

89　Personal communication, 1983.

90　Interview with Dr W. Wall, 1983. Symposium on child guidance, *British Journal of Educational Psychology*, 1953.

91　A. Yates and D. Pidgeon, *Admission to Grammar School*, 1957.

92　Interview, A. Hutchings (General Secretary, Assistant Masters' Association), 31 July 1983.

93　R. Gould, *Chalk up the Memory*, 1976, pp. 106–7.

94　T. Cazalet-Keir, *From the Wings*, 1967, p. 192. H. Smith, 'The problem of "Equal Pay" . . .', *Journal of Modern History*, December 1981.

95　F. Blackburn, *George Tomlinson*, 1954. Interview, A. Yates. Tomlinson was the most interested of all the Ministers of Education, and had considerable local experience on the AEC.

96　H. Ree, *Educator Extraordinary*, 1973, p. 132–9.

97　*TES*, Summary of Development Plans, 10 and 24 May 1947. By the 1950s city children had become the disadvantaged in public commentary, although of course this may not necessarily reflect a real change.

98　Centre for Contemporary Cultural Studies, *Unpopular Education*, 1981, University of Birmingham.

99　P. Vernon (ed.), *Intelligence Testing and Schemes for Secondary Education*, 1952 (a reprint of several pieces in the *TES* which expressed concern about coaching).

100　A. J. P. Taylor, *English History, 1914–1945*, Oxford, 1964, pp. 568.

Acknowledgements

I should like to thank Dr Gillian Sutherland, Dr Peter Searby and Dr Joan Austoker for reading this piece and providing much helpful criticism. Faults remaining are my own responsibility. All places of publication London unless otherwise stated. The work for this piece was a part of the ESRC project on Mental Testing in England and Wales, 1940–70, on which I worked 1982–85. I am grateful for the council's support.

Henry Pelling

The impact of the war on the Labour Party

It is customarily assumed that the five years and eight months between the outbreak of war with Nazi Germany in September 1939 and the final collapse of that power in May 1945 was an epoch of ever-increasing radicalism, both for the British electorate and for the Labour Party itself. Professor Richard Titmuss rather implied this when he wrote in his *Essays on the Welfare State* that:

The aims and context of social policy, both in peace and war, are . . . determined – at least to a substantial extent – by how far the co-operation of the masses is essential to the successful prosecution of the war. [1]

Both Professor Arthur Marwick and Dr Paul Addison have maintained in their respective works on this period that this co-operation was indeed essential, and that the consequent outcome was a government of the left. But both authors recognise that experience in office in the coalition government had made the Labour leaders more cautious than they would otherwise have been: Dr Marwick comments that 'Middle-class radicalism and official trade unionism were much stronger influences than left-wing Socialism', and Dr Addison speaks of an 'Attlee consensus' to which the Conservatives, when they returned to office in 1951, also subscribed. [2] Nor can any general law of 'radicalisation as a result of mobilisation' be regarded as valid solely on the basis of the war's impact: we may recall that at the end of the First World War the electorate voted for a substantially Conservative Parliament, albeit under the leadership of Lloyd George, the wartime Prime Minister. It would be truer to say that the regime which enters the war is usually discredited at the war's end, probably because of its supposed lack of adequate provision for the armed forces in the final pre-war years.

Before the Second World War, to be sure, it looked as if the Labour

Party would be unable to break out of a minority role in British politics. Although the 1935 general election confirmed its position as the only main challenger for the left-wing vote, in that election it secured only 154 MPs – less than a quarter of the total membership of the Commons. At that time the party seemed to have many of the characteristics of a party which did not expect to win elections: it had changed its leadership only a few weeks before the general election was called, Lansbury having resigned and been replaced by Attlee on a temporary basis; and it suffered from a good deal of internal factionalism, and found its major policy demand – collective security through the League of Nations – 'scooped' by Stanley Baldwin, the Prime Minister.[3] The prospects of the party improved somewhat with the adoption at the 1937 conference of an 'Immediate Programme' of nationalisation for a single term of office: this included all the major measures of the post-war Labour government except for iron and steel, which in any case was not to be fundamentally reorganised before the Labour government left office in 1951. But at the conference it was for the first time agreed to allow the constituency parties to elect their own separate representatives to the National Executive, and this at once led to the appearance in this category of Sir Stafford Cripps, Professor Harold Laski and D. N. Pritt – all advocates of close collaboration with the Communist Party, and Pritt indistinguishable from an actual card-carrying member.[4] The trade union leadership of the party at this time often sounded at least as hostile to the National Government as the constituency party members: at the 1939 conference Ernest Bevin was to be heard emphasising that he was

. . . anxious to prevent this Movement fighting for the preservation of the Paris Bourse, the London Stock Exchange, the Amsterdam Exchange, and Wall Street.[5]

And Herbert Morrison moved at the same conference a resolution condemning the government's introduction of conscription: the resolution was carried by more than three to one.[6] Meanwhile Cripps and two other Labour MPs, Aneurin Bevan and G. R. Strauss, were expelled from the party for advocating the policy of a 'popular front' in alliance with Liberals and Communists, and (in Cripps's case) for circulating a memorandum proposing this to all affiliated organisations.[7]

It was not until the crisis of late August 1939, when the Nazi–Soviet pact was announced, clearly foreshadowing the impending attack on Poland, that the Labour Party and the movement at large shook off its hostility to the government at least to the extent of supporting, and in the crisis of early September demanding, an early declaration of war.

The Labour leaders refused to join a reconstituted War Cabinet under Neville Chamberlain's premiership, for party divisions were still acute: but, with the Liberals, Labour accepted an electoral truce whereby the main parties undertook to refrain from opposing the candidate of any retiring member's party at by-elections occasioned during the war. This in no way limited the cut-and-thrust of political disagreement.

In the winter of 1939–40 pacifist feeling was still strong inside the Labour Party, and it was reinforced by the anti-war attitude of the Communists and 'crypto-Communists', the latter being Labour Party members who, whether under Communist Party instructions or not, consistently supported Communist policies without openly joining the Communist Party. When Soviet troops invaded Finland in November 1939, for instance, there was widespread sympathy in Britain for the latest victims of aggression; but D. N. Pritt, although a member of the Labour Party National Executive, attempted to justify the role of the Russians. In March 1940 he was expelled from the Labour Party, and the University Labour Federation, which represented students of Labour sympathies, was disaffiliated for the same reason.[8] Henceforth socialist organisation in the universities was for many years weakened by division between 'socialist' – i.e. Communist-controlled or influenced–societies and Labour Clubs supporting the Labour Party.

When in May 1940 the Commons divided on an issue of confidence in the Chamberlain government's handling of the war, and the normal government majority was seen to have dropped significantly, Chamberlain decided to resign and to make way for Churchill, a leader more acceptable to the opposition parties. At this point Attlee and Greenwood, the leader and deputy leader of the Labour Party, were invited by Churchill to join his small War Cabinet; and many of their colleagues were also invited to join the new administration. Although Attlee and Greenwood were ready to accept the invitation, they did not do so at once but made sure that both the National Executive and the annual Conference, which were conveniently meeting at the same time, it being the Whit weekend, were fully consulted and in agreement with their acceptance of office. In addition, a special meeting of the National Council of Labour – the body that represented the General Council of the Trades Union Congress as well as the Parliamentary Labour Party and the National Executive – was hastily summoned to endorse the commitment.[9] This illustrated the leadership's caution and carefulness in committing the entire Labour movement to their entry into office in a broad-based coalition headed by a Conservative leader long regarded as the bitter enemy of the movement but recognised as a formidable fighting man – Winston Churchill. But the Labour leaders' caution was understandable in the light of the amendments made to the party constitution after the break with Ramsay MacDonald in 1931, the last leader to have favoured a coalition government, whose action had led to a split in the party and his expulsion from membership.

In succeeding years of wartime the annual conference continued to take place, though not at the seaside and not usually for a full week. The conference of 1944 had to be postponed owing to the difficulties of travel, which were imposed in the spring and summer of that year when the Allied invasion forces used Britain as their base for the 're-entry' into France: it was finally held in December.[10] Meanwhile, at the end of October 1944, in moving a resolution for the annual prolongation of Parliament, Churchill had declared, 'I have myself a clear view that it would be wrong to continue this Parliament beyond the period of the German war'.[11] This was at a time when the resistance of Japan was expected to continue for anything up to eighteen months later. Churchill called for a return of all party agents who were in the armed forces, and found that they were overwhelmingly Conservative. This may have led him to exaggerate the extent to which Labour Party organisation had been maintained during the war, while Conservative Party organisation had languished:

Many of the trade union leaders wanted of course to go to the front, but the whole process of organising our production . . . forbade their release. At the same time they maintained – and who could blame them? – their party affiliations; and once our mortal danger had passed these increasingly took on a partisan character. Thus on one side there had been complete effacement of party activities, while on the other they ran forward unresisted.[12]

It was certainly true that there were very few Labour Party full-time agents in the armed forces, but one major reason for this was that there were so few of them even in peacetime, and, of those who existed, many were above the age of military service. The Labour total in 1939, as listed in the annual conference report of that year, was 133, compared with a Conservative total of well over 450 in 1937.[13] As for wartime political activity, this was naturally inhibited for all the main parties by the electoral truce. Thus in the period when Labour was still in opposition in the early part of the war – September 1939 to May 1940 – there were twenty-one by-elections, but only six Labour candidates were put up and they of course were for the previously Labour-held seats: two of these were unopposed and the other four faced candidates of fringe groups, who did not poll well. In general, political propaganda was already difficult in this 'phoney' war period, and a number of full-time agents found their appointments terminated, though some special 'war grants' were paid by the central party organisation. [14]

With the formation of the coalition in May 1940, the central organisation was itself weakened by the absorption of the two leading officers of the Research Department into the government: Arthur Greenwood took office in Churchill's Cabinet and Grant McKenzie was recruited to assist Attlee in the latter's government tasks. During the Battle of Britain and the succeeding period of the so-called 'blitz' – the night bombardment of cities throughout the autumn and winter of 1940–41 – it became still more difficult to conduct party activity. Individual membership declined by a quarter – from 408, 844 in 1939 to 304, 124 in 1940 – and by the end of 1941 it was down by a further third – to 206, 622. [15] Late in 1941 a memorandum to the National Executive indicated, as might have been expected, that the main area of loss of membership was London and the home and eastern counties, where it had been most necessary to evacuate the population. The memorandum listed a formidable catalogue of difficulties which were being encountered:

1 Operation of the Military Forces Acts.
2 Recruitment and geographical transference of labour, including an increasing number of women workers.
3 Tempo of work - overtime, night and weekend shifts.
4 The blitz and blackout.
5 Lack of meeting places and facilities for social gatherings, meetings, etc.
6 Evacuation.
7 Occupation of the more responsible party workers on civil defence duties and national work, including Air Raid Precautions, fire-watching, Home Guard, salvage drives, war savings groups, Women's Voluntary Service, etc.
8 Number of constituency and borough party agents ceasing agency work and taking wartime employment.

From 1940 political activity was damped down not only by the maintenance of the electoral truce but also by a suspension of local government elections. Accompanying all this was 'the transference of public interest from politics to war news and war strategy'. [16]

After Hitler's invasion of Russia, however, which also meant a slackening of air attacks upon Britain, the decline in individual party membership was stemmed and a gradual revival took place. At the end of 1942 the total was 218,783 and at the end of 1943 235,501.[17] Owing to the increased employment on war work, trade union membership had in any case been on the increase. By the end of 1941, with the entry of the United States into the war as a belligerent, the prospects of a favourable outcome seemed to be ensured and discussion could begin in earnest about post-war reconstruction. When the government actually lost a seat at Maldon in Essex on 25 June 1942 to a left-wing independent, Tom Driberg, Attlee dismissed it as 'a mere expression of discontent'. It was true that it followed close on a humiliation for British arms – the loss of the fortress of Tobruk in North Africa and the withdrawal of the Eighth Army to the Egyptian frontier. Attlee commented at the 1943 party conference, 'As a matter of fact you can see the votes at by-elections going up and down in accordance with the progress of our armies in Africa'.[18]

But already at the time Attlee was speaking the situation was changing again. Sir Richard Acland and a group of colleagues, mostly middle-class socialists, had established a new party called Common Wealth which undertook to challenge Conservative candidates at by-elections.[19] There was nothing to stop Labour voters from supporting such rebels against the party truce in the privacy of the ballot box, although party members who publicly supported Common Wealth candidates suffered expulsion. But the seats that Common Wealth began to win were often seats which Labour would have stood little chance of winning even under the most favourable conditions. For instance, Eddisbury in Cheshire, a largely rural constituency, was won by John Loverseed, a man who had the unique distinction of having served as an air force pilot in both the Spanish civil war and the Battle of Britain. This success took place in March 1943; it was repeated in January 1944 by a less remarkable candidate at a similar rural constituency in Yorkshire – Skipton. Neither of these seats was to return a Labour candidate even under the exceptionally favourable circumstances of July 1945.

This left-wing revival among the electorate took place at a time when some devoted socialists were becoming disillusioned with the prospects of actually accomplishing any sort of social revolution during the war itself. George Orwell, for instance, had written in 1940, 'Either we turn this into a revolutionary war, or we lose it'. (He was to apologise for this braggadocio two years later.)[20] The standpoint that he held, however, went all the way to the top. The injunction that Churchill gave Hugh

Dalton, in asking him to oversee the Special Operations Executive, was 'to set Europe ablaze'.[21] It did not come to much: but it was perhaps essential before Britain obtained major allies to believe that somehow a revolutionary movement could be incited to grow in occupied Europe. Except in the mountainous Balkans, this did not prove possible: and it has more recently been argued that resistance was 'seldom effective, sometimes stultifying, frequently dangerous, and almost always too costly'.[22] Nor was there any likelihood of a spontaneous revolt against the Nazi regime in Germany – not even after the overthrow of Mussolini in Italy in the summer of 1943. On the other hand, people in Britain grew increasingly impressed by the success of the Soviet troops on the eastern front. The King himself, sensing the popular mood and indeed sharing it, marked the victory of the Red Army at Stalingrad by presenting to the Soviet government the 'Sword of Stalingrad' as a symbol of British respect. It was assumed, perhaps naively, that the Russian successes were due to what Dalton called 'a planned economic life, unhindered by sectional interests'.[23]

The Labour Party's political revival was also advanced by the publication of the Beveridge report on Social Insurance and Allied Services, on 2 December 1942. The report had initially been commissioned by Arthur Greenwood when he was in the War Cabinet: its purpose had been to recommend measures to consolidate existing welfare provisions, which tended to vary from one scheme to another. But the character of the report as it turned out in the end owed a great deal to Sir William Beveridge himself, who determined to make a 'crusade' out of it for the sake of the achievement of social reform. He thus took as his starting point three major reforms which had not yet been accepted by the government, namely the establishment of family allowances, the creation of a national health service, and the maintenance by government policy of a 'high and stable level' of employment.[24]

When the Beveridge report was debated in the Commons in mid-February 1943 Churchill himself was ill and the government's case was argued by Sir Kingsley Wood, the Chancellor of the Exchequer, a Conservative, and Sir John Anderson, the Lord President, who was a former civil servant elevated to ministerial rank. Although in fact they accepted all three Beveridge 'assumptions' on behalf of the coalition government, the impression they gave was one of hesitancy and caution; and the result was that the Parliamentary Labour Party, for the one and only time during the coalition years, decided to put down an amendment to the government motion and thus divide the House. Of the 121 members who voted for the opposition amendment the very great majority – indeed, a majority of the total Labour Party in the House – were Labour members. Meanwhile the Beveridge report secured widespread publicity in the press and aroused much discussion both in the armed forces and in the public at large. The action of the Parliamentary Party was very embarrassing for the Labour Ministers, who of course could not join their colleagues in the opposition lobby; but it did more than anything else in wartime to identify the Labour Party with the widespread popular desire for social reform in the post-war world.

At the subsequent party conference the National Executive made a point of reasserting its adherence to the electoral truce. In a statement to the conference the executive acknowledged the important role of the Ministers in preparing plans for the armistice, for the rehabilitation of world trade and commerce and for the reconstruction of Britain herself. A resolution to maintain the truce was carried by an overwhelming majority.[25] At the same time the executive resisted a renewed attempt by sympathisers for the affiliation of the Communist Party. The attempt had been strengthened by the respect and admiration for Russian arms that had been aroused by Russian resistance on the eastern front. But J. S. Middleton, the Labour Party General Secretary, had set out in a series of published letters to Harry Pollitt, the Communist secretary, the arguments against allowing Communist affiliation: they were largely based upon the fact that the Communists adhered to the Communist International, based in Moscow, and were bound to obey its orders.[26] Shortly before the conference, however, to the chagrin of the executive, Moscow decreed the disbandment of the International. At the conference the executive spokesmen had to retailor their remarks to suit this new situation. But, although the Mineworkers' Federation supported the proposal, it was defeated by a majority of almost three to one.[27] An attempt to recognise Common Wealth as suitable for affiliation was rejected without a vote.[28]

Nevertheless, the party contained not a few who disapproved of the caution of the Labour leadership in retaining the electoral truce yet apparently obtaining so few significant concessions in respect of policy from the coalition government. In an article published in America Harold Laski attacked both Attlee and the trade union leadership:

In my view it is clear that the party is very much in search of a leader, very anxious, if it is to make an adequate showing at the next general election, over the fact that it needs a symbol of more meaning to the mass electorate than Mr Attlee.

He added, incautiously, 'There is hardly any aspect of policy today in which trade union leaders are not a brake on the wheel'.[29] Laski's attack was drawn to the attention of the executive at its ensuing meeting, and a statement was issued formally repudiating it.[30] But the executive also turned its collective mind to the task of responding to a resolution at the conference which had been sponsored by the Preston Trades Council, drawing attention to the deficiencies of the party in facing a general election, and asking that the machinery should be improved so that the party might 'make a determined bid for a Labour majority at the next General Election'.[31] This galvanised the National Agent, R. T. Windle, into making plans for an individual membership campaign early in 1944;[32] and it led to the executive summoning a conference of trade union officers so as to encourage them to contribute to a general election fund and to increase the proportion of their contracting-in membership – which was much less than half the total membership they reported to the Trades Union Congress. In addition, arrangements were made to reinforce the party's regional councils; and three-year grants were to be paid from the general election fund to enable constituency parties to employ full-time agents.[33]

The membership campaign was reported to be 'developing satisfactorily' at the National Executive's organisation sub-committee meeting in June 1944, but MPs were reported to be reluctant to travel long distances during the Normandy invasion period, and 'preoccupation with invasion fears and worries' led to a 'damping down' of activity.[34] All the same, constituency party membership rose that year to 265,763, an increase of well over 10% on 1943.[35] With the sudden break-out of the armies from the Normandy bridgehead, it looked as if what Churchill called the 'German war' was about to come to its conclusion; and, as we have seen, in October 1944, when the Commons once more renewed the electoral truce for a year, it was Churchill himself who said that this would be the signal for the dissolution of the coalition.

Already almost a year earlier Churchill had recognised that the enemy collapse in Europe might come at any time. After the Italian surrender in the summer of 1943 he privately reckoned the chances of a similar German collapse at six to four against; and he recognised, partly under pressure from Attlee and others on the Labour side, that he ought to appoint a senior Minister to co-ordinate the planning of reconstruction.[36] In November Lord Woolton, a man of no party affiliation but who had been a successful Minister of Food, was appointed to the task, and was given a seat in the War Cabinet. Woolton took on to his staff a small group of civil servants who had been working out the implications of the Beveridge report, and also the Uthwatt report on land values.[37] As it turned out, the prolongation of the war enabled the plans to be quite far advanced before the final collapse of German resistance in May 1945. In 1944 R. A. Butler, the President of the Board of Education, enacted a new Education Act which gave aid to Church schools in a new compromise and made provision for the raising of the school leaving age to fifteen at the end of the war and to sixteen at some date thereafter. And in October that year Sir William Jowitt of the Labour Party was appointed to head a new Ministry of National Insurance.

It should not be thought that Labour Ministers were concerned only with domestic policy, although Morrison was Home Secretary, Bevin was Minister of Labour, and Dalton (from early 1942) President of the Board of Trade. Attlee served as chairman of the Armistice Terms and Civil Administration Committee of the Cabinet, set up in November 1943. In April 1944 it was renamed the Armistice and Post-war Committee: Ernest Bevin was among its seven permanent members.[38] This meant that senior Labour leaders were brought to deal with the problems of the post-war treatment of Germany and the need for providing occupation forces. Both Dalton and Alexander, the First Lord of the Admiralty, argued at meetings of the committee that Germany should be deprived of war-making industries, though not to the extent of the 'pastoralisation' proposed by Henry Morgenthau, the US Secretary of the Treasury, and accepted for a time by Churchill and Roosevelt at their meeting at Quebec in September 1944.[39]

Foreign policy questions were also discussed by the War Cabinet as a whole. In July 1944 Attlee presented a paper on 'Foreign Policy and the Flying Bomb', which pointed out that it would henceforth be impossible for Britain to rely upon the English Channel as a defence against her enemies:

From our point of view, Norway, Denmark, Holland and France are necessary outposts of Britain and, in as much as Britain is now as she has been for a hundred years a shield for the U.S., outposts of America as well. Their defence is necessary to our defence and without us they cannot defend themselves.[40]

In April 1945 Attlee prepared a memorandum for the Cabinet to the effect that his committee favoured the retention of compulsory military service after the war. But Bevin indicated that the Labour Ministers would need to consult the National Executive of the party and the General Council of the Trades Union Congress before finally committing themselves.[41] This was done in May 1945, before the dissolution of the coalition.[42]

It has been argued that there was a cleavage between the Labour Ministers and the extra-parliamentary party on these issues.[43] It is true that some members of the party were inclined to take a 'soft' line towards Germany: prominent among them were Philip Noel-Baker and Richard Stokes, both of them middle-class members of the party. But opposing them were associates of a group calling itself 'Fight for Freedom', who felt that it would be necessary to deal harshly with Germany at the end of the war. This group was quite influential among leading trade unionists; and at the 1943 annual conference of the Labour Party they carried an amendment against an attempt by Stokes to reject the liability of 'the German people as a whole for the atrocities committed under Nazism'. The vote was carried against Stokes by a majority of well over two to one;[44] but Noel-Baker later argued in a letter to Attlee that 'the overwhelming majority of the Constituency Party delegates were against "Fight for Freedom" and Vansittartism'. Lord Vansittart, a former Foreign Office official, had written a pamphlet entitled *Black Record* blaming the Germans for a record of barbarism going back to the era of the Roman Empire. Noel-Baker continued in his letter to Attlee: 'In the card vote, however, they [the constituency party delegates] were heavily outvoted by the Trade Union delegates, and in particular by the Miners' Federation and the Transport and General Workers.'[45] Three months later, after the Trades Union Congress meeting at Southport, Noel-Baker reported that the Miners and the Transport Workers had changed sides and rejected the 'Fight for Freedom' standpoint.[46]

In any case the resolution of the party conference of 1943 gave Hugh Dalton, who was on the side of the 'anti-Germans', and was chairman of the party's International Committee, the opportunity to draft a statement on the 'International Post-war Settlement' emphasising German responsibility for the war and the need for her to pay reparations to the Allies. The statement conceded that there were many 'good' Germans but commented that 'they are singularly ineffective in restraining the bad Germans'.[47] Naturally Noel-Baker, whom Dalton described as 'a terrible old Genevan Tory', was very critical;[48] but Dalton managed to silence Harold Laski, another potential opponent on the committee, by putting in a strongly pro-Zionist paragraph about Palestine. Dalton's opponents were weakened by a general recognition that the Russians were also in favour of a strong line against Germany.

The draft statement had to undergo some further minor amendment, but was substantially accepted by the executive. Its approval at the conference in December 1944 was moved by Attlee himself, and carried with little opposition. Dalton wrote in his diary, 'I have got my way on all essentials'.[49]

The realism of Labour's attitude towards foreign policy was reinforced by Bevin's insistence, both at meetings of the National Executive (to which he was specially invited) and at the 1945 Labour Party Conference at Blackpool that it was essential to continue with military service while Britain retained the responsibility for maintaining occupation forces in Germany and elsewhere. Bevin said:

> We must introduce . . . another National Service Act for a limited period until we know exactly what is going to happen . . . We must continue the obligation to serve until we have brought home the men who have been fighting. That is a definite obligation upon us. We cannot say what the occupation of Germany will involve at the moment, or what will be our obligations in the East and at home.[50]

By approving Bevin's statement the conference committed itself to accepting National Service in peacetime for the first time ever.

The Labour Party entered the election campaign with more advantages than it realised. Few of its members, remembering the success of Lloyd George in 1981, expected to win against the personal appeal of Winston Churchill, who was regarded almost universally as the principal saviour of the country, not only in the crisis of 1940 but in the years of partnership with foreign allies. Yet Labour had a double advantage with the electors: its leaders had served with complete loyalty in the coalition, and had thereby secured valuable experience of government, mostly, to be sure, on the home front; but the party in Parliament had also by its single rebellion in 1943 made it clear to all that it was dissatisfied with the coalition's progress towards social reform. A final essential advantage for the party manifested itself in the general election campaign, when Attlee, for so long the 'unknown Opposition Leader', came to notice as a sober and responsible figure apparently capable of assuming the reins of government.

Throughout the war (except during the worst days of the blitz) the Gallup Poll had been assessing the popularity of the government, and of Churchill himself as Prime Minister. Churchill's personal popularity had been vouched for invariably by above 75% of the respondents, and the government, though poorly regarded during the setbacks to British arms in 1942, after the battle of El Alamein was never below 70%.[51] In 1943 the pollsters began to ask people how they would vote 'if a general election were held tomorrow'. The results, which were regularly published in the Liberal newspaper the *News Chronicle*, showed that there was a Labour lead over the Conservatives of 10% or more. The Liberal Party obtained only about 9% of the voters' support, and Common Wealth merely 1% or 2%.[52] It was easy, however, to discount this evidence at a time when opinion polls were in their infancy, at least so far as credibility was concerned, and when it was universally thought that support would return to Churchill as soon as his formidable oratorical skills were thrown in on one side of the party contest. As for the evidence of the by-elections, Attlee himself had discounted it in 1943:

I suppose every electioneer knows that at a by-election every person with any kind of grievance tends to vote against the Government . . . We should be very ill-advised to build too much on by-election votes.[53]

It was thus with some caution that Labour Ministers – who stood to lose their salaries in the event of the party's defeat – approached the question of the break-up of the coalition. Attlee thought that the coalition should continue until after the end of the war with Japan, however long that should take – and, as we have seen, it was expected to take another eighteen months after the collapse of Nazi Germany. He seems to have taken this view because he was perturbed about the growing power and intransigence of the Soviet Union, whose diplomats he had encountered at the foundation conference of the United Nations in San Francisco in April 1945.[54]

Thus on the eve of the Labour Party Conference at Blackpool in May 1945, which he hurried back from America to attend, Attlee called on Churchill at Downing Street and discussed with him the possibility of maintaining the coalition for a further period. He recommended an amendment to Churchill's published statement to the other party leaders suggesting this course, to say that the government would 'In the meantime . . . together do our utmost to implement the proposals for social security and full employment contained in the White Papers which we have laid before Parliament'.[55] Bevin and Dalton agreed with Attlee's views, although at this late stage they were doubtful whether the National Executive would agree. We now know that Attlee did in fact put the case to the executive, but that only three of its members, all trade union representatives, agreed with him.[56] When the majority executive recommendation – to withdraw from the coalition and fight an early general election – was put to the conference, it was accepted with only two dissentients.[57] The break-up of the coalition and Churchill's formation of a 'caretaker' government, consisting largely of his Conservative supporters together with just a few non-party men, followed almost at once. None of the Labour leaders felt that they should disobey the ruling of Conference that they should return to opposition: and some of them, most notably Morrison, were obviously relishing the prospect of the return to party politics.

As early as February Morrison had been elected chairman of the party's Campaign Committee, which was a sub-committee of the National Executive.[58] With the aid of his colleagues and the drafting assistance of the party's newly appointed research secretary, Michael Young (formerly secretary of the independent research organisation Political and Economic Planning) he prepared a manifesto entitled *Let us Face the Future*.[59] In this document the case for the nationalisation of key industries was argued on practical grounds in each instance: thus 'public ownership of the fuel and power industries' would 'bring great economies in operation and make it possible to modernise production methods and to raise safety standards'; 'public ownership of inland transport' would mean 'co-ordination of transport services by rail, road and canal'; and the iron and steel industry would become efficient 'only if public ownership replaces private monopoly'. Nevertheless the manifesto was in respect of nationalisation little more than an elaboration of the party's one-term programme as accepted at the 1937 conference, with the addition of iron and steel, which had been included as a concession to a radical resolution proposed by Ian Mikardo at the 1944 conference and carried against the advice of the platform. Of course the proposals of the Beveridge report also now came in for mention.

The references to foreign policy were, no doubt intentionally, vague: the manifesto called for the 'consolidation' of the 'great war-time association of the British Commonwealth with the USA and the USSR'. To suggest that on past form 'the Tories' could not be relied upon to maintain the association with Russia, the document added:

Let it not be forgotten that in the years leading to the war the Tories were so scared of Russia that they missed the chance to establish a partnership which might well have prevented war.[60]

Sympathy for the Soviet Union was a major advantage to the Labour Party during the campaign, because there had been widespread admiration of the achievements of the Red Army, not only in maintaining a successful resistance for almost four years but also in crowning that resistance with the capture of Berlin in spring 1945. For weeks on end in 1942 and 1943 and early 1944, before the Western Allies had launched their invasion of Normandy, the progress of the battle on the eastern front had been the principal item in the national newspapers, whatever their political complexion. The Ministry of Information had also played a leading part in lauding the military qualities of the Soviet ally, and indeed many other of its domestic accomplishments: in February 1943 it organised a meeting at the Albert Hall to celebrate the twenty-fifth anniversary of the foundation of the Red Army. This was a most unusual indication of the strength of public feeling, for it was apparently motivated, so far as the Ministry was concerned, by the desire to 'steal the thunder' of the Communist Party and prevent that body from obtaining the credit for the popular enthusiasm. [61] The government was evidently worried by Home Intelligence reports to the effect that there was an almost 'unanimous belief that the success of the Russian armies is due to the political system of that country'. [62] To some extent, the Communist Party of Great Britain benefited from this: its membership trebled after the German invasion, reaching a peak of about 56,000 in 1943. [63] But the impact on the Labour Party, which no longer needed to be slightly ashamed of its 'socialist' label, was also almost certainly of a positive character.

Nor did Labour suffer to the slightest extent in popular esteem from its link with the trade unions. This was because owing to wartime censorship there had been little in the newspapers about industrial disputes. The strikes in the shipyards, which held up the construction of new warships vital for the battle of the Atlantic, would have been heartily unpopular had they been publicised, and some of the adverse publicity would have reflected upon the party. [64] It is true, though, that the general level of strike action was low during the war: the number of working days lost in all six years was less than that lost in just two years (1917 and 1918) of the First World War. [65] The fact that Bevin, the leading figure in British trade unionism, had joined the government as Minister of Labour and was doing what he could to limit industrial conflict encouraged the sense among the public that the unions as a whole were behaving responsibly in the nation's crisis. Since the unions were tied so closely to the Labour Party, this was important for the party's standing in the election.

When the National Executive came to choose speakers for its ten BBC broadcasts, it could call upon a wide range of ministerial talent. None of the speakers spoke more than once, but they included several senior

Ministers, Attlee beginning the series and Morrison concluding it. The Conservatives, on the other hand, were anxious to stress the importance of Churchill's leadership, and he delivered four of their ten broadcasts; the Conservative manifesto was also linked with his name, being entitled *Mr. Churchill's Declaration of Policy to the Electors.* It was evidently the Conservative intention to associate their campaign as closely as possible with the personality of the wartime leader. There was clearly a danger for the Labour Party that its candidate for the premiership would not 'emerge' as a potential leader; this was reinforced by the fact that the Labour manifesto, *Let us Face the Future,* did not even mention his name.

In spite of this, Attlee, who had played a part during the war which was very largely behind the scenes – he had been Deputy Prime Minister and chairman of innumerable Cabinet committees – did 'emerge' during the campaign as a figure of importance, and this was largely an accidental result of Churchill's tactics in conducting his own campaign. When Churchill gave his first broadcast, suggesting that the Labour Party might have to resort to 'some form of Gestapo, no doubt very humanely directed in the first instance', the electors were bound to regard it as a gross exaggeration;[66] Attlee, following the next night, could readily ask his audience to distinguish between 'Winston Churchill, the great leader in war of a united nation, and Mr Churchill the party leader of the Conservatives'.[67] A few days later, when Churchill invited Attlee to accompany him to the Potsdam conference – which was due to meet before the election result would be known – Harold Laski, as chairman of the National Executive, warned Attlee publicly that he should go 'in the role of observer only', because Labour would expect to have a distinctive foreign policy thereafter.[68] Churchill at once sought to exploit this potential rift among his opponents, but Attlee replied firmly to the effect that as leader of his party he was free to make commitments on its behalf.

In the last days of the campaign Churchill returned to the attack, pointing out the danger to the parliamentary leadership of the Labour Party posed by the National Executive; but Attlee replied patiently, explaining the constitutional position of himself and his colleagues as he saw it; naturally his supporters – with the exception of Laski himself – did not gainsay his arguments, and on the whole the electorate took little interest in the discussion. As the Nuffield historians of the election put it, 'There can be little doubt that Mr Attlee had the better of these exchanges'.[69] They might also have noted that they played an important part in bringing Attlee more fully to the notice of the electors. Attlee finally discovered that he was a figure of importance in British politics when he went to Potsdam with Churchill in July, and found that he was greeted with more warmth by the British forces in Berlin than Churchill himself. He wrote to his wife, 'I got a lot of cheers & shouts of "Good Old Clem" from the troops watching'.[70]

Churchill gave Attlee one last boost when they were both back in London and the election results – postponed for three weeks owing to the need to bring from abroad the postal votes of the forces serving overseas – were at last declared. Churchill had been thinking of delaying his resignation, even if defeated, until after the weekend; but the results were so devastating to his party that on the very evening of the declaration of most of them – 26 July – he decided to go to the palace, resign his commission as Prime Minister, and invite the King to send for Attlee. He called on the King at 7.00 p.m.; at 7.30 p.m. Attlee drove up, to be invited to take Churchill's place.[71] This rapid development quelled the movement, which had been proceeding behind the scenes, to replace Attlee with a more obviously partisan anti-Churchillian such as Morrison.[72]

Although the Labour victory was an overwhelming one in terms of parliamentary seats – 393 out of a total of 640, whereas the Conservatives and their allies obtained only 213 – the proportion of the voters who voted Labour was still less than half, at 47·8%. The Labour Party gained substantially on this occasion from the 'first past the post' electoral system and from the unequal size of the constituencies, whose boundaries were overdue for redistribution. In an appendix to the Nuffield study of the election David Butler showed that the average size of Labour-won constituencies was 51,000 electors, compared with Conservative-won at 57,000.[73] It was apparent that Labour had done well in the old inner cities, which the population had been leaving in the previous decade, partly owing to the growth of suburbs, partly owing to the effects of wartime bombing. Indeed, the redistribution of boundaries that took place in 1948 was reckoned in the subsequent elections to have cost the Labour Party between twenty and forty seats.[74]

Labour's newly-elected Members of Parliament contained many of a different type from the old hands of the 1935 Parliament. Owing to the successes in constituencies previously thought unlikely prospects, where many of the candidates were young middle-class aspirants, the character of the party changed and the proportion of trade union nominees, most of them at least in late middle age, declined. Trade union-sponsored MPs, who in the 1935 Parliament had accounted for more than half the party, were now less than a third of the total.[75] On the other hand the number of university graduates greatly increased: many of them had served in the forces, usually as officers, and several had been temporary civil servants. The change did not mean that the new recruits to Parliament were any less committed to socialism: indeed, many of them probably understood its teachings even better than had the bulk of MPs of the pre-war era. Their commitment to the nationalisation programme of *Let us Face the Future* was fully demonstrated when they revealed their opposition to any attempts to 'water down' the principle of public ownership, as over civil aviation in 1945–46 and over iron and steel in 1947.[76] But this is not the place to discuss the details of post-war politics. It only remains to emphasise that the new Parliamentary Labour Party was socially far more representative of the country as a whole than the party of 1935 onwards, and that its leadership, which had had the experience of participation in government during the war, was able to assume the reins of office without any of the difficulties that Ramsay MacDonald encountered in forming his minority governments in 1924 and 1929. What Dr Addison has appropriately described as the 'Attlee consensus' had arrived, and prevailed thereafter for almost a generation.

Notes

1 R. M. Titmuss, *Essays on the Welfare State*, new edn, 1963, p. 86.

2 Arthur Marwick, *Britain in the Century of Total War*, 1968, p. 330; Paul Addison, *The Road to 1945*, 1975, ch. X ('Attlee's consensus').

3 On this see C. T. Stannage, *Baldwin thwarts the Opposition*, 1980.

4 *Labour Party Conference Report* (henceforth *LPCR*), 1937, p. 181.

5 *LPCR*, 1939, p. 243.

6 *Ibid.*, pp. 281–9.

7 *Ibid.*, pp. 44–53 and 226–36.

8 National Executive Committee (henceforth NEC) Minutes, 20 March 1940; *LPCR*, 1940, pp. 20, 161–7.

9 NEC Minutes, 10, 11 and 12 May 1940; Joint Meeting with General Council of TUC, 12 May 1940; and *LPCR*, 1940, pp. 123–34 (13 May 1940).

10 For the postponement decision see NEC Minutes, 16 May 1944.

11 Quoted W. S. Churchill, *The Second World War*, VI, 1954, p. 510.

12 *Ibid.*, p. 509.

13 *LPCR*, 1939, pp. 365–8; John Ramsden, *The Age of Balfour and Baldwin, 1902–1940*, 1978, p. 239.

14 *LPCR*, 1940, p. 28.

15 *LPCR*, 1942, p. 26.

16 Memo on 'Individual Membership', NEC Minutes, 26 November 1941.

17 *LPCR*, 1944, p. 30.
18 Attlee, in *LPCR*, 1943, p. 127.
19 On Common Wealth see Addison, *Road to 1945*, pp. 159–60.
20 George Orwell, *Collected Essays, Journalism and Letters*, III, 1968, 294.
21 Hugh Dalton, *Memoirs, 1931–1945: the Fateful Years*, 1957, p. 366.
22 Alan Milward, in Stephen Hawes and R. White (eds.), *Resistance in Europe*, 1975, p. 203.
23 Dalton, *Fateful Years*, p. 409.
24 On the making of the Beveridge report see José Harris, *William Beveridge*, Oxford, 1977, ch. 16.
25 *LPCR*, 1943, p. 132.
26 *Ibid.*, pp. 9–18.
27 *Ibid.*, p. 168.
28 *Ibid.*, p. 153.
29 *Daily Telegraph*, 3 August 1943.
30 NEC Minutes, 25 August 1943.
31 *LPCR*, 1943, pp. 134–5.
32 NEC Minutes, 24 November 1943.
33 *Ibid.*; *LPCR*, 1944, p. 14.
34 NEC Minutes, 28 June 1944.
35 *LPCR*, 1945, p. 17.
36 Dalton, diary, 23 October 1943, British Library of Political and Economic Science.
37 Earl of Woolton, *Memoirs*, 1959, p. 264.
38 T. D. Burridge, *British Labour and Hitler's War*, 1976, p. 126.
39 *Ibid.*, p. 137.
40 C. R. Attlee, 'Foreign Policy and the Flying Bomb', 26 July 1944, quoted Burridge, *British Labour*, p. 144.
41 Burridge, *British Labour*, p. 156.
42 NEC Minutes, 9 and 21 May 1945; TUC *Report*, 1945, p. 173.
43 M. R. Gordon, *Conflict and Consensus in Labour's Foreign Policy, 1914–1965*, Stanford, Cal., 1969, p. 84. On this see also Neil Diamond, 'Labour and the International Post-war Settlement, 1940–45', Leeds University M Phil thesis, 1974.
44 *LPCR*, 1943, p. 188.
45 Noel-Baker to Attlee, 13 September 1943, Labour Party file, Attlee papers, Bodleian Library.
46 *Ibid.*; TUC *Report*, 1943, pp. 329–33.
47 Quoted J. T. Grantham, 'Hugh Dalton and the international post-war settlement', *Journal of Contemporary History*, XIV, 1979, p. 716.
48 *Ibid.*, p. 717.
49 *Ibid.*, p. 725.
50 *LPCR*, 1945, p. 117.
51 See Pelling, *Britain and the Second World War*, 1970, p. 307.
52 *News Chronicle*, 23 August 1943.
53 *LPCR*, 1943, p. 127.
54 Chuter Ede, diary, 24 May 1945, BL Add. Mss. 59701; Dalton, *Fateful Years*, p. 457.

55   *LPCR*, 1945, p. 87.

56   Dalton, *Fateful Years*, p. 458.

57   *LPCR*, 1945, p. 87.

58   NEC Minutes, 28 February 1945.

59   Michael Young, in John Pinder (ed.), *Fifty Years of Political and Economic Planning*, 1981, p. 96.

60   The manifesto is reprinted in F. W. S. Craig, *British General Election Manifestos, 1918–1966*, Chichester, 1970.

61   Ian McLaine, *Ministry of Morale*, 1979, pp. 203, 206.

62   *Ibid.*, p. 207.

63   Pelling, *British Communist Party*, 1958, p. 192.

64   P. Inman, *Labour in the Munition Industries*, 1957, pp. 96, 394.

65   Figures from *Ministry of Labour Gazette*, quoted Pelling, *History of British Trade Unionism*, 3rd edn, 1976, pp. 294–5.

66   *Listener*, 7 June 1945.

67   Quoted R. B. McCallum and A. Readman, *British General Election of 1945*, 1947, p. 143.

68   *Ibid.*, p. 145.

69   *Ibid.*, p. 175.

70   Attlee to Mrs Attlee, 21 July 1945, Attlee personal papers in possession of Mr Kenneth Harris, consulted by courtesy of Mr Harris.

71   McCallum and Readman, *op. cit.*, pp. 245–6.

72   See, e.g., Dalton, *Fateful Years*, pp. 468, 473.

73   McCallum and Readman, *op. cit.*, p. 287.

74   H. G. Nicholas, *British General Election of 1950*, 1951, p. 4.

75   Martin Harrison, *Trade Unions and the Labour Party*, 1960, p. 267.

76   On this see Hugh Dalton, *Memoirs, 1945–1960: High Tide and After*, 1962, pp. 61, 252–3.

II Social structure

J. M. Winter

The demographic consequences of the war

There have been many substantial studies of the demographic consequences of the Second World War in European States, but none exists with respect to Britain.[1] In part, this reflects the relatively less traumatic effect of the conflict on British society.[2] This country did not escape the horrors of aerial bombardment, but there is a clear distinction between living through the Blitz and enduring the cycle of violence and deprivation linked to military operations, occupation, resistance, and liberation on the Continent.

It is therefore surprising that, in some important respects, demographic developments in the period of the Second World War in Britain bear a striking resemblance to those on the Continent. This suggests, first, that underlying demographic trends in motion before the war determined movements in vital statistics in several European countries in this period; and, secondly, that the upheaval of the Second World War drew Britain into a wider, Western European, phase of economic and social reconstruction, the ramifications of which are reflected in demographic history.

Consequently, this chapter will examine both the peculiarities of the British and the affinities between demographic developments in this country and abroad. First, we will sketch movements in vital statistics in Britain. Secondly, we will set these data in an international context. Thirdly, we will try to account for demographic continuities with respect to mortality decline, and demographic discontinuities with respect to nuptiality and fertility trends in Britain during and after the Second World War.

1. *Vital statistics in the period of the Second World War*
(a) Nuptiality. Let us begin with nuptiality. Just as in the 1914–18 war,[3]

there were three phases in the history of marriage in Britain during the Second World War. The first was a surge in marriages in 1939 and 1940. As we can see in Table 1, the marriage rate in England and Wales in 1938 was 17·6 per 1,000. In the following two years the marriage rate rose substantially, reaching the highest figure ever recorded, 22·5 per 1,000 in 1940. In the First World War a similar marriage boom occurred early in the war. But it is important to note that in 1914–15 military recruitment was still voluntary and centred on unmarried men. Since conscription antedated the outbreak of war in 1939, the question of liability for military service with respect to marital status simply did not arise. It is probably more sensible to suggest that, in both conflicts, thousands of people decided to marry while they still had the chance. In this war, as in others, the basic unit of survival was apparently two.

Table 1 Marriage rates, birth rates and fertility rates, England and Wales, 1935–50.

Year	Marriage rate[a]	Birth rate[a]	Total fertility rate[b]	Gross reproduction rate[b]	Net reproduction rate[c]
1935	17·2	14·7	1·75	0·85	0·79
1936	17·4	14·8	1·77	0·86	0·80
1937	17·5	14·9	1·79	0·87	0·81
1938	17·6	15·1	1·85	0·90	0·83
1939	21·2	14·8	1·83	0·89	0·82
1940	22·5	14·1	1·75	0·85	0·79
1941	18·6	13·9	1·73	0·84	0·78
1942	17·7	15·6	1·91	0·93	0·87
1943	14·0	16·2	2·02	0·98	0·92
1944	14·3	17·7	2·24	1·09	1·02
1945	18·7	15·9	2·04	0·99	0·94
1946	18·1	19·2	2·49	1·21	1·14
1947	18·6	20·5	2·70	1·31	1·24
1948	18·2	17·8	2·39	1·16	1·11
1949	17·1	16·7	2·26	1·10	1·05
1950	16·3	15·8	2·18	1·06	1·02

Source. (*a*) B. Mitchell, *Abstract of British Historical Statistics*, Cambridge, 1962, tables 10, 16; B. Mitchell and H. G. Jones, *Second Abstract of British Historical Statistics*, Cambridge, 1971, tables 8, 14. (*b*) J. M. Winter and M. S. Teitelbaum, *The Fear of Population Decline*, 1985, appendix A. (*c*) United Nations Demographic Yearbook, 1954, table 21.

The second phase of wartime nuptiality extended from 1941 to 1944. In this period the marriage rate fell sharply, reaching 14·0 per 1,000 in 1943, which was almost identical to the lowest level recorded during the First World War. The absence of men on active service accounts for this downward trend in both conflicts.

The third phase can be dated between 1945 and 1948 and constitutes an end-of-war and post-war marriage boom. Clearly, deferred marriages from the second phase of the war were solemnised in this period. By 1949 the marriage rate was about where it had been a decade earlier. We shall return to the question of nuptiality later, since these aggregate data do not reveal important changes in marital behaviour which took place at this time.

(b) Fertility. The trajectory of birth rates during the Second World War was quite different from that of marriage rates. The surge of marriages in 1939–40 was not followed either immediately or within a year by a surge in births. Just as in the First World War, the first phase of the 1939–45 war was marked by a depression of the birth rate below pre-war levels. But after 1941 the birth rate in England and Wales rose substantially, reaching 17·7 per 1,000 in 1944, fully 20% higher than the average for 1935–38.

This minor wartime 'baby boom' was followed by a more substantial one, extending from 1945 to 1948. On one level, this third phase of fertility was in part one of recovery of deferred births. But as we can see in Table 1, data on total fertility rates (the sum of age-specific fertility rates for women in their child-bearing years) and on gross and net reproduction rates (the number of female children produced by women during their child-bearing years, either uncorrected or corrected for mortality) suggest that a more fundamental change in demographic behaviour had taken place during and after the war.

Demographers use a rough rule of thumb that a total fertility rate of 2·1 implies that a population is just replacing itself. A figure below that is designated below-replacement; a higher figure, above-replacement. Similarly a figure of 1·00 is used as a divide in gross and net reproduction rates; in the long term a society with a net reproduction rate above 1·00 will grow; one with, say, 0·80 will eventually and slowly diminish. As we can see Table 1, the pre-war period was clearly one of below-replacement fertility, while the post-war period was one of above-replacement fertility, however it be measured. Again, we shall return to this important question below.

(c) Mortality. Civilian death rates rose during the Second World War in Britain. For example, in 1938 the crude death rate stood at 11·6 per

1,000. That figure was exceded in every year in the succeeding decade, with the worst figure registered for 1940. (See Table 2.) Of course this question is complicated by conscription, military casualties and civilian casualties of military operations. We shall discuss the components of mortality rates in more detail below. But initially we can see from the figures in Table 3 that much better progress was made during the war with respect to infant and maternal mortality than with respect to mortality rates as a whole. After setbacks in 1940 and 1941 the infant mortality rate dropped steadily both before and after the end of the war. By 1945 the infant mortality rate was fully 20% below pre-war levels; by 1950 the pre-war rate had been nearly halved. (Table 3.)

These gains were attributable both to a decline in the mortality of infants after the first month of life (post-neonatal mortality) and to a decline in mortality in the earliest stages of infancy. For example, while the infant mortality rate in 1946 stood at 76% of the pre-war figure, that for post-neonatal mortality stood at 68%, and that for perinatal mortality (stillbirths plus week-one deaths per 1,000 live and stillbirths) stood at 73%. (Table 3.) This suggests that there was an improvement in conditions affecting, on the one hand, pregnancy and the management of delivery and, on the other, the survival chances of infants in later stages of the first year of life.

These gains, while impressive, were exceeded by those related to maternal health. The data in Table 3 suggest that in the years surrounding the Second World War there occurred a fundamental transformation in the risks associated with child-bearing. These data are not strictly comparable with other mortality rates, for two simple reasons. First, the denominator of the rate does not accurately reflect the true number of women at risk of dying from causes associated with pregnancy and child-bearing. No demographer has yet discovered how to find out how many women become pregnant in any one year, and thus we must use, *faute de mieux*, the number of live and stillbirths as a surrogate for a true measure of population at risk. Secondly, the hidden agenda of all studies of maternal mortality is the history of abortion, the frequency of which under conditions of illegality is extremely difficult to measure. Some discretionary misreporting of causes of death probably occurred, further distorting the data. Consequently we must treat these statistics with extreme care and as only very rough approximations of the risk associated with child-bearing in this period.

But, however we hedge our findings with qualifications, it is still apparent that the most spectacular gains in survival rates in these years

Table 2 Crude death rates, infant mortality rates, stillbirth rates, perinatal mortality rates and maternal mortality rates, England and Wales, 1935–50.

Year	Death rate[a]	Infant mortality rate[b]	Month 1 mortality rate[b]	Months 1–12 mortality rate[b]	Still-birth rate[c]	Perinatal mortality rate[c]	Maternal mortality rate[d]
1935	11·7	57·0	30·4	26·6	40·7	61·9	5·29
1936	12·1	58·7	30·2	28·5	39·7	60·8	4·92
1937	12·4	57·7	29·7	28·0	39·0	60·2	4·57
1938	11·6	52·8	28·3	24·5	38·3	58·6	4·22
1939	12·1	50·6	28·3	22·3	38·1	58·5	3·99
1940	14·4	56·8	29·6	27·2	37·2	57·7	3·37
1941	13·5	60·0	29·0	31·0	34·8	54·7	3·47
1942	12·3	50·6	27·2	23·4	33·2	52·1	3·10
1943	13·0	49·1	25·2	23·9	30·1	47·9	3·00
1944	12·7	45·4	24·4	21·0	27·6	44·5	2·50
1945	12·6	46·0	24·8	21·2	27·6	45·2	2·33
1946	12·0	42·9	24·5	18·4	27·2	44·3	1·90
1947	12·3	41·4	22·7	18·7	24·1	40·3	1·52
1948	11·0	33·9	19·7	14·2	23·2	38·5	1·33
1949	11·8	32·4	19·3	13·1	22·7	38·0	1·21
1950	11·6	29·6	18·5	11·1	22·6	37·4	1·15

Source. (a) Mitchell and Jones, Abstract, table 10; (b) Registrar General's Statistical Review of England and Wales, 1951, table LX. (c) Registrar General's Statistical Review of England and Wales, 1950, table XIX. (Perinatal mortality equals stillbirths plus week-one mortality per 1,000 live and stillbirths.) (d) Registrar General's Statistical Review of England and Wales, 1950, table XI. (Maternal mortality due to all causes, per 1,000 live and stillbirths.)

Table 3 An index of death rates, England and Wales, 1935–50 (1935–38 = 100).

Year	Crude death rate[a]	Infant mortality rate[b]	Month 1 mortality rate[b]	Months 1–12 mortality rate[b]	Still-birth rate[c]	Perinatal mortality rate[c]	Maternal mortality rate[d]
1939	101	89	95	83	97	97	84
1940	121	101	100	101	94	95	71
1941	113	106	98	115	88	91	73
1942	103	89	92	87	84	86	73
1943	109	87	85	89	76	79	65
1944	106	80	82	78	70	74	53
1945	105	81	84	77	70	75	49
1946	100	76	83	68	69	73	40
1947	103	73	77	70	61	67	32
1948	92	60	66	53	59	64	28
1949	99	57	65	49	58	63	25
1950	97	52	62	41	57	62	24

Source. (a) Mitchell and Jones, Abstract, table 10; (b) Registrar General's Statistical Review of England and Wales, 1951, table LX. (c) Registrar General's Statistical Review of England and Wales, 1950, table XIX. (Perinatal mortality equals stillbirths plus week-one mortality per 1,000 live and stillbirths.) (d) Registrar General's Statistical Review of England and Wales, 1950, table XI. (Maternal mortality due to all causes, per 1,000 live and stillbirths.)

occurred with respect to maternity. While it is clear that the overall decline had begun prior to the war, the gains made during the war itself are remarkable. In 1939 the maternal mortality rate for all causes stood at about 4 per 1,000 births. In 1946 the rate had reached 1·90, and descended to 1·15 by 1950. In the course of a decade the risks associated with childbirth had been reduced by 75%. This is well in advance of all other improvements in life expectancy in this period, and requires separate discussion below.

(d) International migration. When we turn to the question of British migration we confront a much less unsettled terrain. The Second World War constituted much less of a discontinuity in the history of migration than did the First World War. The 1914–18 conflict ended an extraordinarily turbulent phase of out-migration from Europe as a whole and from Britain in particular. In the years 1910–14 there was a net outflow of over 650,000 migrants from Britain. After the armistice out-migration resumed first at a much slower rate and then was reduced to a trickle by changes in the political and economic climate in receiver States.[4] In addition, after 1933 there was an additional inflow of refugees from Nazi Germany, which further helps account for the fact that in the four years preceding the Second World War there was a net inflow of about 50,000 people to this country.

After 1945 the country again exported more migrants than she imported, but the outflow was, after 1946, at the modest level of the mid-1920s. What had changed over the war years, though, was the age structure of emigrants. Before the war over 35% of all male emigrants were in the age group eighteen to twenty-nine. After the war only 23% were in this age bracket. In contrast, whereas about 19% of male emigrants were under the age of seventeen before 1939, fully 31% were in this group after the war. The average age of female emigrants also declined over the war decade.[5]

These statistics make sense when set against the backdrop of labour scarcity in the post-war years. After 1945 job opportunities for young men in this country were unusually good. In addition, difficulties in finding shipping space or appropriate housing in receiver countries were persistent and discouraging. The prospects for unmarried men to earn a good living in Britain were probably better than they had been for at least a generation.

At the same time, many women who had married servicemen from abroad during the war left Britain after 1945. This helps account for the decline in the average age of female migrants. But thousands of British couples with young dependents also decided to find new homes, particularly in Canada, Australia and South Africa. It is their demographic profile which we see in the overall data on the age structure of migrants.

In strictly demographic terms, the most important implication of the age structure of migration is its effects on nuptiality. And here both the relatively small numbers involved and the decline in the proportion of young men of marriageable age among them suggest that migration had a slight but positive effect on nuptiality in Britain.

2. *International comparisons*

When we survey international demographic developments in the Second World War it is apparent that most British trends are not at all unique. This is most clearly the case with respect to nuptiality. The crude marriage rate simply tells us about the frequency of marriage. But of far greater demographic importance is the question of the timing of marriage, since a shift of a few years in the age of first marriage can have far-reaching effects on population growth rates. [6]

A glance at Table 4 will show that such a change took place in the period of the Second World War in most parts of Western Europe and the United States. For example, in Britain in 1931, 42% of all women in the twenty-five to twenty-nine age group were still unmarried. Two decades later only 22% were unmarried. This suggests that, whatever the level of the crude marriage rate, British women were marrying earlier after the war than before it. The same clear divide occurs in the history of American nuptiality in this period: the proportion still single in the twenty-five to twenty-nine age group in 1951 is exactly half that in 1930. Similar trends occurred in the Netherlands, Sweden and Switzerland, while in France pre-war nuptiality patterns survived the war period intact.

Another way of demonstrating this significant demographic development is to use an index of nuptiality developed by demographers at the Office of Population Research at Princeton University. They have followed the great French demographer Louis Henry in seeking to measure European fertility against the pattern set by one particular community with the highest fertility rates on record – the Hutterites of the mid-western American states and bordering Canadian provinces. An index of nuptiality, $I(m)$, is a fertility-weighted summary measure

Table 4 Proportions single at specified ages in several European countries in the period of the Second World War.

Country	Year	Men			Women		
		20–24	*25–29*	*45–49*	*20–24*	*25–29*	*45–49*
France	1936	0·79	0·35	0·10[a]	0·49	0·23	0·13[a]
	1949	0·81	0·39	0·12[a]	0·54	0·22	0·11[a]
Britain	1931	0·86	0·41	0·12	0·74	0·42	0·17
	1951	0·77	0·35	0·10	0·53	0·22	0·16
Netherlands	1930	0·90	0·49	0·11	0·75	0·38	0·15
	1951	0·89	0·48	0·09	0·71	0·31	0·13
Sweden	1930	0·94	0·67	0·17	0·80	0·52	0·23
	1945	0·87	0·52	0·17	0·64	0·30	0·21
Switzerland	1930	0·93	0·60	0·14	0·82	0·48	0·19
	1950	0·86	0·50	0·13	0·66	0·31	0·19
USA	1930	0·71	0·37	0·11[b]	0·46	0·22	0·09[b]
	1951	0·52	0·20	0·08[b]	0·31	0·11	0·07[b]

Notes. (a) Forty to forty-nine. (b) Forty-five to fifty-four.
Source. J. Hajnal, 'The marriage boom', *Population Index*, xix (1953), table 3.

of propensity to marry, which sets the Hutterite experience as 1·000 and permits comparisons over time and space. For example, as in Table 5, $I(m)$ for Belgium in 1910 was about half that of the Hutterites, while $I(m)$ for Scotland was lower, roughly two-fifths of the Hutterite schedule.

Using this index, we can see that nuptiality rates rose substantially in the decades surrounding the Second World War. The absence of full data for 1940 make strict comparisons impossible, but, taken together with the statistics in Table 4, it is apparent that the institution of marriage went through a substantial revival in this period. In 1930 $I(m)$ for England and Wales stood at about 0·5; by 1960 the figure was 0·7. A similarly impressive increase in Scottish $I(m)$ occurred over this interval. Less marked, though parallel trends, can be noted for most other European countries.

These statistics constitute what the noted demographer John Hajnal has called the end of the 'European marriage pattern', dating roughly from 1740 to 1940, under which Europeans tended to marry late and a substantial proportion of women never married at all.[7] This key feature of the demographic history of Western Europe vanished in the years surrounding the Second World War. To what extent this change was war-related is a question we shall discuss below, but at this point it is clear that we cannot accept strictly British explanations of movements in nuptiality in Britain which so clearly parallel developments in many other countries.

Table 5. An index of nuptiality, $I(m)$,* for several European countries, 1910–60.

Country	1910	1920	1930	1940	1950	1960
Belgium	0·502	0·477	0·577	–	0·605	0·697
England and Wales	0·472	0·485	0·507	–	–	0·703
France	0·605	0·541	0·616	–	–	0·645
Germany	0·523	–	0·527	–	–	0·686
Italy	0·535	0·497	0·515	0·522	0·539	0·581
Netherlands	0·475	0·488	0·506	–	–	0·636
Portugal	0·488	0·468	0·486	0·495	0·524	0·561
Scotland	0·390	0·403	0·419	–	–	0·658
Switzerland	0·459	0·413	0·417	0·471	0·517	0·564

$$* \ I(m) = \frac{\sum m(i)F(i)}{\sum w(i)F(i)}$$

where, for each age group (i), $m(i)$ is the number of married women, $w(i)$ is the total number of women, and $F(i)$ is the age-specific marital fertility rate for Hutterite women married in the years 1921–30.

Source. S. C. Watkins, 'Regional patterns of nuptiality in Europe, 1870–1960', *Population Studies*, xxxv (1981), table 1.

This point can be made in another way. A very wide range of law and custom governed divorce in Europe in the period. This makes it even more significant that divorce rates rose simultaneously in many European countries in the years surrounding the war. We are still dealing with relatively small numbers of divorces, but divorce rates (divorces per 1,000 married couples) doubled not only in England and Wales over the years 1939–41 and 1944–46 but also in France, Finland and Sweden over roughly the same period. It is apparent that people throughout Europe were getting into and out of marriage with greater frequency after the Second World War than before it.[8]

If the history of nuptiality in this country cannot be written without an international perspective, the same is true of the history of fertility in the Second World War. We have noted the striking rise in total fertility rates and in gross and net reproduction rates for Britain during and after the 1939–45 conflict. But it is important to recognise how similar the trend is to developments in many other countries at the same time.

In the aftermath of the war there were two kinds of 'baby booms'. The first and more robust variety occurred in the United States and in a number of countries of white settlement, Canada, Australia and New Zealand. Their total fertility rates in the period 1920–83 are illustrated in Fig. 1. In Fig. 2 we present data on fertility over this period in England and Wales, Scotland, France and Germany, with the American data superimposed on them. It is apparent that Western European countries went through not a 'baby boom' but a 'boomlet': Fig. 1 suggests the Matterhorn; Fig. 2, the foothills of the Alps.[9]

Still, while not approaching the amplitude or duration of the American 'baby boom', the European surge in fertility in the post-1940 period is clear enough. Equally apparent is the simultaneity of the end of the post-war period in the history of fertility. After 1964 fertility in virtually every Western European country began a sharp decline which, more or less, has persisted to this day.[10]

Demographers are far from agreed as to the causes of the onset and demise of the 'baby boom', and we shall return to some interpretations below. But, again, it is apparent that explanations of fertility trends relying primarily upon the peculiarities of the British simply will not do.

The same is true with respect to mortality trends. Despite wide fluctuations in wartime,[11] the decline in stillbirth rates and in infant mortality rates in Britain is mirrored by similar trends in other European countries at this time. For example, the stillbirth rate in France stood at $30 \cdot 5$ per 1,000 live and stillbirths in 1938; a decade later the figure was $19 \cdot 9$. Data for Denmark and Sweden show the same trajectory.[12] Similarly, maternal mortality rates dropped in other countries as precipitately as they did in Britain in this period.[13]

It is only with respect to trends in international migration that we must clearly distinguish between British and European developments. This country had the good fortune to avoid the displacement of populations which took place on a gigantic scale in continental Europe during and after the Second World War.[14] There were literally millions of people scattered across Europe, many without hope or destination, trying to pick up the threads of their lives after 1945. Leaving aside the question of the scale of civilian casualties, to which we shall refer below, the movement and repatriation of survivors after VE day complicate the post-war demographic history of Europe in a way that precludes direct comparison with that of Britain.

Figure 1

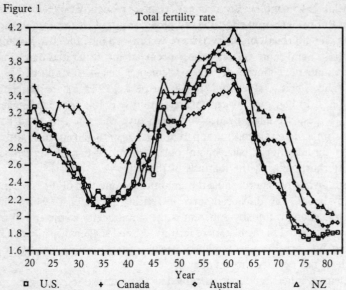

Total fertility rate

□ U.S.   + Canada   ◇ Austral   △ NZ

Fig. 1 Total fertility rates, 1920–83: Australia, Canada, New Zealand, USA.
Source: M. S. Teitelbaum and J. M. Winter, *The Fear of Population Decline*,
New York, 1985, figs. 4.1–2.

Figure 2

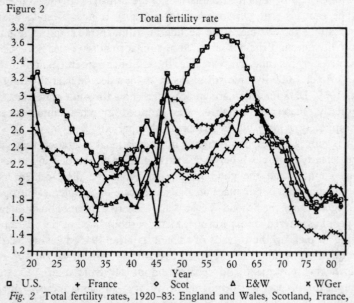

Total fertility rate

□ U.S.   + France   ◇ Scot   △ E&W   × WGer

Fig. 2 Total fertility rates, 1920–83: England and Wales, Scotland, France,
West Germany, USA. Source: as Fig. 1.

With this notable exception, it is still possible to argue that Britain and Europe went through a set of major demographic changes together, as it were. The remainder of this chapter is directed to unravelling the origins, both domestic and international, of these developments.

3. *Direct demographic effects of war: war losses*

War losses of British forces in 1939–45 were roughly a third of those in the 1914–18 conflict. Whereas over 700,000 men died or were killed on active service in the Great War, 264,000 perished a generation later. Since approximately the same number of men served in both world wars, it meant that the risk a soldier faced of getting killed in the second was between a third and a half that faced by men in uniform in the earlier conflict. No doubt this arose out of changes in tactics and an improvement in medical care for wounded men.

The more prominent part played by the Royal Navy and RAF in the Second World War is reflected in the fact that death rates were higher in both these service arms than in the army. This is in striking contrast to the figures for the 1914–18 war, when death rates in the army were double those in the navy and six times those in the RFC/RAF.[15]

The fact that trench warfare did not recur in 1939–45 is also reflected in the statistics of proportions wounded. In 1914–18 over 30% of all men who served in the army were wounded at least once; in 1939–45 the figure mercifully dropped to about 6%. Percentages missing and taken prisoner in the two wars were roughly similar.[16]

To this total of the human costs of the Second World War we must add over 30,000 men who died on service in the merchant navy and fishing fleet and approximately 4,000 people who died while on service in the Women's Auxiliary Forces, in civil defence work or in the Home Guard. This figure must be increased by the toll of civilian lives lost through bombing. Over 60,000 people were killed and 80,000 wounded in air raids.[17]

In sum, the obliteration of the distinction between civilian and military targets meant that the war cost Britain approximately 360,000 lives. If we take casualty statistics for the First World War as a base figure, we can conclude that direct British war losses in 1939–45 were about 50% lower.

4. *Indirect demographic effects of war: mortality decline, 1940–51*

It is clear in the case of the First World War that the war economy created conditions which made this country a healthier place in which to live.[18]

Table 6 Casualties suffered by British forces in the Second World War.

Branch of service	Served	Killed	% killed	Wounded	% wounded	Missing and POW	% missing and POW	Total	% casualties
Army	3,788,000	144,079	3·80	239,575	6·32	185,847	4·91	569,501	15·03
Navy	923,000	50,758	5·50	14,663	1·59	8,221	0·89	73,642	7·98
RAF	1,185,000	69,606	5·87	33,771	2·85	19,851	1·68	112,296	9·48
Total	5,896,000	264,443	4·49	277,077	4·70	218,671	3·71	755,439	12·81

Source. W. Franklin Mellor (ed.), *Casualties and Medical Statistics,* (1972), table 6, p. 836.

As Richard Titmuss pointed out thirty years ago, the same was true with respect to the 1939–45 war.[19]

One way to demonstrate this fact is to examine patterns of female mortality. This enables us to avoid the difficulties which arise from the unusual masculine age structure among the civilian population during the war. We shall proceed first to examine the cause structure of mortality decline in the war decade, and secondly to discuss the special features of maternal mortality, the decline of which was particularly sharp.

(a) The cause structure of mortality decline, 1940–51. It is only in recent years that demographers have begun to investigate the cause structure of mortality with the precision already devoted to the age structure of mortality. Inaccuracies in cause-of-death diagnoses and substantial variations in completeness and modes of classification undoubtedly exist and ensure that any statistical analysis using cause-of-death data will contain a wide margin of error. The most successful attempt to overcome the problems and to develop a model of causes of mortality over time is that of Preston, who accumulated and analysed data on mortality in 162 countries over the period 1860 to the present. He developed a twelve-part classification of causes of death based on etiological rather than anatomical criteria and then distributed among these twelve categories all causes of death enumerated in the International Classifications of Causes of Death, produced between 1909 and 1955.[20] He then calculated age-specific and cause-specific death rates for each country at decennial or quinquennial intervals. These permitted an elaborate analysis of the contribution of different causes of death to overall mortality decline over time.

With some qualifications,[21] this approach is of considerable value to the demographic historian. Among the collection of life tables Preston and his colleagues produced are two referring to England and Wales in 1940 and 1951. These enable us to specify which diseases contributed most to female mortality decline in the years during and after the Second World War.

There are, though, two drawbacks to the use of these data. First, the inclusion of the post-war years makes it difficult to separate the effects of war from the effects of time. Still, no one at the time ignored the fact that post-war conditions were a direct result not only of the economic burdens but also of the political achievements of the struggle against Hitler. It is only the legal purist who insists upon restricting the survey of the effects of war to wartime and not one day more. The second difficulty is more serious. By starting in 1940 we incorporate data on a society facing the Blitz. This will inevitably increase the death rate due to causes associated with violence and thereby unbalance the cause structure of mortality as a whole. But, once we take this distortion into account, it is still possible to draw some important inferences from this statistical exercise.

Our results are set out in Tables 7–9, which describe the extent and components of female mortality decline in England and Wales during the war. In Table 7 we present age-specific death rates for all causes. In Table 8 we present cause-specific death rates for all ages. Table 7 shows that standardised female mortality declined by about 26·3% in the period. This is higher than the decline registered during the First World War.[22]

Table 7 The age structure of mortality decline, female population of England and Wales, 1940–51, all causes.

Age at start of interval	Death rates			
	1951	1940	Decline 1940–51	Decline 1940–51(%)
0	0·02631	0·05000	0·02369	47·38
1	0·00126	0·00448	0·00322	71·88
5	0·00045	0·00180	0·00135	75·00
10	0·00037	0·00131	0·00094	71·76
15	0·00064	0·00232	0·00168	72·41
20	0·00089	0·00286	0·00197	68·88
25	0·00115	0·00287	0·00172	59·93
30	0·00147	0·00301	0·00154	51·16
35	0·00191	0·00364	0·00173	47·53
40	0·00269	0·00467	0·00198	42·40
45	0·00428	0·00662	0·00234	35·35
50	0·00645	0·00957	0·00312	32·60
55	0·01015	0·01387	0·00372	26·82
60	0·01638	0·02201	0·00563	25·58
65	0·02795	0·03529	0·00734	20·80
70	0·04818	0·05837	0·01019	17·46
75	0·08523	0·09781	0·01258	12·86
80	0·14414	0·15852	0·01438	9·07
85+	0·25442	0·25692	0·00250	0·97
All (crude)	0·01176	0·01286	0·00110	8·55
All (standardised)	0·00932	0·01264	0·00332	26·27

Source. S. Preston, N. Keyfitz and S. Schoen, *Causes of Death: Life Tables for National Populations* (New York, 1972).

Table 8 The cause structure of mortality decline, female population of England and Wales, 1940–51.

Cause	Death rate (standardised)			Case A Decline due to each set of causes (%)	Case B Decline due to each set of causes (without 10–12) (%)
	1951	1940	Decline		
All	0·00932	0·01264	0·00332		
1. Resp. TB	0·00017	0·00042	0·00025	7·53	13·02
2. Other infec. and paras.	0·00012	0·00040	0·00028	8·43	14·58
3. Neoplasms	0·00145	0·00155	0·00010	3·01	5·21
4. Cardiovascular	0·00461	0·00472	0·00011	3·31	5·73
5. Infl., bronch., pneum.	0·00117	0·00182	0·00065	19·58	33·85
6. Diarrhoeal	0·00006	0·00013	0·00007	2·11	3·65
7. Certain degen. diseases	0·00026	0·00053	0·00027	8·13	14·06
8. Maternal	0·00002	0·00007	0·00005	1·51	2·60
9. Certain infants' diseases	0·00028	0·00043	0·00015	4·52	7·81
10. Motor vehicles	0·00005	0·00007	0·00002	0·60	
11. Violence	0·00023	0·00080	0·00057	17·17	
12. Unknown and other	0·00091	0·00172	0·00081	24·40	

Source. See Table 7.

It is clear, though, that mortality decline was concentrated at certain ages. In particular, infant and child mortality was reduced substantially. For example, the death rate for girls aged five to nine was reduced by 75%. After the age of forty, much smaller gains were registered, and relatively little change occurred in the survival rates of the elderly.

Table 8 is a more sophisticated measure of mortality decline. The data therein are standardised, in order to take into account the fact that the age structure of the population in 1940 and 1951 was quite different. We present two measures of the cause structure of mortality decline. The first (A) includes all causes of death. The second (B) excludes three categories: (1) violent deaths, which, as we noted above, obviously reflected the unusual circumstances of 1940; (2) deaths due to motor vehicle accidents, which also reflect exogenous developments; and (3) the miscellaneous category of deaths due to unknown or obscure causes. These must be set aside to get a clear idea of epidemiological trends in this period.

Once this is done, we can see that the most important contribution to overall mortality decline was made by the category of respiratory diseases, including bronchitis, pneumonia and influenza. In the more restricted survey of causes of death (case B) this one set of causes contributed a third of the overall mortality decline. Of importance were smaller, though tangible, contributions of the general category of infectious and parasitic diseases, which include most children's disorders ($14 \cdot 6\%$), the polyglot category of certain degenerative diseases, including the largely adult complaints of cirrhosis of the liver, nephritis and diabetes ($14 \cdot 1\%$), and respiratory tuberculosis ($13 \cdot 0\%$).

We can draw two other inferences from these data. The first is that although maternal mortality rates declined drastically the number of deaths due to this cause was so small as to affect the overall pattern of female mortality in only a very modest manner. In addition, the categories of certain diseases of infancy, largely related to prematurity and birth defects, and of diarrhoeal diseases, which affect the very young and the very old, made only small contributions to overall female mortality decline.

The contrasts between the effects of the two world wars on the cause structure of mortality decline are presented in Table 9. In the period surrounding the 1914–18 conflict, respiratory diseases were not the 'leading sector' in mortality decline. Indeed, female mortality due to this set of causes actually rose over those years, even when we discount mortality due to the 'Spanish flu' of 1918–19. Instead, other infectious and parasitic diseases played the dominant role in the period of the First World War that respiratory diseases did in the Second. When we add the data Preston provided for an aggregate population of 162 nations, we can see that the role played by influenza, bronchitis and pneumonia in England and Wales between 1940 and 1951 was characteristic of most countries' experience of mortality decline.

Table 9   The cause structure of mortality decline, female population of England and Wales, 1912–21, 1940–51, and in 162 populations.

Cause	Decline due to each set of causes (%)		
	1940–51	*1912–21*	*162 pops.*
Resp. TB	7·53	4·30	10·60
Other infec. and paras.	8·43	30·60	14·00
Neoplasms	3·01	–	–
Cardiovascular	3·31	28·80	1·80
Infl., bronch., pneum.	19·58	–	24·30
Diarrhoeal	2·11	14·50	10·40
Certain degen. diseases	8·13	13·80	1·70
Maternal	1·51	0·40	2·00
Certain infants' diseases	4·52	0·60	4·20
Motor vehicles	0·60	3·50	–
Violence	17·17	27·90	0·40
Unknown and other	24·40	–	33·10

Source. See Table 8; and J. M. Winter, *The Great War and the British People* (1985), table 4·7.

The prominence of the category of respiratory diseases in overall mortality decline is surprising, given that there was a surge in tuberculosis mortality in the years 1940–42 and that there was an outbreak of epidemic influenza in 1951.[23] The terminal dates of our enquiry suggest a rough stability in the course of respiratory diseases over the war decade; but such was not the case.

There are three central reasons why respiratory diseases led overall mortality decline in these years: the first relates to the war; the second, to progress in chemotherapy; and the third, to longer-term trends in nutrition and standards of living. First, by 1951 much of the environment of war-related stress and overcrowding associated with a recrudescence of respiratory tuberculosis and with reduced resistance to other infections[24] had disappeared. Secondly, and of perhaps even greater importance, is the fact that by the late 1940s a chemotherapeutic revolution had occurred in the treatment of infectious diseases. Some of these developments were war-related, such as Florey's work on penicillin; others were not, such as Waksman's discovery and development of streptomycin.[25] But, whatever their origins, these drugs, and others like them, radically altered the impact of these diseases, in both their epidemic and their endemic forms.[26]

For this reason it is not possible to separate the effects of medical treatment from short-term or long-term environmental improvements in the history of mortality decline after the 1930s. On the one hand the associations between morbidity and mortality attributable to respiratory diseases and poverty, malnutrition and poor housing did not vanish.[27] Indeed, the correlation between the mortality structure of men by occupation and their wives was so strong as to suggest that it was environment rather than occupation which was decisive in determining risk of infection and chances of recovery.[28] Furthermore, access to medical care in general and chemotherapy in particular was (and is) not socially uniform. The better-educated demand more and get better treatment today; there is little reason to doubt that such was the case forty years ago.[29] But, on the other hand, chemotherapy was unmistakably effective in countering bacterial infection. It is perhaps best, therefore, to conclude that while medical intervention played a decisive role in the control of infectious diseases, their overall decline was a long-term phenomenon, reflecting both the positive features of specific wartime experiments in social policy,[30] as well as several generations of improvements in nutrition and overall living standards.[31] What the economy of the Second World War did was to accelerate the trend further, and so add to the overall momentum of mortality decline as a whole.

(b) The decline of maternal mortality, 1940–51. The need for caution in attributing mortality decline solely to changes in chemotherapy is equally clear in the case of maternal mortality. On the one hand the discovery and application of the drug prontosil to cases of puerperal sepsis (childbirth fever) in 1935–37 coincides with the precipitate decline in the trend of maternal mortality. But, on the other, there is evidence that the maternal death rate was actually beginning to decline in the years just prior to the introduction of effective chemotherapy.[32] Furthermore, it is difficult to establish precisely when the drug prontosil (or indeed other drugs) were produced and distributed in sufficient quantities to

account for the clear change in trend which occurred in the years just prior to the Second World War. [33] Some medical opinion has it that the decline in maternal mortality rates after nearly a century of stability demonstrates what is known as a threshold effect: that is, slow incremental improvements in health had to reach a certain point before resistance to infection changed dramatically. That point was reached in the later 1930s, coinciding with independent medical developments. [34] This view has the advantage of accounting for the relatively late decline in maternal mortality rates, fully thirty-five years after the decline of infant mortality rates and seventy after the decline of crude death rates as a whole.

For these reasons it is perhaps best to adopt a multi-causal explanation of the decline of maternal mortality in the period. This is not to deny the importance of the introduction of sulphonamides after 1936 or of penicillin after 1944. [35] It is rather to suggest that short-term and long-term developments in social conditions and social policy complemented improvements in chemotherapy in such a way as to produce the steep decline in maternal mortality rates shown in Tables 2–3.

During the war itself the development of the blood transfusion service helped reduce mortality due to haemorrhage. An extension of antenatal care and an increase in rates of attendance in antental centres early in pregnancy increased the likelihood of the disclosure and treatment of toxaemias of pregnancy. In addition, the provision of emergency maternity homes for evacuated mothers led to a major increase in institutional (as opposed to domiciliary) deliveries, and as Ann Oakley has recently noted, the experience of evacuation helped create a climate of opinion based on the belief that 'instead of relying on "the family" to provide for individual health and subsistance needs, the government had to step in and do so instead'. [36]

This consensus was reinforced by the beneficial effects of wartime food policy, which, as we have noted elsewhere, was in large part responsible for the gains in infant mortality in the later years of the 1939–45 war. [37] Unlike social policy in the 1914–18 war, there was after 1940 conscious and deliberate planning to ensure that the burden of wartime conditions would not fall on the shoulders of the nation's mothers. Consequently the positive features of the National Milk scheme and rationing as a whole in improving the health of mothers and in reducing anaemias, deficiency diseases, and other conditions associated with maternal morbidity and mortality, were intended and largely successful results of the mobilisation for war.

Some Scottish evidence suggests that women in social classes IV–V (wives of semi-skilled and unskilled workers) benefited most from these developments.[38] The same was probably true in the rest of Britain.[39] It is in this broader context, therefore, that we must place the 50% decline in maternal mortality rates in the war years, and the further 25% decline in the five years after VE day.

5. *Indirect demographic effects of war: the rise of fertility, 1940–64*

We have already referred to the striking discontinuity between the 1930s and 1940s with respect to period total fertility rates and net and gross reproduction rates. We have also noted a major rise in nuptiality rates over the same period. The question remains as to the place of the Second World War in this reversal of earlier demographic trends.

Two accounts of the post-war 'baby boom' have dominated research and writing in this field. One is associated with the work of Richard Easterlin and may be termed the relative income approach in fertility movements; the other is the work of Gary Becker and his associates, and may be termed the 'new home economics' approach. Both are based largely on American data, but have relevance for developments in other countries.

We shall summarise these interpretations, and then suggest that they suffer from two serious deficiencies. First, they tend to collapse the sociology of fertility into the economics of fertility. Secondly, they ignore the significance of the wartime upheaval in changing attitudes to marriage and the family. We shall suggest that fertility movements between 1945 and 1964 constitute a broad cultural reaction to the disturbances of 1939–45 which marked the outlook and aspirations of an entire generation in Europe and the United States. Once this generation's child-bearing years were in large part over, the earlier decline in fertility was resumed, and was reinforced by the appearance of effective contraceptive devices and more liberal abortion laws. The period of the war appears, in this context, less as the opening of a new phase in demographic history and more as an important, though temporary, deviation from a trend towards family limitation set in the 1870s and likely to continue for the foreseeable future.

First, let us consider the two economic explanations of fertility before turning to the hypothesis we shall advance. The central argument of Richard Easterlin is that the baby boom was a generational phenomenon. The generation of child-bearing age in the post-war period were born in the 1920s and 1930s, when fertility had reached record lows. As a result, these were small cohorts which, despite the trials of the Depression and the Second World War during their childhood and adolescent years, faced only limited competition for the available educational and occupational 'slots'. Hence, in Easterlin's view, these generations experienced relatively high achievement and earnings (relative to their older peers) and hence had an 'optimistic' view of the future that stimulated earlier marriage and higher fertility.

Easterlin's hypothesis is based on the central assumption that adult aspirations are formed in adolescence by people living in parental households. Young married adults, he argued, developed a sense of 'relative income', which is a way of seeing the distance between their aspirations (reflecting their parents' earnings) and their own expected earnings. When their relative income rises they will be prepared to have more children. Such was the case, he believes, in the 1950s, when aspirations formed in the previous generation of austerity and warfare were realised or exceeded by a substantial part of the population.

In contrast, when the same age groups perceive a fall in 'relative income', as in the 1960s, young couples will tend to restrict their fertility. Such a decline in relative income can result from the maturation of large birth cohorts, as when the children of the baby boom entered a labour market tightening because of abundant labour supply.[40] While based largely on American data, Easterlin's work has also provided a framework for the analysis of international demographic trends in the post-1945 period.[41]

An alternative economic interpretation has been developed by Gary Becker, again on the basis of American data.[42] What is termed (ironically) the 'new home economics' approach is in effect an argument about the opportunity costs of child-bearing as the key variable in fertility swings. Thus in the late 1940s and 1950s the demobilisation of millions of soldiers led to a drop in demand for female labour and a consequent decline in relative wages for women. This served to reduce the potential income women (and their families) lost by choosing to stay at home and raise children rather than to go out to paid work. It was, therefore, a perfectly rational economic choice for couples to arrange their labour resources around larger families and not around full-time employment for both husbands and wives. By the mid-1960s, the argument proceeds, the situation had been reversed. Increased demand for female labour raised the absolute and relative rewards of work, and thereby raised the opportunity cost of maternity. The result was a substantial decline of fertility.

It is best to see these interpretations as complementary rather than contradictory,[43] but both are based on the premise that strategies of family formation are essentially exercised in economic rationality. There is, no doubt, some truth in this perspective, though empirical studies have not yielded decisive evidence to confirm either approach to the economic determinants of fertility in this period.[44] But Easterlin and Becker seem to share an unnecessarily limited way of looking at decisions which involve complex and profoundly important normative and cultural questions. In the context of this preliminary sketch of the demographic consequences of the war it is perhaps best to point out some of the features of a broader cultural interpretation.

It is based on the premise that the wartime and post-war increases in nuptiality and fertility reflected a change in attitudes towards family life in general and child-bearing in particular. What John Hajnal called the 'marriage boom' of the post-war years may have been as much a response to the special conditions of a world at war as a function of longer-term economic or demographic pressures. It seems perfectly rational (not to say human) that people in many countries deeply affected by the war came to place a higher value on domesticity in the midst of international chaos. In this context families could well have appeared as a 'haven in a heartless world' to a generation raised in the shadow of the Second World War.

As is apparent in Fig. 3, the change was largely one of women opting for married life in much greater proportions than was the case in the interwar years. Male nuptiality fluctuated radically in the war period, but the proportion of men 'never marrying' (that is, not married before the age of fifty) in the 1950s and 1960s was not much higher than that of the 1920s and 1930s. The real change occurred with respect to women's marriage patterns. There is a clear break in levels of female nuptiality in the period of the Second World War: in the interwar years nearly 20% of women effectively avoided the institution of marriage; in the post-war period only about 5% did do so. Given the fact that marriage was more universal, and that women entered into it earlier in their child-bearing lives, a rise in fertility was probably inevitable before reliable contraceptives were available.

It would be foolish to deny that there were some straightforward material explanations for these changes. One was the appearance of a scheme of family allowances both during and after the war. Another was the complex machinery of war pensions, which discriminated against unmarried couples. A third was the easing of divorce laws and the

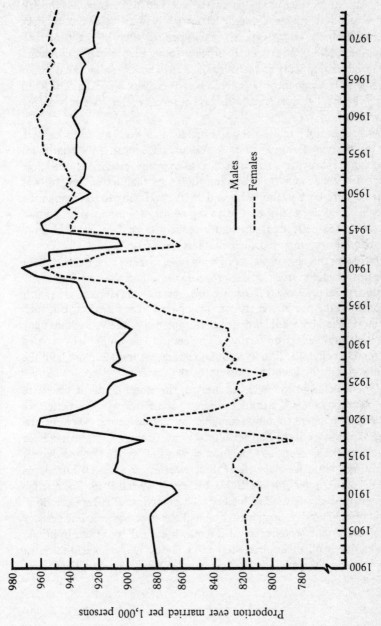

Fig. 3 Proportion ever married by exact age fifty, according to period gross nuptiality tables, England and Wales, 1900–74. Source: S. M. Farid, 'Cohort nuptiality in England and Wales', *Population Studies*, XXX, 1976, p. 149.

consequent increase in divorce rates after 1945.[45] A fourth was the exit of women war workers from the labour force, in the context of military demobilisation. Of course, this also happened after 1918 without any long-term effects on fertility. Suffice it to say that virtually all studies of trends in nuptiality and fertility since 1870 have been forced to accept that strictly economic interpretations can 'explain' trends in fertility in only the most general way;[46] the case of fertility after 1945 is probably no exception.

Consequently it may be best to conclude that women's attitudes were at the heart of fertility trends in this period, and that their attitudes embodied more than a reflex reaction to economic conditions. We know that the female cohorts producing the larger families of the post-war period were born in the 1920s and 1930s.[47] Having lived through the war as children, adolescents or young adults, a substantial proportion came to see early marriage and relatively large families in a more favourable way than did their mothers' generation.

No doubt this change was a profound relief to many men worried about the disturbance of traditional sex roles by the influx of women into heavy industry and the army. Pro-natalist propaganda and campaigns to return women to the home after the war may have had some effect. But such rhetoric had abounded throughout Europe before the war without any demonstrable effect on fertility. The central question is why women responded after 1940; to look for an answer, we must explore both the cultural and the economic history of the period.

The conclusion to which we are led, therefore, is that if we are to reconstruct women's attitudes to family and fertility in this period we must supplement purely economic by reconsidering some of the special features of the Second World War. The stress of a struggle for survival, the tensions of separation and loss of loved ones, the despair of military disaster and defeat: these were experiences all Europeans shared, to a greater or lesser degree, between 1939 and 1945. The reaction against this dark period of history took many forms. All we can do in this brief chapter is suggest that one of the least noticed, but perhaps most important, was the revival of family life which took place in Britain and in many other countries after 1940. Herein may lie one of the most fundamental, though indirect, demographic consequences of the Second World War.

Notes

1   See P. Vincent, 'Conséquences de six années de guerre sur la population française', *Population*, I, 1940; H. Bauermann, 'Demographic changes in postwar Germany', *Annals of the American Academy of Political and Social Sciences*, CCLX, 1948; J. N. Biraben, 'Pertes allemandes au cours de la deuxième guerre mondiale', *Population*, XVI, 1961; G. Frumkin, 'Pologne: six années d'histoire démographique', *Population*, IV, 1949; X. Lannes, 'Les Conséquences démographique de la seconde guerre mondiale en Europe', *Revue d'histoire de la deuxième guerre mondiale*, V, 1955; Z. Stein *et al.*, *Famine and Human Development: the Dutch Hunger Winter of 1944-45*, Oxford, 1975; B. Urlanis, *Wars and Population*, Moscow, 1971; D. Kirk and E. Huykk, 'Overseas migration from Europe since World War II', *American Sociological Review*, XIX, 1954; anon, 'The demography of war: Germany', *Population Index*, XIV, 1948.

2   H. M. Pelling, *Britain and the Second World War*, 1970.

3   J. M. Winter, *The Great War and the British People*, 1985, ch. 8.

4   N. Carrier and J. R. Jeffery, *External Migration: a study of the available statistics, 1815-1950*, General Register Office Studies in Medical and Population Subjects No. 6, 1953, pp. 34-8.

5   Carrier and Jeffery, *External Migration*, table J2.

6   *Cf.* E. A. Wrigley and R. S. Schofield, *A Population History of England, 1541-1871*, 1981.

7   J. Hajnal, 'European marriage patterns in perspective', in D. Glass and D. Eversley (eds), *Population in History*, 1965, pp. 101-47.

8   *United Nations Demographic Yearbook, 1954*, table 34.

9   J. M. Winter and M. S. Teitelbaum, *The Fear of Population Decline*, New York, 1985, ch. 4.

10   *Ibid.*, ch. 5.

11   J. M. Winter, 'Unemployment, nutrition and infant mortality in Britain, 1920-1950', in J. M. Winter (ed.), *The Working Class in Modern British History*, Cambridge, 1984, fig. 1.

12   *United Nations Demographic Yearbook, 1954*, table 23.

13   S. Preston, N. Keyfitz and R. Schoen, *Causes of Death*, New York, 1972, for standardised maternal death rates.

14   J. B. Schechtman, *Post-war Population Transfers in Europe, 1945-1955*, New York, 1952.

15   Winter, *The Great War*, table 2.2.

16   *Ibid.*, table 2.3.

17   W. Franklin Mellor (ed.), *Casualties and Medical Statistics*, 1972, table 11.

18   Winter, *The Great War*, ch. 7.

19   R. M. Titmuss, *Problems of Social Policy*, 1950, ch. 25.

20   Preston, Keyfitz and Schoen, *Causes of Death*; S. Preston, *Mortality Patterns in National Populations*, 1976.

21   See Winter, *The Great War*, p. 119.

22   *Ibid.*, table 4.3.

23   *Registrar-General's Decennial Supplement of England and Wales, 1951: Occupational Mortality*, Part II, Vol. 1, *Commentary*, 1958, p. 51.

24 A. S. MacNalty (ed.), *The Civilian Health and Medical Services*, 1953, I, pp. 90–113.

25 Sir M. Burnet and D. O. White, *The Natural History of Infectious Disease*, Cambridge, 1972, p. 174; S. A. Waksman, *The Conquest of Tuberculosis*, 1964.

26 E. D. Kilbourne, 'Epidemiology of influenza', in E. D. Kilbourne (ed.), *The Influenza Viruses and Influenza*, 1975, pp. 483–538; W. I. B. Beveridge, *Influenza: the Last Great Plague*, 1977.

27 W. Pagel *et al.*, *Pulmonary Tuberculosis*, 1964, p. 472.

28 *Decennial Supplement, 1951*, Vol. 1, p. 52.

29 See the Black report on *Inequalities in Health* (1980).

30 On which see Titmuss, *Social Policy, passim*.

31 Winter, 'Unemployment', pp. 282 ff.

32 C. A. Douglas, 'Trends in the risks of childbearing and in the mortalities of infants during the last 30 years', *British Journal of Obstetrics and Gynaecology*, LXII, 1955, pp. 216–31.

33 Thanks are due to Ann Oakley for advice on this point and for access to her files on maternal mortality.

34 A. Loudon, 'Maternal mortality', paper delivered to the Centre for Economic Policy Research seminar on 'Health and Unemployment', 1 February 1985.

35 J. Webb and P. Weston-Edwards, 'Recent trends in maternal mortality', *Medical Officer*, LXXXVI, 1951, pp. 201–4; W. Taylor and M. Dauncey, 'Changing pattern of mortality in England and Wales. II. Maternal mortality', *British Journal of Preventive and Social Medicine*, VIII, 1954, pp. 172–9.

36 A. Oakley, *The Captured Womb: a History of the Medical Care of Pregnant Women*, Oxford, 1984, p. 121.

37 Winter, 'Unemployment', p. 289.

38 J. M. Munro Kerr, R. W. Johnstone and M. H. Phillips, *Historical Review of British Obstetrics and Gynaecology 1800–1950*, 1954, p. 272.

39 *Decennial Supplement, 1951, Occupational Mortality*, Part I, table 36, p. 34.

40 R. A. Easterlin, *Birth and Fortune: the Impact of Numbers on Personal Welfare*, 1980.

41 J. Ermisch, *The Political Economy of Demographic Change*, 1983; R. A. Easterlin and G. A. Condran, 'A note on the recent fertility swing in Australia, Canada, England and Wales, and the United States', in H. Richards (ed.), *Population, Factor Movements and Economic Development: Studies presented to Brinley Thomas*, Cardiff, 1976.

42 G. Becker, 'An economic analysis of fertility', in National Bureau of Economic Research, *Demographic and Economic Change in Developed Countries*, Princeton, N.J., 1960.

43 W. C. Sanderson, 'On two schools of the economics of fertility', *Population and Development Review*, II, 1976, pp. 469–77.

44 See Ermisch, *Political Economy*, for one such attempt.

45 O. MacGregor, *Divorce in England*, 1958, pp. 36–7.

46 M. S. Teitelbaum, *The British Fertility Decline*, Princeton, N.J., 1984, conclusion.

47 S. M. Farid, 'Cohort nuptiality in England and Wales', *Population Studies*, XXX, 1976, pp. 137–51.

Penny Summerfield

The 'levelling of class'

Many historians subscribe to the idea that the Second World War was a 'leveller of classes'. Above all, Arthur Marwick depicted the war as a time when the gulf between classes narrowed. He attributed the change to the opportunities for participation in areas of work, politics and social life usually reserved for members of a single class which arose as a result of the labour shortage and political pressure associated with the war.[1]

This interpretation is influenced by the earlier writings of Stanislas Andrzejewski[2] and of R. M. Titmuss, who wrote, 'Mass war, involving a high proportion of the total population tends to a levelling in social class differences'.[3] Marwick argued that the 'relative changes' were greatest for the 'working class', which experienced a significant reduction in class differences *vis à vis* the 'middle class', even though the position of the 'upper class' was not much altered. He supported his argument with evidence of changes in the political position of the working class due to such things as the participation of trade union leaders and Labour politicians in government and with examples of new working-class self-images in wartime. Though indicative of change, however, this evidence does not represent a complete substantiation of the contention that a 'levelling of class' specifically benefiting the working class was achieved during the war. Discussion of the issue requires, first and foremost, clarification of the concept 'class'.

The definition of 'class' is itself a contentious issue.[4] But an omission from Marwick's account which is common ground in other discussions of class is a serious attempt to grapple with class as an economic relationship, whether in terms of income, occupation or ownership of capital. There is, of course, more to class than 'stratification' according to these criteria, notably 'consciousness of the nature and distribution of power in society' and 'sensations of collective identity of interest among individuals' which give rise to class consciousness and political and industrial organisation and action.[5] A full investigation of 'the levelling of class' in the Second World War would embrace changes in both social stratification and class consciousness and activity, and if the hypothesis that wartime participation led to 'levelling' is right one would expect to find both a reduction in the degree of stratification and a weakening of the political identity of separate social classes.

My intention here is to address only the first part of the hypothesis. This does not mean that I attribute exclusive importance to 'objective' economic indicators of class rather than to 'subjective' experiential ones relating to perception, consciousness and political expression, but it seemed important to tackle the issue of economic stratification in order to redress the balance of previous writing, and the matter became so complex and intriguing that I decided to devote this chapter to it.

The question of changes in social stratification before, during and after the war has been discussed, particularly in the 1950s and '60s, by historians and sociologists interested in the course of social change during the twentieth century. They can be divided into three camps: those who believed that levelling took place in the Second World War and was permanent; those who argued that by some criteria levelling can be seen to have taken place but that it was not necessarily permanent; and those who concluded that no levelling took place at all.

D. C. Marsh's book *The Changing Social Structure of England and Wales* presents a case for permanent levelling over the period in which the Second World War occurred. Writing in 1958, Marsh concluded from his survey of income data based on tax returns that 'the gap between the very rich and the very poor is much smaller than it was even thirty years ago, and in money terms the inequalities in the distribution of income are less marked'.[6] Two and a half times as many incomes came within the tax ranges in 1950 as in 1920, embracing half the adult population, compared with about a quarter in 1919–20. A larger proportion came into the higher range of incomes over £500 (8% compared with 2%), and a smaller number declared themselves to be in the highest tax bracket, of incomes over £20,000. As far as accumulated wealth was concerned, in both 1930 and 1950 the vast majority of estates assessed for death duties were in the lower ranges, under £5,000, and only a small number were in the highest ranges over £100,000. The main change was in the range between these two figures, in which more than twice the number of estates were left in 1950 compared with 1930.[7] This apparent evidence of expansion of numbers in the middle income brackets and improvement in the position of those at the bottom gave rise to both optimism and alarm in the late 1940s and '50s. The optimism was voiced by those who saw the war and, particularly, post-war reconstruction, as ushering in a period of rising affluence and social stability.[8] The alarm was expressed by those such as Roy Lewis and Angus Maude who feared that the lowest income groups were making gains at the expense of 'the middle classes', whose drive and initiative were being fatally weakened as a result.[9]

In fact, of course, analyses of money incomes based on tax returns have well known imperfections. Tax returns tell us nothing about the incomes of those below taxable levels, who constituted half of income earners even in 1950, and, as many critics have pointed out, returns may not be accurate and will almost certainly not reflect 'hidden' income such as occupational perquisites most likely to benefit the higher-income earners.[10] Further, tax returns are taken to represent individually earned and consumed incomes, and it is rare for any attempt to be made to assess how many individuals in fact contributed to and lived on each income: wives (whether earning or not) and dependants such as children are invisible. Finally, the usefulness of tax returns for comparisons of income over time is severely limited by the changing value of money. G. D. H. Cole argued in 1955 that the fact that the value of money diminished in the period 1930 to 1950 by a factor of between two and three, while tax thresholds remained the same, 'accounts for a large part of the increase in the total number of incomes over £250, and also for a large part of the shift from lower to higher income grades'.[11] Thus Marsh's failure to take account of *real* incomes greatly exaggerates the 'levelling up' of incomes over the period of the war.

Work on income changes by Dudley Seers in the late 1940s came to more qualified conclusions. Seers made a crude division of income-earners into 'working-class', i.e. all wage-earners and non-manual workers with salaries of less than £250 per annum, and 'middle-class', i.e. all other salaried non-manual employees, and then used technically complex methods of attaching correct weightings to class-specific indices of pay and prices in order to assess changes in the real incomes of these two classes.[12] Seers claimed that after the war (1947) wages took up a larger proportion of the national income than salaries, which, coupled with the faster rise in the middle-class than in the working-class cost-of-living index, meant that the gap between the real net incomes of the two classes had narrowed. Comparing aggregates, Seers concluded that the real net incomes of the working class had risen by over 9%, and those of the middle class had fallen by 7%, between 1938 and 1947.[13] As far as causes were concerned, Seers explained the improved working-class share partly as a result of the rise in the national product during the war, and partly as a result of fiscal changes, including subsidies, which gave the working class 59% of post-tax incomes in 1947 compared with 55% in 1938. This led Seers to point out that the wartime redistribution of income could be 'largely reversed by fiscal means (e.g. by lowering the standard rate of income tax, reducing food subsidies, etc.)'. He suggested that such changes were already beginning with tax changes in 1947, the reduction of subsidies and the government policy of 'wage stabilisation'.[14]

The upshot of Seers's arguments was that the future of the wartime redistribution of income was dependent on State action, a conclusion at which others arrived by different routes. For example, after observing that higher income groups retained less of their income than they had pre-war, G. D. H. Cole argued in 1955 that 'the effect of taxation on the distribution of real incomes has clearly been very substantial',[15] and later writers such as Westergaard and Resler noted that the more progressive direct taxation of the 1940s indeed reduced the share of top and middle incomes in the post-tax total between 1938 and 1949, while government controls over the cost of necessities – notably food, housing and fuel – during the war 'favoured those on low and moderate incomes'. These authors argued that the removal of controls after the war led to disproportionate increases in the price of these necessities, and that the reduction of the share of the richest 20% in post-tax income was slight after 1949: 'The effect of this reversal of trends is to sharpen the contrast between the equalising tendencies of the decade of war and post-war "social reconstruction", and the stability or accentuation of income inequality from around 1950.'[16]

Thus the conclusion of these authors, led by Seers, on the subject of the levelling of class in the Second World War differed from that of Marsh. The examination of real, post-tax incomes produced a more convincing case for levelling during the war than that which Marsh presented, but the stress on fiscal policy suggested that wartime levelling was not permanent, but was being reversed in the 1950s by government action. On the other hand, two aspects of this body of work may have led to overstatement of the degree of levelling during the war. Firstly, the data used were aggregates rather than *per capita* incomes. The relative growth of the group earning either wages or salaries under £250, compared to that earning larger salaries, may have been important in pushing up the proportion of national income going to wages as opposed to salaries.[17] Secondly, this division of the recipients of income into wage and salary earners, manual and non-manual workers, members of the working and of the middle classes, is arbitrary and may have obscured both overlap between the two groups and stratification within them. We shall return to these points later in the discussion of levelling.

Of course, levelling of earned income is not all there is to levelling of social strata, let alone of social classes. Several authors have seen the situation with regard to property as ultimately more decisive. Thus T. B. Bottomore wrote, 'the inequality of incomes depends very largely upon the unequal distribution of property through inheritance, and not primarily upon the differences in earned income'.[18] For the class position of wage-earners to change, then, does not require simply enlargement of earnings, but the kind of consistent saving which would allow them to acquire and pass on property. 'Levelling', by this argument, is meaningful only if it is seen as a change in the distribution of property owners in society.

Most authors agree that the belief held by some public figures, particularly Liberal spokesmen, in the 1930s, that there was a widespread distribution of small savings and property in the working class, was erroneous.[19] However, the shift from high levels of unemployment and underemployment in the 1930s to full employment, overtime work and rising wage rates during the war caused some investigators to ask whether this situation was transformed between 1939 and 1945. Notably, Charles Madge, a sociologist, undertook to discover the truth about working-class accumulation during the war. He expected to find widespread and extensive working-class saving caused by the pressure, on the one hand, of improved earnings coupled with a limited supply of consumer goods due to shortages and rationing, and, on the other, of the official wartime campaign to promote savings as a counter to inflation. He therefore thought he would find a process of 'levelling up' within the social structure as more members of relatively low-income groups joined the ranks of small property holders.[20]

Madge reported that 'a great campaign' had been launched since 1939, to persuade people to save in three principal ways, through Trustee Saving Banks, by buying National Savings Certificates through the Post Office and through Savings Groups, which were usually based in the work place, where a fixed deduction from the member's pay was made each week. The government had spent £834,100 on this campaign by June 1941. Madge found that the campaign had been successful in increasing the number of savers. There was considerable regional variation, but in the towns which Madge looked at, between 10% and 30% more families were saving by the new methods in 1942 than had been before the war, and they included those usually outside 'the orbit of national savings', such as 'families at low income levels and secondary earners'. This wartime saving was in addition to traditional methods of working-class saving, such as contributions to industrial assurance, pension funds, trade union subscriptions and voluntary health insurance, which Madge said were 'relatively unaffected by the war', and which would not lead to a change in the class position of the saver.[21]

Nevertheless, although there was an absolute increase in the number of working-class savers, Madge concluded from his survey of a large sample of households in Glasgow, Leeds and Bristol that the new savers represented a tiny proportion of the working class as a whole. Madge concluded that 'a large proportion of wage-earners' savings are due to a small proportion of wage-earners'; to be precise, among Leeds wage-earners 31% of national saving came from 3% of families. Forty-four per cent of families had no savings at all, and the majority of the rest (38% of the total) saved less than 5s a week. The median weekly amount saved was 3s 4d, while the most popular single figure was 1s.[22]

Madge found that patterns of saving were in some respects not surprising. National saving behaved as a luxury – that is, the proportion saved rose rapidly as income increased, whereas the proportion saved in the form of insurance behaved as a necessity, decreasing slightly as income rose. But beyond this the relation between income and saving was less straightforward. Madge did not look simply at the income of the 'chief wage-earner' of a household, but took account of the entire income and outgoings of each housekeeping unit, from which he calculated its 'excess income', that is, the money beyond that necessary to satisfy its basic needs in terms of housing, food, fuel and clothing. He found, at both low and high levels of 'excess income', only a weak relation between excess income and national saving; for example, just seven out of seventy-one Leeds families with excess incomes below £1 5s did 57% of the saving at this level. 'Heavy' saving of over 13s a week, likely to lead to significant capital accumulation on average began with a gross family income of more than £6 10s, but even here 'not all the heavy savers have so much as £2 10s in excess income. Neither are all those who have £2 10s excess income heavy savers'.[23] Even in this sub-group, savers were a minority. Madge commented, 'National saving is much more strongly concentrated than insurance saving, mainly because saving, apart from for a definite security purpose, is a new thing for the majority of wage-earners'. [24] He concluded (in 1943) that this meant that even 'if real incomes continue to rise and there is a progressive redistribution of incomes, the wage-earning class will not advance as a class towards middle-class standards'. [25] Rather, the small group of '*rentier* proletarians', whose growth the war had stimulated, would continue the process of accumulation and try to assimilate with the middle class. Madge thought that the principal methods of doing this were by acquiring property or a small business (such as a shop), or investing in education for children with a view to their joining the ranks of the black-coated or professional salariat.

Even within the minority group of savers, however, such upward social mobility was not the universally held objective. The interviews conducted in the course of his enquiry led Madge to conclude that most savers were motivated firstly by the fact that large consumables (like furniture or motor cycles) were not available in wartime but might be afterwards, and secondly by the not unconnected 'fear that present earning capacity may not last'. [26] Many of Madge's respondents expected and dreaded a post-war slump, but their desire to 'put something by' to meet such an emergency did not represent an urge to change their class position, nor did the amounts they typically saved warrant such a result.

Madge thought that wartime unpredictabilities themselves encouraged 'mild hoarding', but questioning in Glasgow suggested that not more than a quarter of manual and black-coated workers kept reserves at home, typically behind the clock or in a jar on the mantelpiece, and the amounts put by were usually under £2. Madge was adamant that the apparently numerous 'suitcases full of ancient crumpled notes' deposited by workers in the Glasgow Savings Bank when the town was blitzed were 'exceptional'. [27] In this context it is worth noting that Madge's own methodology would tend to exaggerate rather than diminish the proportion of savers in his samples. He based his findings on budgets voluntarily kept by his respondents, and, as Seers pointed out, 'only the more literate and more careful would keep budgets, and there is reason to expect a correlation between ability to keep budgets and care in arranging outlay'. [28] The fact that only a tiny proportion of these budget-keepers were amassing war savings which might permanently alter their class position is therefore the more remarkable.

Madge's investigation of working-class patterns of saving and spending tends to make Seers's presentation of the improved aggregate share of the working class in national income as a form of 'levelling' look somewhat misleading. Madge showed that, as far as working-class experience was concerned, its rising share of the national income did not signify a trend towards economic equivalence in terms of property ownership. Indeed, the achievement of social mobility through the accumulation of savings appeared extremely limited. In addition, Madge's work emphasised that there were many divisions within the class of manual workers. It is relevant to our discussion to consider whether a 'levelling' process occurred as between these different groups within the working class during the war, or whether pre-war sub-groups continued to exist and new ones were created.

Looking first at the overall picture, the numbers of those in paid employment rose during the war, from 19,473,000 in 1938 to a peak of 22,285,000 in 1943, composed of 15,032,000 men and 7,253,000 women (compared with 14,476,000 men and 4,997,000 women in 1938).[29] This expansion of the labour force obviously meant an improvement in living standards for the nearly 3 million people who in 1938 had been outside paid employment (e.g. housewives, schoolchildren and those unemployed). Average earnings rose, according to official figures, by 80% (from 53s 3d in October 1938 to 96s 1d in July 1945).[30] On the other hand, hours worked also went up – from an average of 46·5 per week in 1938 to 50 in 1943, falling to 47·4 in July 1945 – and so too did the cost of living. The official figure for the rise in the working-class cost of living index was 31% between 1939 and 1945,[31] although Seers criticises this for underweighting some items of working-class expenditure, notably alcohol and tobacco, and put the increase between 1938 and 1947 at 61%–62%.[32] Either way, these averages suggest that full employment made manual workers better off than they had been pre-war.

However, they are no more than averages. Earnings during the war varied greatly between men and women, and between different industries, as they had done before it. If there was any 'levelling' of the differences between men and women it was very moderate. Women's average weekly earnings in manual work were 47% of those of men in 1938 and 52% in 1945.[33] As this suggests, few women received equal pay with men, in spite of the 'dilution agreements' which were supposed to guarantee women on 'men's work' the full male rate after a certain length of time. Both private employers and government Ministries were loath to give women '100%' and exploited clauses in the agreements stating that, to qualify, women must do the work 'without additional supervision or assistance'.[34] However, by far the most important means by which the gender differential was maintained was the classification of work as either 'men's' or 'women's'. Employers endeavoured to place any jobs women did in the 'women's work' category, where lower wage rates applied, and the trade unions pressed for as much work as possible to be labelled 'men's work', in which case it would be paid at men's rates and the women doing it would be regarded as temporary.[35] According to the official historian, in September 1942 three-quarters of women in munitions 'came under the women's schedule as performing women's work'.[36] This did not only mean that the economic position of male and female wage earners remained sharply differentiated. It also meant that there could be wide differences in what women earned within a single factory, according to whether they were paid at men's or women's rates.[37] Age made a difference, too. The average earnings of girls under eighteen were the lowest of any group throughout the war. In addition, women's earnings in different industries diverged increasingly. In 1938 women's average weekly earnings in six industrial groups were within 3s 3d of each other, the lowest being textiles at 31s 9d and the highest transport at 34s 11d. By 1945 the differential was 26s, with women transport workers' average earnings standing at 81s 7d and clothing workers' at 55s 7d.[38]

To some extent this is accounted for by differences in union bargaining power in the different industries, since women's hourly pay, bonuses and piece rates were mostly fixed at a proportion of those of men. Like women, male workers in textiles, clothing and food, drink and tobacco received lower earnings than workers in other industries in 1938, and the differential widened during the war. However, the top male earners in 1945 were in metals, engineering and shipbuilding. Their average earnings of 133s exceeded those of male workers in chemicals by 10s 2d and in transport by 20s 2d. In contrast, the earnings of women transport workers exceeded those of women engineering workers by 12s 6d. The tendency among employers to confine women to 'women's work' in engineering and metals, together with divisions in policy towards women between the unions involved (notably the craft and the general unions), may go some way to explaining why, in contrast to the situation for men, engineering and metals were not the industries in which women's average earnings were greatest by the end of the war.

Far from industrial workers' earnings levelling during the war, differentials widened. To put a figure on this in the case of men, the gap between the highest and the lowest average earnings had been 12s in 1938 whereas in 1945 it was 28s 5d[39] (over twice the amount Madge thought necessary for significant saving). Further, within the 'best paying' industries – engineering and metals – earnings varied very greatly, and union efforts to maintain differentials were, if anything, more successful than counter-pressures to reduce them.

Earnings varied not only between grades and skill categories of men, but also between districts, mainly owing to factors like local union strength, the level of organisation among employers, the degree of technological change in the particular branch of the industry and the position with regard to labour supply.[40] For example, earnings in Midland aircraft and engineering factories were relatively high before the war, and in the context of labour shortage arising during rearmament and the rapid expansion of production during the first years of the war, unions succeeded in pushing them up higher.[41] Much engineering work was organised as piece work, the rates for which were settled job by job. Some skilled craftsmen on time rates, such as tool-room workers, were given guarantees that their earnings would not be allowed to fall below those of the most productive piece workers. In addition, in both the engineering and the aircraft industries, there was a system of bonus payments. Before the war these bonuses were typically 25% to 30% of time rates; by spring 1940 they had risen to 40%–50% in the north-west region, while in the Midlands they were as much as 100% and by 1942 one Coventry motor factory was reported to be paying an average bonus of 324%, with a top figure of 581%. Not surprisingly, Coventry engineering workers rejected the employers' offer to fix the bonus at 100%![42]

The particularly high earnings of men in the Midland engineering and aircraft factories gave rise to national concern. It came not so much from employers, whose anxiety to limit the size of their wage bills was less pressing in wartime because they could pass on their labour costs to the government, but more from various government departments dealing with the control of labour. For example, the Ministry of Labour was concerned about the difficulties of transferring skilled men from the Midlands to new factories in other districts where rates were lower, the Ministry of Supply was worried about the impact of high engineering wages in private firms on the expectations of its workers in Royal Ordnance Factories, and the Select Committee on National Expenditure was worried about the negative effects on productivity of very high earnings.[43] Its suggestion that £12 – to £15 a week constituted a threshold beyond which a man lost interest in increasing his efficiency underlines the great divergence of earnings among manual workers in wartime.[44] Expressed in shillings, these sums are 240*s* and 300*s*, compared with average male earnings in engineering in 1941 of 112*s* 2*d*, average female earnings in engineering of 48*s* 1*d*, average male earnings throughout manufacturing of 99*s* 5*d* and equivalent female earnings of 43*s* 11*d*.[45]

Whether this small minority of men with exceptionally high wartime earnings should be regarded as having 'levelled up' to the middle class is another matter. Most of the social surveys of the 1940s used an income of £250 a year, or £5 (i.e. 100*s*) a week as the approximate dividing line between the working and middle classes, by which criterion such men would qualify as 'middle-class'. However, Madge believed that skilled men earning spectacularly large amounts in new industries tended not to be regular savers, but enjoyed the 'windfall' while it lasted, especially if they came from a background of unemployment in the 1930s.[46] They therefore did not, in general, accumulate capital which could have assisted their assimilation into the middle class.

Further, in the debate of the 1950s and '60s on the class position of manual workers with high incomes, numerous sociologists argued against seeing working-class affluence alone as sufficient to close the gap between classes. For example, W. G. Runciman pointed out that the conditions under which a manual worker earned a relatively high income differed sharply from those of a non-manual worker at the same level of income, in terms of the overtime and piece-work components, the meals, furnishings and sanitation available in the workplace, rights to holidays and pensions, chances of promotion and the degree of security in the employment.[47]

It would be fascinating to draw up a balance sheet of these aspects of manual and non-manual work in wartime. In the absence of the kind of research which would permit such precision, it can be said that there was improvement in some of these areas for some manual workers, while some non-manual workers, evacuated to temporary office accommodation, for example, may have been worse off than pre-war. Most obviously, the number of workplace canteens expanded from about 1,500 pre-war to 11,800 in 1944 under a requirement in the Essential Work Order, and the Ministry of Labour also urged employers to improve lavatory facilities and to employ a works doctor or nurse. The occurrence of change was patchy, however. For example, the increase in the number of workplaces with canteens by over 10,000 must be set against the total of 67,400 undertakings covered by Essential Work Orders in 1944, and against the fact that in no industry did more than half the workers use the canteens. Married women workers in particular missed out because of the tendency to use the lunch hour for shopping.[48]

Any improvements in workplace conditions need to be seen in the context of the increasing organisation of manual work on a piece-work basis (which brought with it greater pressure), the long hours expected and infrequent holidays.[49] The chances of promotion for a male manual worker (e.g. from machinist to setter, setter to chargehand and so to overseer, foreman and manager) may have been slightly greater in wartime, with the expansion of workforces and introduction of new processes, though the same may have been true for salaried workers (moving, for example, from clerical to administrative or managerial grades). But security of employment for manual workers lasted for only as long as the war effort required a particular type of production, as the transfers and lay-offs from engineering and Royal Ordnance factories in 1944–45 demonstrated.[50]

Thus I am arguing here that widening differentials in wartime both caused the working class to become more heterogeneous, and did not automatically lead to the 'levelling up' of the best paid manual workers into 1944–45 demonstrated.[50]

Undoubtedly, government departments would have liked there to have been a levelling of income among manual workers, and pressed for it when they could, as in the case of the Royal Ordnance Factories, where the Ministry of Supply did achieve some degree of standardisation between districts, if not between grades of worker. The upward movement of earnings stabilised in the Midlands during the war, though not because of government intervention. Rather, the explanation lies in the fact that the pace of technological change slowed somewhat, so there was no longer a constant process of fixing new prices, and communist shop stewards tended to work against disruption in the shops after the entry of Russia to the war in June 1941, while in other districts growing militancy and a mounting propensity to strike in 1943–44 may have made earnings less stable.[51]

But differentials between grades of workers and between districts continued throughout the war and after it. The official historian wrote, 'In June 1953 weekly earnings in the Coventry district averaged more than 43s 0d above those in any other district even though hours worked there were comparatively short'.[52] In other branches of the munition industries the regional pattern of differentials was different; for instance, in shipbuilding, earnings were particularly high in London and Southampton, and the best-paying Royal Ordnance Factories were in London and South Wales. Although greater geographical uniformity was achieved in these industries than in the case of the motor and aircraft branches of engineering, differences remained between the earnings of time and piece workers (particularly between those of machine setters on time rates and dilutees on piece rates in ROFs), between the rates of adults and apprentices, and between those of men and women, and frequently caused contention. [53]

To sum up, the division of industries into 'essential' and 'non-essential' and the combination in the former of labour shortage, 'dilution', the premium on 'skill', and growing union strength, coupled with the government's fear of strikes, in the context of major local differences dating from before the war, ensured that the war had the opposite effect on manual workers' earnings to 'levelling'.

Another aspect of the distribution of income within the working class is its allocation between and within households. It is possible that the overall rise in working-class earnings during the war led to 'levelling' in this respect. Madge's data on working-class spending patterns provide a basis for discussion of this question.

Commenting on expenditure trends since 1904, Madge wrote, 'The most striking change in the pattern of demand is the great decline in the proportion allotted to food, and the corresponding increase in the proportion allotted to "other items" '. [54] The war accelerated, though it obviously had not initiated, this trend. 'Other items', which were mainly 'non-essentials' like alcohol, tobacco and entertainment, rose from 30% of working-class budgets in 1938 to 34% in 1942, and the proportion spent on food fell by 3% (from 40% to 37%), [55] even though (in spite of relatively heavy subsidies, price control and rationing) food had risen by 22% in the working-class cost-of-living index between 1939 and 1941. [56]

Authors of social surveys agree that a major factor explaining the declining proportion of working-class expenditure on food was the reduction in family size during the twentieth century. The war made a special contribution to this, with particularly low birth rates 1939–41, though during 1942–45 there was something of a recovery. [57]

However, there were of course wide variations in family size, as there had been pre-war. In wartime, as before, an increase in the number of children heralded the decline of the family's standard of living, a point graphically illustrated by the finding of the Wartime Social Survey in 1942 that the heaviest users of credit facilities were families with three or more children under fourteen. [58] It follows that the majority of three-child families (75%) had no National Savings. [59] Madge observed that working-class families with five or six non-earning children were almost invariably in relative poverty, regardless of the skill status of the main wage-earner. He wrote, 'If one arranges a random sample of wage-earning families in order of effective wealth, skilled, well-paid workers with children will come lower down than unskilled, low-paid workers without any children'.[60]

A survey of 'The British Household' in 1947 found that in fact a higher proportion of households of the middle-income group of 'better paid unskilled operatives', 'lower paid skilled operatives' and 'lower paid clerical workers', with a basic weekly wage rate of £4 to £5 10s, had children under fifteen than any other income group. Twenty-four per cent had two or more children, compared with 15% in the group of lower-paid unskilled operatives immediately below them and 20% in the group of better-paid skilled and clerical workers, and lower-paid managerial and professional workers, above them. The households of the middle group were also more overcrowded than those of the other groups. Thirty-three per cent had more than one person per habitable room, compared with 24% in the group below, 17% in the group above, and 4% in the top income group.[61] The larger than average family size of the middle group, then, limited the potential for 'levelling up' offered by its improved wartime earnings.

The uneven distribution of income per head of the working-class population due to family size was further intensified by uneven distribution within families. Madge noticed that wage-earning husbands quite frequently did not share the rise in their incomes with their wives and children. In none of the seven towns he looked at did a majority of husbands hand over all their weekly earnings to their wives, and in most only a small proportion (under 15%) did so. The dominant pattern was for husbands to give wives a fixed sum as a result of an 'actual or implicit bargain . . . driven at intervals', and in some towns, notably Glasgow, a majority of husbands kept their wives in the dark about the wartime increase in their earnings. It was here that Madge 'came across evidence of revolt against the whole system' of housekeeping 'allowances'.[62] Madge wrote, 'fortunately the deceptions occurred mainly at the higher income levels', meaning by the word 'fortunately' that actual undernourishment of wives and children due to the husband's contribution of too low a figure to meet the rising cost of living was limited to a minority.[63] But his findings nevertheless suggest that in the majority of families in Glasgow, and possibly elsewhere, the husband neither declared his income accurately nor passed on a rising proportion of his rising earnings to his wife.[64] Thus, far from there being any

'levelling' in the household distribution of income, the economic gulf
between husbands and wives actually widened.

The households in which the wife was most likely to share the benefit
of her husband's wartime earnings were those in which incomes were
pooled and then distributed according to need. Though nowhere
universal, Madge found that this pattern was most prevalent in Leeds
and Blackburn, where 24% and 49% of families pooled their incomes.
The benefits to wives and children are reflected in the proportions of
family income allocated to housekeeping and husband's pocket money,
which were 65% and 17% in Leeds, in contrast to 58% and 27% in
Glasgow, where only 14% of families pooled their earnings.[65]

The extent of pooling appears to have been a very local matter, only
partly determined by the degree to which it was customary for women,
including wives, to do paid work. Madge noticed that in Bradford only
15% of families pooled their incomes, in contrast to the high figure of
49% in Blackburn, even though there was a high female participation
rate in both towns. In spite of the rising numbers of married women
in war work (43% of women workers were married in 1943, compared
with 16% in 1931),[66] Madge did not observe an increase in the habit
of pooling, and was emphatic that the wife's economic position remained
highly inequitable.[67]

Having said this, there is no doubt that women's earnings made a
significant contribution to family incomes in wartime. It could be that
the rising share of total personal allocated income going to the lower
income groups in the 1940s, which Seers depicted, was a result less of
'redistribution' (which, as we have seen, was how it was interpreted)
than of the greater extent of paid employment among the wives of lower-
income than higher-income husbands during and after the war. It would,
of course, be difficult to determine this accurately.[68]

The idea of extensive social mixing among women workers, much
vaunted in wartime progaganda, is a confusing factor when considering
which class benefited more from women's work. It is usually suggested
that women from upper and middle-class families took wartime jobs
beneath their social status for the duration.[69] The Wartime Social Survey
report *Women at Work* contains evidence that 28% of women who had
worked pre-war in the white-collar category 'professional, administrative
and clerical' took manual jobs of various types. However, they formed
no more than 7½% of the total number of women manual workers of
all types in the sample, and the report commented that most of these
ex-white-collar women had been clerks,[70] whose class position was in

any case somewhat intermediate, especially after a decade in which opportunities for the daughters of manual workers to obtain their first job in white-collar work had increased rapidly.[71] This evidence, plus information on the educational backgrounds of women factory workers, strongly suggests that social mixing among women war workers, and the social levelling implied by it, has been exaggerated.[72]

The most compelling evidence against social mixing, however, is the attempt by the Wartime Social Survey to classify women workers in wartime industries by the income of the 'chief wage-earner' in the woman's household, which revealed that a higher proportion of women war workers were in households in which the 'chief wage-earner' received up to £5 a week than the proportion of such households in the population as a whole (87%, compared with 75%). The WSS concluded that 'Women in the higher income groups have gone into other forms of National Service and that the group from which the greatest proportion of working women has been drawn is that of the semi-skilled and skilled workers with wage rates of £3 12s 0d to £5 0s 0d'.[73] In view of the evidence which we have already reviewed about the large family size of precisely this middle group and its tendency towards financial shortfall, it makes good sense that wives and daughters from such households filled the factories in greater proportion than they occurred in the community at large.

The WSS evidence also lends substance to the view that women's wartime paid employment contributed more to the increase in the share of the working class in national income than to that of the middle class. The forms of National Service chosen by the majority of women whose husbands or fathers were in the middle-class income groups were either relatively low-paying, as in the case of the women's auxiliary services and the Women's Land Army, or entirely voluntary, like the Red Cross and the Women's Voluntary Service. Participation of this sort in the war effort would have added little to middle-class aggregate income, and thus would have assisted 'levelling' – ironically, in view of the resentment which middle-class women's preference for exemption from paid work and for involvement in voluntary work provoked among some working women, who saw it as a sign of 'inequality of sacrifice'.[74]

However, it is difficult to assess the extent of working-class women's contribution, either in terms of the financial effects on individual families, or in terms of the proportion of families affected in each working-class income group, given the invisibility in survey data of working women's earnings.[75] One can only return to the WSS statement that the majority of working women came from homes classified as belonging to the middle-income bracket of the working class, and official evidence that the overall average earnings of women workers were 64s in 1944.

Whether the addition of this average sum to the budget of working-class homes either did no more than pull a family out of debt or succeeded in pushing it into the narrow ranks of upwardly mobile savers must have depended on how many mouths there were to feed in the household, the extent of additional expenditure on nurseries, laundries and other facilities for the domestic work which the wife was no longer doing unpaid, and the proportion of the couple's joint income which they chose to spend on those 'other items' to which, as we have seen, the working class had been devoting an increasing proportion of its expenditure since 1904, a trend which the war intensified.

Madge repeatedly stated that, after they had given their wives an allowance or paid for their board and lodging if they were single, men spent the surplus of their increased wartime earnings on such 'non-essential' items of consumption. Though critical when such spending was at the expense of the well-being of wives and children, he was mainly concerned to show that alcohol and tobacco were more important to the vast majority of working men than were savings: 'National savings is . . . considered more of a luxury than tobacco and alcohol in that, when there are more mouths to feed, it is the former and not the latter which are dispensed with.'[76]

Women were, of course, not immune to these pleasures, and many started smoking cigarettes for the first time during the war, but Madge said that 'the great bulk of the spending on tobacco and alcohol is contributed by husbands and other male earners'.[77] In contrast, 'most of the spending on "Entertainment" comes from female earners'. Madge thought the reasons for increased spending on these items were primarily social and narcotic, though he hinted that for men there was an element of compensation for 'giving up' the bulk of their income for housekeeping.[78] One may add that, for both men and women, beer, cigarettes and cinemas offered some solace in the face of the immeasurably discomforting aspects of war: the blackout, bombardment, long hours of work, the difficulties of travel and the anxiety of separation.

Such reasons for spending a rising proportion of income on 'non-essentials' evidently outweighed the relatively rapid rise in cost. The price of tobacco doubled between 1939 and 1942, and the price of beer went up steeply, unchecked by the government (and underweighted in the government's calculation of the working-class cost-of-living index) because of its value as a source of revenue. [79]

Of course, the working class was not alone in its consumption of tobacco and alcohol, nor in its need for consolation. But according to Seers it devoted a larger proportion of its total expenditure to these things than did the population as a whole: 5% on tobacco and 7% on alcohol, compared with a global figure of just over 4% on each. A more direct comparison with middle-class spending shows that nearly half working-class expenditure on 'other items' went on drink and tobacco, compared with under a fifth of middle-class expenditure. [80] It is almost irresistible to conclude (with Madge) that most male members of the working class were drinking and smoking their wartime 'excess incomes' rather than using them as a means by which to 'level up' socially, because for the majority such a shift in class position had very little meaning. [81]

We have established, I hope, that there was a great deal of variety in the economic circumstances of working-class families during the war. Whether both husband and wife were earning, the occupations and industries in which they worked, the region in which they lived, the number of dependants and the method by which income was allocated in the household were important determinants of the capacity of a family to generate 'excess income'. But, even when all these circumstances were favourable, spending rather than accumulation was the norm, even (or especially) in the face of wartime shortages.

Individuals living outside family households tended to be particularly disadvantaged, in economic terms. Pensioners had been a relatively poor sub-group before the war which, because of its dependence upon a fixed income at a time of rising cost of living, became worse off during the war, in spite of a patchily applied Exchequer supplement to old age pensions on a 'household needs' basis after January 1940. [82] Nevertheless, Madge showed that 'single' pensioners were falling into heavier debt during the war than those living in 'mixed pensioner families'. [83]

The same contrast occurred in the economic circumstances of servicemen's wives. A private soldier's wife with two children received a total allowance of 32s in 1939, which rose to 33s in 1940, 38s in 1941 and 43s in 1942. [84] But Madge discovered a sharp contrast in standard of living between the 20% of service wives in his sample with no children, living with their parents and working, who were saving heavily (to the tune of 27s a week), and the 20% of service wives at the other extreme, who did not live with other adults, were not doing paid work and had children to support, who were falling heavily into debt (to the tune of 15s 6d per week). [85]

A large proportion of service wives were dependent on credit buying (nearly 53% compared with 38% of a sample of working-class women), though it is not surprising that the Wartime Social Survey found that they were the main group to which shopkeepers were reluctant to give credit and landlords loath to let rooms.[86] Nor is it surprising that servicemen's wives were keen to find paid work and were often given priority for places in wartime nurseries.[87] As 'the new poor' of the war, whose plight was caused by their husbands' service in defence of the country, they commanded considerable sympathy from members of the public who did not stand in a direct financial relationship with them. Public pressure resulted in a 'rise' to an allowance of 60*s* for the service wife with two children.[88] Though an improvement, this was still below the woman's average wage of 64*s*.

Servicemen and women themselves (whatever their class) were, of course, a relatively low-paid group. They had little chance of amassing savings during their period in the forces, even though part of a pay rise in January 1942 took the form of a post-war credit of 6*d* a day.[89] Madge would not have considered this a high saving. It represented 3*s* 6*d* a week, and about £9 a year. However, there were opportunities in the forces for men and women to 'level up' in non-financial ways, for instance raising their status by becoming noncommissioned or commissioned officers, and acquiring skills ranging from clerical and administrative to technical, which may have opened up new job prospects in the post-war world. The financially disadvantaged position of the private soldier also applied to the officer, who received more pay and allowances but was still at an income level well below a middling white-collar salary. There was much complaint in 1941–42 that officers' pay was so inadequate that it needed supplementing with a private income simply to cover mess bills, uniform and other essentials.[90] Officers' wives received larger allowances than privates', but their incomes were still relatively low in the wartime context.[91] Much the same stratification must have existed where officers' wives were concerned as Madge depicted for servicemen's wives, the best-off being those without children who were living with relatives, and the worst-off those struggling to make ends meet on their own with children.

Servicemen of all ranks and their wives may have experienced quite considerable 'levelling', in the sense of sharing a similar economic position, depressed in comparison to their civilian pre-war peers. Ironically the service hierarchy, which was apparently maintained as energetically among service wives as within the services themselves, countered with sharp status differentiation this economic levelling.

Up to this point in the discussion the 'middle class' had been largely neglected, because interest has focused on the question of whether the rise in the working-class share of the national income meant for that class (or a substantial part of it) a process of permanent 'levelling up', either as between the working class and the middle class or within the ranks of the working class. It has not been possible to be definitive, but the suggestion here is that permanent levelling up affected only a tiny group of self-denying savers, and that the war may have increased differentials between groups of workers and between husbands and wives, rather than diminishing them. It is now time to examine the other side of the coin of Seers's findings on the working-class aggregate income. Did the relative fall in the middle-class share of national income mean that the middle class (defined as non-manual workers with an income over £250 p.a.) experienced permanent 'levelling down'?

To recap, Seers wrote that between 1938 and 1947 the salary bill had 'risen by only just over fifty per cent, compared with a near doubling of most other forms of income'. When taxes and the cost of living were taken into account, this meant that 'the real net incomes of the working class had risen over nine per cent, and those of the middle class had fallen over seven per cent'.[92] Seers stated that outside these aggregates there were wide differences in the income position of different groups within the middle class, but though he presented evidence about differences in the middle-class cost of living he omitted evidence about income differences.

Guy Routh, however, looked at trends in average earnings in the various occupational classes used in the census, over a longer period than that of the war itself. He found that 'the only really big changes' between 1910 and 1960 were the declining differentials of three occupational classes – professionals, clerks and foremen – between 1935 and 1955. The income of all three groups had been 'levelled down' towards the average for men and women in all occupational classes, although the extent of the fall varied and in some cases the differential was still extensive. For instance, 'higher professionals' enjoyed incomes nearly three times the average, even though this represented a fall of 26% compared with their position in 1935/36. The relative drop had been particularly severe for men and women in the 'lower professional' group, though clerks of both sexes were the non-manual group with the lowest earnings. The occupational group 'managers and administrators', in contrast, improved its position.[93] Thus, as in the working class, so in the middle class, the picture was not one of overall levelling, but of differing fortunes for different groups.

Of course, it may be misleading to look at change over the period 1935–55, since by then the effects of war may have been overtaken by subsequent developments. But Routh provided some details on the relative movement of average manual earnings and the salaries of various classes of civil servants, which show the period 1938–40 to have marked the beginning of the fall of non-manual pay in relation to manual earnings and 1944 to have marked its nadir.[94]

Undoubtedly, the shortage of manual labour in the munition industries and the improved leverage of the trade unions immediately before and during the war had much to do with the overall narrowing of differentials between non-manual and manual occupations. However, Routh stated that changes in the averages of occupational groups were only partly caused by changes in the pay of individual occupations, and were also caused 'by changes in the numbers occupied in occupations at different levels of pay'.[95] Elsewhere he suggested that the apparent reduction in the average pay of the non-manual industrial employee population in 1938–40 'could have been brought about by the substitution of female for male labour'.[96] In other words, because of the influx of women at low rates of pay, and the outflow of men, the earnings averages of various non-manual occupational groups were depressed. Routh unfortunately did not subject this suggestion to careful scrutiny, and the necessary research is a larger project than can be undertaken here. It is made particularly difficult by the absence of an occupational census for the war. However, using the rather unsatisfactory Industrial Classificiation some suggestions can be made.

Workers in national government can be taken as primarily 'non-manual'. The wartime influx of women into this group was extreme. The total in 1945 was 1,214% what it was in 1939, whereas the number of men was 174% of the 1939 figure, making the proportion of women rise from 14% to 54% of the total number of workers in national government. By comparison, the total number of insured women in industry in 1945 was 128% of the number in 1939, and the proportion rose from 28% to 39%.[97]

It does look possible, then, as Routh suggested, that the extensive substitution for men in white-collar work of women, employed by custom in different grades from men and at lower rates of pay, made a significant contribution to the reduction of the differential between civil service non-manual salaries and average manual earnings.

Earlier, however, we suggested that the wartime earnings of women in manual work may have made a significant contribution to aggregate working-class income, even though women's average manual earnings were only just over half those of men. Why did the increased number of white-collar women not augment middle-class earnings in the same way? The issue hinges on where low-paid non-manual workers, especially women, are placed in terms of class. Routh simply compared all civil service salary earners with wage earners, but Seers took as his criterion for membership of the middle class 1938–47 non-manual workers with incomes of £250 or above. This would disqualify numerous male clerks, whose average pay in 1938 was £192 p.a. (rising to approximately £224 in 1942), almost all women clerks, whose average was £99 (rising to approximately £115), and many women in the lower professions, whose average was £211 (rising to approximately £246).[98] By his own declaration Seers cannot have included the salaries of low-paid white-collar workers, particularly those of the numerous women entering this section during the war, in his estimate of the middle-class share of national income, but subsumed them in aggregate 'working-class' income.[99] In Seers's work, then, the wartime influx of women to white-collar work assisted the levelling up of the working class, whereas in Routh's work the low salaries of such women contributed to the levelling down of the salariat.

All this points to the difficulty of using income and occupational criteria of 'class', as well as to the particular problem of locating white-collar women workers in the class structure.[100] It also supports the idea of the growth of a 'cross-class' group of low salary earners and better-paid manual workers, which George Orwell described as an 'intermediate stratum at which the older class distinctions are beginning to break down',[101] and which excited both him and G. D. H. Cole, who thought it would swell the ranks of Labour voters.[102] However, harmonious assimiliation within the 'intermediate class' after the war was not guaranteed, notably when it came to housing. Referring to the feelings of manual and low-paid non-manual groups, a Middlesbrough planner wrote in 1948, 'there is a good deal of evidence that mixing of social classes and other groups . . . creates social friction', and he recommended separate housing provision.[103]

Let us look, finally and very briefly, at the extent to which the middle class was accumulating savings during the war. Though unfortunately we do not have details of middle-class patterns of saving of the kind Madge collected from the working class, both he and Seers made some suggestive comments.

They both argued that during the war the middle class (or, as Madge emphasised, its wealthier sections) saved money which would normally have been spent on 'other items', notably motor cars, education and domestic help.[104] Certainly expenditure on large 'luxury' items dried up during the war. For example, that on 'cars and motor cycles' fell from £152 million in 1938 to nil in 1943.[105] In addition Seers noted that shortages, subsidies and rationing meant that the goods which members of the middle class bought during the war were cheaper than the sort of things they had bought pre-war. Further, they stood to benefit from the 'undistributed profits' of wartime, which enforced the saving of dividends and increased the value of shares.[106]

Madge viewed wealthier middle-class families as 'pertinacious savers' by dint of both their 'high excess incomes' and their 'outlook and upbringing', and attributed to them the bulk of the money raised by National Savings and the sale of Defence Bonds.[107] If indeed they were saving heavily in wartime, they would have increased the property differential between themselves and other middle-class as well as working-class groups. In a 'hidden', or at any rate individualised and private way, then, the narrowing of income differentials such as those of 'higher professionals' may have been offset by wartime savings, and the improvement in the position of 'managers and administrators' may have been even greater than it appeared. This is ironic in that levelling of consumption during the war was a major component of the popular impression of the 'levelling of class'.[108]

What can we conclude from this review of surveys and accounts pertinent to the issue of the 'levelling of class'? I should like to end by drawing together three main points.

Firstly, permanent 'levelling up' of the working class, as depicted by both defenders of middle-class status and advocates of a 'classless' society in the 1940s and '50s, is thrown in doubt by the absence of any guarantee of the permanence of relatively enlarged working-class incomes and by the beginnings in the late 1940s of the reversal of fiscal policies which had favoured the working class during the war.

Secondly, on the other hand, there were certainly wartime changes in social stratification, and there is no doubt that some groups of manual workers improved their pay position markedly, relative both to other groups of manual workers and to some groups of salaried workers. In addition, it seems that working-class women undertook paid work to a greater extent (and at higher levels of pay) than women of the middle class, apart from those in the latter group who entered low-salary white-collar jobs, whose class position is one of the unresolved problems of stratification theory. All the same, there were wide variations in the income levels of different working-class groups – for example, aircraft workers and servicemen's wives – and little sign of any 'levelling' within the working-class household. Likewise, some middle-class groups, such as 'managers and administrators', fared better than others, such as 'professionals'.

Thirdly, evidence of differences in saving patterns within and between classes suggests that when class is seen in relation to property, rather than income, the war gave rise to very little movement out of the working class via accumulation, and it may even have encouraged the widening of property differentials, both within the middle class and between it and the working class.

Finally, it must be emphasised that much of the above is, of necessity in view of the available data, tentative. It is intended as an antidote to a focus entirely upon images and attitudes, and indeed has at some points suggested that popular contemporary ideas of the way levelling would be achieved in wartime (e.g. by drawing women of all classes into paid industrial work and by establishing equality of consumption) may have been quite mistaken, in terms of underlying economic tendencies conducive to levelling, as opposed to appearances of equality. This chapter, then, is offered as a challenge to previous interpretations and it is hoped that it will both provoke debate and stimulate further research.

Notes

1 Arthur Marwick, *Class, Image and Reality in Britain, France and the U.S.A. since 1930*, Collins, London 1980, ch. 11.

2 Stanislas Andrzejewski, *Military Organisation and Society*, Routledge, London, 1954.

3 R. M. Titmuss, 'War and social policy', in *Essays on 'The Welfare State'*, Allen & Unwin, London 1963, p. 86.

4 For a stimulating discussion of the way recent historians have used 'class' see R. S. Neale, *Class in English History, 1680–1850*, Blackwell, Oxford, 1981.

5 Neale, *Class*, p. 132.

6 D. C. Marsh, *The Changing Social Structure of England and Wales, 1871–1951*, Routledge, London, 1958, p. 220.

7 Marsh, *Changing Social Structure*, pp. 218 and 223.

8 See discussion in J. Westergaard and H. Resler, *Class in a Capitalist Society: a Study of Contemporary Britain*, Heinemann, London, 1975, p. 32.

9 Roy Lewis and Angus Maude, *The English Middle Classes*, Phoenix House,

London 1949. See also discussion in W. G. Runciman, *Relative Deprivation and Social Justice: a Study of Attitudes to Social Inequality in Twentieth-century England*, Penguin, Harmondsworth, 1972, p. 94.

10 See, for example, Richard M. Titmuss, *Income Distribution and Social Change: a Study in Criticism*, Allen & Unwin, London, 1962, ch. 3 and 8.

11 G. D. H. Cole, *Studies in Class Structure*, Routledge, London, 1955, p. 75. Cole's reservations are supported in A. H. Halsey (ed.), *Trends in British Society since 1900: a Guide to the Changing Social Structure of Britain*, Macmillan, London, 1972, p. 75.

12 Dudley Seers, *Changes in the Cost-of-living and the Distribution of Income since 1938*, Oxford University Institute of Statistics, Blackwell, Oxford, 1949, pp. 5 and 8. Westergaard and Resler refer to Seers's work as 'probably the most comprehensive examination of the 1940s shift' in incomes, *Class*, p. 55.

13 Seers, *Changes*, p. 65.

14 *Ibid.*

15 Cole, *Studies*, p. 76. See also Halsey, *Trends*, tables 3.15, p. 95.

16 Westergaard and Resler, *Class*, pp. 54–5, and tables 1 and 2, pp. 39–40. T. B. Bottomore also believed this to be so. See *Classes in Modern Society*, Allen & Unwin, London, 1965, p. 34: 'between 1939 and 1949 redistribution may have transferred some ten per cent of the national income from property owners to wage earners; but . . . since 1949 there has again been growing inequality'.

17 Seers is explicit on how he arrived at figures for the total wage and salary bills (see *Changes*, pp. 59–65), but surprisingly silent on the issue of the calculation of the size of the two groups. In the absence of an occupational census for the war period, and in view of the presentation of all employment data using industrial classifications, it seems that there is no obvious way in which it could be done.

18 Bottomore, *Classes*, p. 16.

19 See discussion in Runciman, *Relative Deprivation*, p. 90, and John Hilton, *Rich Man, Poor Man*, Allen & Unwin, London, 1944, pp. 60 and 68–9. He found that 70% of savings in Post Office accounts were under £25, and 90% of those earning less than £200 rented their accommodation.

20 Charles Madge, *War-time Patterns of Saving and Spending*, National Institute of Economic and Social Research Occasional Papers, IV, Cambridge University Press, 1943, pp. 1, 4, 7, 9.

21 Madge, *War-time Patterns*, p. 41–9.

22 *Ibid.*, pp. 1 and 50.

23 *Ibid.*, p. 69.

24 *Ibid.*, p. 67.

25 *Ibid.*, p. 82.

26 *Ibid.*, p. 73.

27 *Ibid.*, pp. 47–8.

28 Seers, *Changes*, p. 6.

29 Central Statistical Office, *Statistical Digest of the War*, HMSO, London, 1951, table 9, p. 8.

30 Central Statistical Office, *Digest*, table 187, p. 204.

31 *Ibid.*, table 188, p. 204, and table 190, p. 205.

32 Seers, *Changes*, pp. 22–3.

33 Penny Summerfield, *Women Workers in the Second World War: Production*

and Patriarchy in Conflict, Croom Helm, London, 1984, p. 200.

34   The official historian wrote that the practice was 'that the 100 per cent concession should be limited to individual cases', P. Inman, *Labour in the Munition Industries*, HMSO, London, 1957, p. 357.

35   Summerfield, *Women Workers*, ch. 7.

36   Inman, *Labour*, p. 354.

37   Summerfield, *Women Workers*, p. 170.

38   Central Statistical Office, *Digest*, table 189, p. 205.

39   *Ibid.*

40   Richard Croucher, 'Communist Politics and Shop Stewards in Engineering, 1935–46', unpub. PhD thesis, University of Warwick, 1978, ch. 1.

41   Inman, *Labour*, pp. 319–20.

42   *Ibid.*, pp. 320–5.

43   *Ibid.*, pp. 323, 338, 355.

44   Select Committee on National Expenditure, *Fifteenth Report*, Session 1940–1, section 7.

45   Central Statistical Office, *Digest*, pp. 204–5.

46   Madge, *War-time Patterns*, p. 15. See also W. K. Hancock and M. M. Gowing, *British War Economy*, HMSO, London, 1949, p. 330, who corroborate this.

47   Runciman, *Relative Deprivation*, pp. 98–100.

48   Summerfield, *Women Workers*, pp. 19, 100–1.

49   Inman, *Labour*, pp. 396–7; PRO, Lab. 10/281, 'Causes of Industrial Unrest, 1943'.

50   Richard Croucher, *Engineers at War, 1939–1945*, Merlin, London, 1982, pp. 297–9; Summerfield, *Women Workers*, pp. 160–1.

51   Croucher, *Engineers*, ch. 3, particularly p. 168.

52   Inman, *Labour*, p. 327, n. 2.

53   *Ibid.*, pp. 329–30, 340–6, 334; Croucher, *Engineers*, pp. 197–244; Summerfield, *Women Workers*, ch. 7.

54   Madge, *War-time Patterns*, p. 70.

55   *Ibid.*, table XLIV, p. 70.

56   Central Statistical Office, *Digest*, table 190, p. 205. On food subsidies, etc., see Hancock and Gowing, *War Economy*, pp. 167, 333–4, 501–2. Clothes consumed more of working-class expenditure in 1942 than 1938, not surprisingly in view of their steep rise in the working-class cost-of-living index (92% in 1939–42), though clothes rationing (1941) and the Utility clothing scheme (1942) brought clothes' prices down thereafter. There was a small decline in the proportion spent on rent, probably due to rent control under the Rent and Mortgage Interest Restrictions Act, 1939, which held rents to an (official) rise of only 1% in 1939–42. See Hancock and Gowing, *War Economy*, pp. 502–3 and p. 166.

57   Central Statistical Office, *Digest*, table 7, p. 5.

58   Central Office of Information, Wartime Social Survey, Report No. 23, New Series, 42, *Credit Buying*, July 1942.

59   Madge, *War-time patterns*, p. 62.

60   *Ibid.*, p. 16.

61   Central Office of Information, Social Survey, *The British Household*, by

P. G. Gray, based on an enquiry carried out in 1947 (1949), table 5, p. 7, and table 33, p. 24.

62 Madge, *War-time Patterns*, p. 54.

63 *Ibid.*, p. 53.

64 *Ibid.*, pp. 53, 58–9.

65 *Ibid.*, table XXVIII, p. 54.

66 Central Office of Information, Wartime Social Survey, *Women at Work*, by Geoffrey Thomas, June 1944, p. 1; Census of England and Wales, 1931, *Occupational Tables*, I, 1934.

67 Madge, *War-time Patterns*, p. 55.

68 As Westergaard and Resler point out when making a similar point, *Class*, p. 41.

69 Summerfield, *Women Workers*, pp. 55–7.

70 Central Office of Information, Wartime Social Survey, *Women at Work*, table 14, p. 9.

71 E. Gamarnikow *et al.*, *Gender, Class and Work*, Heinemann, London, 1983, ch. 5, 'Trends in female social mobility', by Geoff Payne, Judy Payne and Tony Chapman.

72 Ninety-four per cent of women on assembly and unskilled repetitive work and 96% of machinists and hand-tool operators had received no secondary education, compared with a total of 80% of the age group who had received such education in 1938. Central Office of Information, Wartime Social Survey, *Women at Work*, p. 6; Board of Education, *Report of the Consultative Committee on Secondary Education*, HMSO, London, 1938, table I, p. 88.

73 Central Office of Information, Wartime Social Survey, *Women at Work*, p. 7. The actual proportions given were as follows:

Weekly wage of chief wage-earner	%
Up to £3 12s	29
£3 12s–£5	58
£5–£10	11
Over £10	3 (as in original)

74 Ian McLaine, *Ministry of Morale: Home Front Morale and the Ministry of Information in World War II*, Allen & Unwin, London, 1979, pp. 176–7. Middle-class women showed a preference for the Women's Royal Naval Service and the Women's Auxiliary Air Force rather than the Auxiliary Territorial Service, where the gulf between working-class privates and upper-class officers was thought to present a problem for recruitment. See PRO, Lab. 26/63, Women's Services (Welfare and Amenities) Committee, 'Recruiting of Womanpower', and Central Office of Information, Wartime Social Survey, *An Investigation of the Attitudes of Women, the General Public and A.T.S. Personnel to the Auxiliary Territorial Service*, October 1941.

75 The convention (followed by the Wartime Social Survey) was (and remained) to classify families by the income of the 'chief' wage earner, defined as male. Even Madge, who did attempt to assess complete family incomes, did not record the separate contribution made by wives, and actually blurred it in his breakdown of Glasgow family incomes into husbands 62%, 'other earners

over twenty-one' 26% and juvenile earners 12%. Madge, *War-time Patterns*, p. 53.

76 *Ibid.*, p. 62.

77 *Ibid.*, p. 32. A comparison of the spending of a male and female lodger–earner in Leeds showed that the man spent 8*s* 6*d* on tobacco, compared with the woman's 2*s* 6*d*, 5*s* 1*d* on alcohol compared with 3*d*, and 2*s* 8*d* on entertainment, compared with 2*s* 3*d*. See table XII, p. 33.

78 *Ibid.*, p. 73.

79 *Ibid.*; Seers, *Changes*, p. 23; Hancock and Gowing, *War Economy*, pp. 170, 327, 330.

80 Seers, *Changes*, pp. 22 and 8.

81 See especially appendix II of Madge's book, in which many negative working-class opinions about saving are quoted, e.g. a man whose family generated a considerable 'excess income' but who drank and smoked more than the average said, 'the average man, if he does himself and his family justice, has nothing to save', and a riveter said, 'some people will starve their weans to put money in the bank'.

82 Hancock and Gowing, *War Economy*, p. 169.

83 Madge, *War-time Patterns*, p. 40.

84 Hancock and Gowing, *War Economy*, p. 169, n. 5; R. M. Titmuss, *Problems of Social Policy*, HMSO, London, 1950, p. 162.

85 Madge, *War-time Patterns*, pp. 17 and 39.

86 Central Office of Information, Wartime Social Survey, *Credit Buying*, p. 3. Middlesbrough service wives reciprocated the negativity of landlords by being 'the group most dissatisfied' with their social environment. See Central Office of Information, Social Survey, *Middlesbrough: a Social Survey*, 1948, Part IV, p. 4.

87 Titmuss, *Problems*, p. 414, n. 2; Summerfield, *Women Workers*, pp. 83–4.

88 Hancock and Gowing, *War Economy*, pp. 505–6.

89 *Ibid.*, pp. 325, 340, n. 4, p. 505. It was alleged by the government that a private's total pay and allowances, including payments in kind and income tax relief, were close to average industrial earnings, but this argument was apparently rather unconvincing to privates themselves.

90 Mass-Observation Archive, Topic Collection: Armed Forces, box 4, file E. Cuttings from *Sunday Express*, 13 April 1941, and other newspapers. An officer's pay at this time was said to be £3 17*s* per week, whereas a male clerk's pay (relatively low down on the salary scale) was about £4 15*s*.

91 The differential provoked adverse comment. For example, a 'teacher and housewife' wrote in her diary in September 1942, 'I can't see why a soldier's child should have 1*s* 0*d* per week increase, but an officer's 1*s* 0*d* per day'. Mass-Observation Archive, Topic Collection: Armed Forces, box 4, file E.

92 Seers, *Changes*, pp. 62 and 65.

93 Guy Routh, *Occupation and Pay in Great Britain, 1906–1960*, Cambridge University Press, 1965, p. 106, and table 48, p. 107. Men in the lower professions earned 115% of the average in 1955/56, a fall of 40% since 1935/36, and women in this group earned 82%, a fall of 37%. Male clerks earned 98% of the average, a fall of 18%, and women clerks earned 60%, a fall of 2%. Male managers improved their position by 3%, earning 279% of average earnings, female

managers earned 151%, an improvement of 45%.

94   Routh, *Occupation and Pay*, p. 124. Manual earnings increased by 30% in 1938–40, whereas the increase for all employees was 14%, and by 1944 manual earnings stood at 182% of the 1938 level, compared with an average of 117% for white-collar civil servants.

95   *Ibid.*, p. 106.

96   *Ibid.*, p. 125, n. 1.

97   Ministry of Labour and National Service, *Tables Relating to Employment and Unemployment in Great Britain, 1939, 1945 and 1946*, HMSO, London, 1947, pp. 4–5. In another relatively 'white collar' industrial category, 'commerce, banking, insurance and finance', the number of men had actually fallen by 1945 to 38% of the 1939 number, whereas the number of women rose to 149% of what it had been, changing the proportion of women from 31% to 63%.

98   Routh, *Occupation and Pay*, pp. 104 and 124.

99   Seers, *Changes*, p. 64.

100   The first jobs of around 35% of the daughters of working-class fathers entering the Scottish labour market between 1939 and 1945 were non-manual. See Gamarnikow, *Gender*, pp. 65–6, especially fig. 5.1. Other authors in the same collection suggest that a high proportion of women in low-paid non-manual work marry men in manual occupations. If this was occurring in the 1930s and 1940s it would again have caused the group of women white-collar workers to straddle the conventional class boundaries. See Gamarnikow, *Gender*, p. 60.

101   George Orwell, 'England, your England', 1941, quoted by Runciman, *Relative Deprivation*, p. 130.

102   Cole, *Studies*, p. 77.

103   Central Office of Information, Social Survey, *Middlesbrough*, Part IV, p. 3. See also H. Orlans, *Stevenage: a Sociological Study of a New Town*, Greenwood, London, 1971, pp. 160–3.

104   Madge, *War-time Patterns*, p. 74; Seers, *Changes*, pp. 41–2.

105   Halsey, *Trends*, table 3.5, p. 87.

106   Seers, *Changes*, pp. 41, 59.

107   Madge, *War-time Patterns*, pp. 74, 50. Both the National Savings scheme and the sale of Defence Bonds were introduced as a form of government borrowing in November 1939. See Hancock and Gowing, *War Economy*, p. 171.

108   McLaine, *Ministry of Morale*, pp. 177–8. 'Home Intelligence' reported in 1941–42 that apparent 'unfairness' in the distribution of consumer goods due to the greater purchasing power of better-off groups 'seemed to rankle increasingly', but McLaine comments, 'As long as the government appeared to be doing its best to impose the burdens of war equally upon all sections of the community, expressions of discontent did not threaten to coalesce into a serious danger to morale and national unity'.

Harold L. Smith

The effect of the war on the status of women

The notion that the Second World War must have had a profound and lasting effect on the lives of British women has continued to shape interpretive studies of the conflict to the present day. No one has done more to draw attention to its effect on society than Arthur Marwick. He maintains that the impact on women is of crucial importance to his general thesis about the relationship between war and social change; in his words, it 'brings one to the heart of the whole question of whether the war brought about significant social and economic changes'.[1] After reviewing the evidence Marwick concludes that the war was a turning point in the emancipation of women; it led to a 'new social and economic freedom' for them, as well as a marked change in their consciousness.[2] Although his analysis places much weight on the changed position of women, especially married women, in the labour force, Marwick also suggests that there were important changes in the attitudes of those not employed outside the home. In contrast to many other historians, he believes that the wartime changes affecting women did not end in 1945, but continued to shape their lives after the conflict.[3]

Marwick's general view of the war's effect on women resembles the position taken by many authors who commented at the time. In studies written near the end of the war Margaret Goldsmith and Gertrude Williams both concluded that there had been a 'revolution' in the position of women. Both believed that the changed status of women workers was the central development in this wartime revolution.[4] Although considerably more cautious, the study conducted by the International Labour Office shortly after the war also noted the altered position of women workers and concluded that in light of the post-war labour shortage it seemed likely that the changes in women's economic status would become permanent.[5]

But by the early 1950s discussions of this issue had become much more sceptical about the lasting effect of the war. Vera Brittain described the belief that the conflict was responsible for women's progress towards equality as an 'illusion': if it had accelerated pre-war processes of change, it had not brought about any 'revolution in values'. [6] While recognising the importance of wartime alterations in women's employment, Alva Myrdall and Viola Klein found that the changes had been a temporary adjustment to an emergency, and that after 1945 there had been a restoration of pre-war patterns. [7] With some qualifications, recent studies by Sheila Lewenhak, Sarah Boston, Penny Summerfield and Harold Smith have presented a similar view. [8]

Central to Marwick's thesis is his belief that war affects society through four main dimensions: disruption, the testing of existing institutions, the participation of previously underprivileged groups in the waging of the war, and as a psychological experience. [9] This approach does draw attention to some important ways in which women were affected. But it will be suggested in the following pages that women did not necessarily react to these stimuli in quite the manner Marwick suggests. His reading of the evidence generally associates change with progress towards the emancipation of women from traditional sex-roles. Inherent within his argument is the assumption that women generally welcomed wartime changes and took advantage of the new opportunities to lead more independent and satisfying lives. In many respects, however, women found the wartime changes undesirable, and responded by seeking to re-establish an idealised version of pre-war relationships.

Marwick's concept of disruption, for example, suggests that women were shaken out of long-established patterns of behaviour, including social relationships. [10] But these innovations often occurred within the context of unpleasant, even life-threatening experiences which influenced how women perceived them. One of the more striking features of the Second World War was its blurring of the distinction between civilians and combatants. German bombing placed civilians in the front line, with the result that for the first time in war women were frequently exposed to the danger of violent death. Of the 130,000 civilian adults killed or seriously wounded, 48% (63,000) were female. [11]

The mass migration of the population was one important way in which the war disrupted the lives of large numbers of women. Partly owing to the fear of enemy air attack, approximately 2,250,000 people moved during the first month of the war; by the end of the conflict there were 60 million recorded changes of address. [12] Many were of mothers evacuated from their homes as part of the government's scheme to remove young children and their mothers from danger areas; about half a million mothers or expectant mothers were evacuated at the beginning of the war. For very large numbers of women, therefore, the war's immediate effect was to transform them into evacuees or the hostesses of evacuees. The latter were recognised by the government as doing essential war work and granted exemption from conscription into industry or the armed forces, but they were given no financial compensation for this additional burden. Instead they received a special word of appreciation from the Queen. For these women the war reinforced their traditional role: their war work consisted of duties traditionally performed by women, and they were rewarded as housewives traditionally have been, with praise rather than pay.

Previous studies of wartime women have focused on those who were working, in part because this has been perceived as an area of considerable change. Inevitably it encourages a distorted image of the war's effect by neglecting the largest category of females: housewives. Even in 1943, at the peak of the mobilisation of womanpower, the number of adult women employed full-time in industry, the armed forces and civil defence was less than the number who were full-time housewives: 7,250,000 as against 8,770,000.[13] While it is true that for many the wartime absence of their husband provided the opportunity to become more independent and exercise greater authority in the family, the change was recognised as a temporary expedient and was associated with an increased level of stress and anxiety.

In concentrating on the positive changes associated with the war insufficient attention is sometimes paid to the fact that the conflict, as one social historian recently put it, 'trampled roughshod through woman's sphere, the home'.[14] The build-up of men in the armed forces meant that wives were separated from their loved ones, and anxious about their safety; many women with pre-school-age children were evacuated from their homes and separated from friends and familiar surroundings; many lost their homes in air raids (two in every seven houses in England were damaged or destroyed); food shortages and rationing made shopping more difficult; the mass movement of domestic servants into other jobs forced middle and upper-class women to shoulder additional burdens, including, in some instances, their own housework; and after August 1942 those not in full-time war work were required to accept fire-watching duties, a job which often meant increased risk of injury during the bombing.[15]

Marwick has suggested that housewives forced to manage the family's affairs while their husbands were away in the armed forces were emancipated by the experience. In support of the claim he cites the following diary entry by Nella Last:

I suddenly thought tonight, 'I know why a lot of women have gone into pants – it's a sign that they are asserting themselves in some way'. I feel pants are more a sign of the times than I had realised. A growing contempt for man in general sweeps over me . . . I feel that, in the world of tomorrow, marriage will be – will have to be – more of a partnership, less of this 'I have spoken' attitude. [16]

It is plausible that in light of the additional responsibilities assumed by wartime wives attitudes like this would have become common among married women. But it appears to be the only example Marwick has been able to find in support of his view. Furthermore, post-war studies of contemporary marriages do not agree that war-generated changes in attitudes had significantly altered relationships between spouses. [17] It seems likely that the pattern associated with the First World War held true for the later conflict as well: wives considered wartime conditions exceptional and, when their husbands returned, reverted to the relationships which they had established prior to the conflict. [18]

The subject of women's employment has contributed more than its share to the mythology of the Second World War. Britain mobilised women much more extensively in 1939–45 than in 1914–18, and far exceeded other belligerents in its use of womanpower. By September 1943 some 7,258,000 women, 46% of those between the ages of fourteen and fifty-nine, were engaged in some form of national service. Virtually all able-bodied single women between the ages of eighteen and forty (90%), as well as 80% of those in this age group who were married but had no children, were involved in the war effort. [19] Marwick claims that this development was the single most important means by which the war emancipated women. [20] His view rests on several assumptions: (1) that their wartime employment was a new experience for most women, (2) that they welcomed the opportunity of paid work and entered the labour force voluntarily, (3) that the war undermined the sex segregation of jobs, and (4) that employment changed the consciousness of women, leaving them permanently dissatisfied with traditional sex roles.

The belief that paid employment was a new experience for most of the women who swelled the labour force seems dubious on several grounds. In 1939 there were about 5 million women employed in industry, commerce and the armed forces; by 1943 the number had increased by 2,250,000. [21] Thus, even if all those who obtained employment after 1939 had never worked previously, only about 31% of the 1943 total could have been new employees. And wartime surveys of women industrial workers suggest that this figure overstates the actual proportion of new entrants to the work force. The 1943 Wartime Social Survey of women industrial workers found that only 28% of those interviewed were not working when the war began; moreover, some of them had worked before 1939 and were re-entering industry. [22] During the inter-war period it was normal for young and single working-class women to work for wages; 75·7% of all single women aged fourteen to twenty-four were employed in 1931. [23] Since they often ceased work after marriage, many wives entering the labour force were clearly returning to paid employment rather than experiencing it for the first time. While some upper and middle-class women were drawn into the labour force for the first time by the war, it is unlikely that the attitudes of the majority of women workers were sharply altered by their wartime employment since paid work was not a new experience for them.

Marwick claims that conscription 'played a relatively minor role in the changes in women's employment during the war' . . . [24] This is a point of some importance, since women who were compelled to take up war work were unlikely to view it as a form of emancipation. The mobilisation of womanpower has often been presented in the context of the belief that the war initiated an unprecedented sense of national unity. Given this assumption, it has seemed plausible to believe that women came forward with only minimal prodding from government. [25] While they were influenced by patriotic feelings, and many believed it their duty to serve their country, it will be suggested in the following pages that coercion was far more important than the traditional view has admitted.

Although the government was reluctant to conscript women into war work, once it recognised that there was no other way of solving the labour shortage it proceeded to apply as much coercion as it thought necessary. The Manpower Requirements Committee's reports late in 1940 were the initial turning point. They projected that about 2 million additional women would be needed in industry, and pointed out that this total could be achieved only by drawing upon the supply of married women. The committee recommended that the government resort to an increased use of compulsion to direct women into the industries where they were needed most. [26] Shortly after this, Ernest Bevin, the Minister of Labour and National Service, obtained the approval of the War Cabinet and Parliament for two measures which in effect established industrial conscription for women. The first of these, the Essential Work (General Provisions) Order, permitted the Minister of Labour to designate certain types of employment as essential work; employees in these designated areas would not be allowed to leave their jobs without permission from the Ministry.[27]

But the Registration for Employment Order became the most important means by which the government sought to increase the supply of womanpower. It authorised the Ministry of Labour to require specified groups of women to register with their local labour exchange as a preliminary to taking up war work; during 1941 only those in the twenty to thirty-one age group were required to register but the following year the scheme was extended to those aged nineteen to forty-one. Some women, such as those with children under fourteen or those with household responsibilities, were granted exemption. Those who registered and were considered suitable for essential war work were required to return later for an interview in which they were advised of the alternative forms of work available to them. If they refused to take one of the recommended jobs the Minister could issue a formal direction requiring them to do so. It would appear that only about 200,000 women were formally directed into industry during the war, while another 2,067 were prosecuted for failing to take up work when directed.[28] But it is likely that many women entered employment after being interviewed because they expected to be directed into essential war work if they did not. The actual number of directions issued is thus less significant than the threat of compulsion. This point was explicitly acknowledged by the official historian of the wartime use of manpower: 'The chief value of the power of direction was in the indirect pressure it could bring to bear.'[29]

Although most women publicly agreed that women should do their part in the war effort, in private many had strong reservations about the government's new policy. By August 1941 500,000 had been interviewed, but only 87,000 had joined the Women's Auxiliary Services or gone to work in the munitions industry.[30] A survey in October 1941 of 1,000 women who were apparently free to accept employment found that 32% did not want to do any type of war work; the majority cited domestic responsibilities or a strong desire not to leave home as the reason.[31] Also contributing to their reluctance was uncertainty over the working conditions they would encounter, what wages they would be paid, and whether they would be able to continue living at home.[32] While accepting the general principle of conscription, some women, presumably mainly middle and upper-class, held back because they feared being forced into factory work. [33]

After reviewing the situation late in 1941, the War Cabinet concluded that in light of the accelerating demand for labour it would be necessary to increase the degree of coercion. Although reluctant to allow military conscription for women, Churchill showed no such hesitation about applying greater coercion to bring more of them into industry. In a memorandum to the War Cabinet he urged that the existing powers for directing women into the munitions industries be used 'with greater intensity'. [34] Even before Churchill's recommendation was presented to the Cabinet the Ministry of Labour had begun to increase the pressure on eligible women to take up war work. Ministry officials interviewing women were instructed that when those eligible were unwilling to take up war work it should be made clear to them that formal directions would be issued 'forthwith'. [35]

In December 1941 the government extended compulsion by introducing military conscription for women. Although the specific purpose of the National Service (No. 2) Act was to allow women to be called up into the Women's Auxiliary Forces, it also had the effect of increasing the flow of women into industry. Those who were called up were allowed (at least until July 1942) to choose whether they wished to serve in the auxiliary forces, in civil defence or in specified types of industry; about one-third of those conscripted chose to accept employment in industry. [36] The women who were conscripted under the Act and who chose to do their service in industry were automatically issued formal directions. This reduced the grounds for appeal, a matter of some importance, since they were pressed by Ministry of Labour officials to accept unpleasant and dangerous work filling shells in Royal Ordnance Factories. [37] Later, in 1943, when the labour shortage had become even more acute, all women conscripted under the Act were directed into industry.

The powers granted the government under the National Service (No. 2) Act were hedged in by various restrictions. Originally only women aged twenty to thirty-one were covered (later the range was extended), married women and women with children under fourteen were exempt, and no conscripted woman could be compelled to use lethal weapons. But even with these limitations on it military conscription stimulated considerable anxiety. Public opinion polls in November 1941 indicated that only a bare majority (52%) of the women polled approved the government's proposal. [38] Mass-Observation noted that, while women's public reactions were favourable, their private responses were much more critical: a poll it conducted late in 1941 found that slightly less than half (49%) of those questioned supported the military call-up for women, while 46% preferred a voluntary system. [39]

Even feminists had mixed feelings. Some took the position articulated by a feminist journal early in 1941 that the 'thing that would guarantee equality for women after the war would be conscription for women now'. [40] But others had reservations about the unequal conditions which would be imposed on the conscripted women. Edith Summerskill, Labour MP, repeatedly raised questions in the Ministry of Labour's Women's Consultative Committee about the wage rates women compelled to take up war work would receive, and insisted that she would support conscription only if the government ensured that they received equal pay for work equal to that done by men. [41] After discussing the issue at great length the Woman Power Committee divided equally for and against a resolution stating that the committee had no objection in principle to conscription. [42] When the matter was discussed by the Ministry of Labour's Women's Consultative Committee late in November, both representatives from the Woman Power Committee expressed support for the measure provided the conscripted women would receive equal pay. [43] But the National Service (No. 2) Bill which the government presented to Parliament made no reference to equal pay. The only organised opposition in the lobby of the House of Commons was conducted by women MPs who opposed the measure because of this. [44]

Although it is often said that the war submerged class divisions in a growing sense of national unity, the debate over conscription indicates that class feeling continued to shape perceptions of public issues. At least some of those supporting conscription for women did so in part because they believed it would increase the likelihood that the burden of war work would be divided fairly between women of different classes. Mass-Observation surveys conducted during 1941 found that many who advocated conscription believed it would force 'idle rich girls' to work. [45] When the issue was discussed by women trade unionists in 1941 conscription was supported on the ground that it would ensure that women 'who had never done a day's work before' would be required to contribute to the war effort. [46] And at the 1941 London Women's Parliament indignation was expressed about middle-class women more concerned with their standards of comfort than assisting the war effort. One delegate concluded, 'If compulsion can get any work out of such women, then let's have compulsion'.[47]

During 1942–43 the government introduced new forms of compulsion which affected categories of women previously untouched by it. In 1942, for example, the Ministry of Labour began applying 'sterner standards' to those previously exempt, especially those who claimed heavy household responsibilities.[48] The Employment of Women (Control of Engagement) Order enabled the Minister of Labour to specify that certain groups could obtain employment only through a labour exchange; originally it applied to those aged twenty to thirty who did not have children under fourteen living with them, but it was later extended to almost all women. The measure was intended to ensure that women changing jobs were shifted into essential war work rather than positions which they might consider more desirable. Also in 1942 the government began to direct women into civil defence; by September 1944 212,340 had entered the civil defence forces in this manner.[49] And, amid considerable criticism, in April 1943 the government began to direct women into part-time work who had previously been exempt from conscription because their domestic responsibilities were too great for them to work full-time. This affected several hundred thousand: the number of female part-time employees increased from about 380,000 in June 1942 to 900,000 by June 1944.[50]

Most accounts have assumed that one of the profound changes brought about by the war was the erosion of the sex segregation of jobs characteristic of the pre-war economy. Under the May 1940 Extended Employment of Women Agreement the unions in the engineering industry agreed that for the duration of the war women would be allowed on to jobs previously reserved for men. Certain conditions were laid down, including rates of pay, but the agreement seemed to remove the biggest barrier to ending the division of jobs by sex in a vital industry. Wartime publicity issued by the government encouraged potential female employees to believe that this was taking place, and contemporary commentators singled it out as one of the major victories that women achieved in the war.[51]

But Peggy Inman cast doubt on this view in her official history of labour in the munitions industry, and her scepticism has been endorsed in a more recent study by Penny Summerfield.[52] Inman concluded that, while the number of women in engineering expanded considerably, only a 'very small proportion' were allowed onto men's jobs.[53] Summerfield and others have drawn attention to the extreme hostility that women dilutees often encountered from male workers, even when the latter were members of a union which had signed the Extended Employment of Women Agreement. This reaction from the men, as well as employers' doubts about women's ability to cope, contributed to the infrequency with which they were employed on skilled men's jobs. In some instances employers downgraded jobs by requiring women to accept assistance even when they did not need it.[54] Often a job was altered by dividing it between two women or introducing new machinery.[55] In some instances a man's job was redefined as women's work, and thus semi-skilled, on the ground that women were doing the same job in another factory elsewhere. A rough indication of the extent to which the influx of women workers continued to experience sex segregation is suggested by the fact that 75% of those in engineering were paid under the special women's schedule for employees classified as doing women's work.[56] The notion that sex segregation was substantially eliminated might best be regarded as a myth, encouraged by government publicity designed to recruit women into industry, and accepted uncritically by some feminists eager to believe that the war was bringing substantial progress toward sex equality.[57]

Marwick places great importance on the notion that the war altered the consciousness of women, making them less willing to accept traditional sex roles and subordination to men.[58] If there was such a change it should have been especially evident among women workers, manifesting itself in a strong desire to remain in paid employment when the war was over. But the evidence from wartime surveys does not support claims that women's attitudes altered. The most comprehensive of these was conducted by the government's Wartime Social Survey late in 1943. A large sample (2,609) of employed women were questioned about their post-war plans; only 25% responded unequivocally that they wanted to go on working.[58] As might be expected, attitudes varied considerably according to the type of employment the women held; among professional and administrative employees 75% expressed a desire to continue working, whereas only 50% of those employed as labourers did. Since a large proportion of the increase in the number of women workers consisted of married women, their responses were particularly interesting. While 29% of the married women workers polled wished to continue working, this preference was considerably stronger among married women aged thirty-five or over. Married women under thirty-five, especially those without children, were far more prone to respond that women should be at home. All the women were asked if jobs should go to the best qualified person after the war, or whether preference should be given to men. Their response seems especially inconsistent with the notion that wartime employment had radically changed their outlook: 44% said the best person should have the job, while 39% replied that preference should be given to men. [59]

Surveys conducted by Mass-Observation and the British Institute of Public Opinion near the end of the war arrived at similar conclusions. Mass-Observation found that less than 25% of the women factory workers it surveyed wished to remain in their present jobs once the war was over. Most were aged thirty-five to fifty, unmarried or widowed, and had been employed before the war. [60] The post-war aspirations of the vast majority of women factory workers were focused on marriage and domestic life; their wartime employment was considered a temporary response to an abnormal situation. One young woman explained:

Of course when we get married I shan't want to work; I shall want to stay at home and have some children. You can't look on anything you do during the war as what you really mean to do; it's just filling in time till you can live your own life again. [61]

A Gallup poll of working women conducted early in 1945 by the British Institute of Public Opinion found that 61% of those polled thought it 'likely' that they would continue working after the war; 39% thought it unlikely. But these totals obscure some important differences. The ones who wanted to go on working were mainly those who had worked prior to the war: 81% of respondents who had been working before the war indicated a wish to continue. A majority of the women who entered the work force during the war planned to leave when it was over: only 39% of the new workers wanted to keep their jobs. Finally, wartime employment apparently brought little change in the attitude of single women towards employment: 66% of the single women working who were polled indicated they intended to stop working as soon as they married. [62]

It is generally believed that one of the most significant lasting changes was the acceptance of married women working outside the home. The 1931 census indicated that only 10% of married women worked for wages, but by 1951 the figure had increased to 21·74%. [63] Since the Second World War substantially increased the proportion of married women who were employed, it seems logical to attribute the change to that conflict.

But even on this point it is possible to overstate the importance of the war. The proportion of married women working had increased considerably during the previous decade; one author has calculated that by 1939 it had risen 4% from the 1931 level.[64] This increase was due in part to long-term changes in the economy which have continued to the present day. It is likely, therefore, that a considerable increase in the number of married women working would have occurred by 1951 even if there had been no war.[65] Moreover, the 1951 census figure almost certainly exaggerates the effect of the war, since part of the increase it indicates came during the post-war period when the Labour government initiated a concerted effort to attract more married women into the work force. It has been estimated that in 1947 about 18% of married women were working; the increase directly attributable to the war therefore may have been as little as 4%.[66]

It has been claimed that the war was a turning point because it removed obstacles to married women's employment, especially the marriage bar. But the relationship between the war and the elimination of the marriage bar is less clear-cut than appears. During the war the marriage bar was suspended for women teachers and civil servants. The government eventually removed it permanently in both areas of employment, but for reasons unrelated to the wartime performance of married women workers.

The removal of the marriage bar for teachers was proposed in an amendment to the 1944 Education Bill.[67] It was opposed by the Secretary of the Board of Education, but after discussion within the government it was agreed to accept the amendment. There is no indication that the war record of married women teachers affected this decision. The factors which did have a bearing on it included the expectation that there would be a shortage of teachers after the war, an awareness that the Education Bill would exacerbate the problem, and a concern that it was undesirable to restrict headmistress-ships to spinsters who had led a life of sexual repression.[68]

At the end of the war the question of whether to restore the marriage bar in the civil service was referred to a civil service committee, but the civil service unions were so deeply divided on the issue that the committee was unable to make a recommendation. When the matter was discussed by the Cabinet late in 1946, Hugh Dalton, the Minister directly responsible for the civil service, recommended that the bar be retained with some modification. But other Cabinet Ministers objected that this seemed illogical in view of the labour shortage and the government's efforts to increase the number of married women working. The Cabinet therefore concluded that when 'the Government were urging industry to retain married women in employment, it would seem inconsistent that they should announce new rules reaffirming the marriage bar . . .', and thus agreed that the bar should be abolished. [69]

Marwick has repeatedly claimed that the war increased the opportunities for married women to work by altering the attitudes of employers. In several studies he states that among private employers at the end of the war there was 'a remarkable swing round in opinion' in favour of employing married women. [70] But the survey he cites in support of this claim actually suggests the opposite conclusion. Apart from Boot's Pure Drug Co. Ltd, all the employers who expressed an opinion on their experience with married women workers during the war stated that married women had 'definite disadvantages' as employees. Of the firms surveyed which had a marriage bar prior to the war, only one, Boot's, stated that it intended to end the marriage bar for its employees. The others, including the four main railway companies, Unilever, Imperial Chemical Industries, the Bank of England, Rowntree & Co. and Cadbury Brothers, all replied that they planned to restore the marriage bar. [71] By 1950 many private employers had removed the marriage bar, but not as a result of the war. A post-war survey of firms conducted by Viola Klein revealed that many regarded the employment of married women 'a necessary expedient to tide them over the post-war labour shortage'. [72]

If it is true, as Richard Titmuss has suggested, that the decline in the birth rate since 1900 has been the single most important factor contributing to women's emancipation, then the Second World War must be regarded as one of the most retrogressive events in the recent history of British women. [73] One of the more striking, although temporary, changes initiated by the war was a drastic reversal in the long-term trend of the birth rate. The birth rate had been declining steadily since the 1870s; in 1941 it reached the lowest point since official records were kept, 13·9 per 1,000 of the population. [74] But the following year it jumped to 15·6 per 1,000, the highest level since 1931, and then continued to rise until it peaked in 1947 at 20·6 per 1,000. [75] Like many other changes associated with the war, however, this reversal was not permanent; after 1950 the birth rate began to fall once again. [76]

The sharp rise in the marriage rate during the war partially explains the dramatic increase in the wartime birth rate. In this respect the war accelerated a tendency which had been previously established. By the end of the 1930s the British marriage rate was higher than it had been since the middle of the nineteenth century. [77] The outbreak of war was accompanied by a record marriage rate in the years 1939–40; after a decline during the middle of the war it soared again from 1945 to 1948.[78] The result was virtually a revolution in the marital status of young women: 42% of all women aged twenty-five to twenty-nine were single in 1931, but by 1951 only 22% of the women in this age group were unmarried. The wartime changes in marriage and birth rates do not seem consistent with the notion that the war emancipated women. Instead, they point towards the conclusion that the war reinforced traditional roles and thereby contributed to the sense of oppression that some women experienced in the post-war period.[79]

While Marwick is correct in suggesting that the war created new pressures for change, what seems most striking is how little the conflict permanently altered the position of women. Why this should have been so is a complex matter, but the following help to explain the surprising degree of continuity: (1) the nature of women's work experience, (2) government policy, and (3) the relative weakness of the British feminist movement.

Feminist historians have been puzzled by the evidence that women's wartime employment brought little change in the consciousness of women workers.[80] But in the light of women's wartime work experiences this does not seem especially surprising. Many women war workers found their jobs frustrating and unpleasant. They were often placed in low-level jobs involving routine repetition work in which, as one female factory worker admitted, 'boredom is our worst enemy'.[81] Others, especially those from a sheltered background, who entered factories found themselves 'plunged abruptly into a world of coarse, ill-bred men and women, whose language was foul and bluer than the bluest sky . . .'.[82] Male white-collar workers, as well as those in factories, often resented women and made them feel unwelcome. One BBC official, asked in 1942 if women might be allowed to become newsreaders, dismissed the idea frigidly: 'I hardly think we are considering women as newsreaders'.[83]

Women who took up war work were well aware that they were considered temporary workers; this sense of impermanence may also have affected the way they felt about their employment. The 1940 Extended Employment of Women Agreement defined the women who entered industry under its provisions as temporary workers, with the clear implication that they would be removed from their jobs at the end of the war. Records were kept of these women, and shop stewards informed them they would be the first to be dismissed when redundancies began to occur.[84] The public debate over the 1942 Restoration of Pre-war

Practices Act also helped spread the conviction among women employees that they would be removed from their jobs when the war ended. [85]

Married women workers experienced additional stress because of the double burden of employment and housework. Wartime conditions reduced the likelihood that their husbands would be available to help with household chores while increasing the amount of time they needed for shopping and travelling to and from work. The rate of absenteeism among women industrial workers was almost twice the men's rate; not surprisingly, it was higher for married than for single women. [86] By 1945 it is likely that many married women shared the attitude of the working wife who confided to Mass-Observation: 'The two jobs of home and work are getting me down . . . what I feel is that when the war is over I'll want a good long rest.' [87]

Government policies also helped ensure that the position of women would not be greatly altered by the war. The government mobilised the nation's womanpower reluctantly, made determined efforts to maintain its pre-war practice of sex differentiation among its own employees, and facilitated the movement of women workers back home once the conflict had ended. When a question about the post-war status of women industrial workers was raised in 1942, William Jowitt, the Minister responsible for reconstruction, candidly admitted that the government was committed to 'putting back the man in his own preferential position' even though it would mean an 'enormous recession of opportunities' for women to work. [88]

One specific means by which working women were encouraged to return to their homes was the rapid reduction in the number of day nurseries after 1945. During the conflict the number of nurseries had increased substantially in order to allow women with young children to enter work. But the Ministry of Health, which was responsible for the nurseries, disapproved of paid employment for mothers with young children and was concerned that the practice might continue after the war. It therefore accepted the nurseries but only as a temporary measure. One Ministry official noted, 'The very fact that a nursery centre is neither a nursery school nor a day nursery would stamp them as a purely temporary expedient to deal with war conditions and would make them easier to get rid of after the war'. [89] Following the war the number of nurseries declined swiftly; by December 1947 only 879 remained, compared to 1,450 in 1943. [90]

In the 1943 Commons debate on womanpower Thelma Cazalet-Keir noted that 'a good many people' were already deeply concerned that women's wartime emancipation and economic freedom would have an adverse effect on the family after the war.[91] Fears that there might be a permanent change in women's role heightened anxiety over the long-term decline in the birth rate. This concern led to the appointment of a Royal Commission on Population in 1944; among the topics civil servants thought it should consider was that of the attraction of employment to women as an alternative to child-rearing.[92] And at least part of the support for the 1945 Family Allowances Act came from people who believed that reform might have a positive effect on the birth rate.[93]

But even more important, because of its influence on the social security system created by the post-war Labour government, was the Beveridge report. In it Beveridge stated explicitly that his proposals were intended to make the position of housewife and mother more attractive in order to ensure that married women would be content with their traditional role. He explained that 'the attitude of the housewife to gainful employment outside the home is not and should not be the same as the single woman . . . housewives and mothers have vital work to do in ensuring the adequate continuance of the British race . . .'.[94] His assumptions about the position of married women drew criticism from feminists: Mavis Tate, Conservative MP and chairwoman of the Equal Pay Campaign Committee, claimed that no more 'reactionary measure in regard to married women had ever been brought forward'.[95] But the position of women in the social security system established by the 1946 National Insurance Act reflected Beveridge's thinking. Wives were made economically dependent upon their husbands, in part by changes which made it more difficult for a working woman to regain her insurance rights if she interrupted her employment after marriage and then wished to return to paid work at a later date. Members of the TUC National Women's Advisory Committee objected that this left married women workers worse off than they had been before the war, but to no avail.[96]

The existence of a vigorous feminist movement would have increased the likelihood of wartime steps towards the emancipation of women becoming permanent. Early in the conflict the war seemed to be stimulating a feminist revival: new feminist organisations, such as the Woman Power Committee and the Women's Publicity Planning Association, were established, and feminists played an important part in the successful campaign to secure equal compensation for war injuries for women.[97] But wartime feminists experienced more defeats than successes. Their efforts to influence government policy on the mobilisation of womanpower were largely deflected by Bevin.[98] A campaign for equal pay was blocked by the War Cabinet and then shelved by the appointment of a Royal Commission. [99]

The difficulties that feminists faced are suggested by the outcome of the most radical wartime feminist reform movement: the Equal Citizenship (Blanket) Bill campaign. The idea of a comprehensive Bill that would end all forms of sex discrimination emerged within the Six Point Group during the debate over the government's plan to conscript women. Dorothy Evans, who chaired the Six Point Group executive committee, wrote to the Prime Minister suggesting that if the government were to eliminate sex differentiation in its 'manpower' policies by extending conscription to women, then it should also eliminate sex-based inequality in other areas, including pay scales and National Insurance benefit rates. [100] When the government did not respond, Evans was asked to prepare a report on the Acts of Parliament which provided the legal basis for existing forms of sex discrimination. In the course of her investigation she conceived the idea of a single Bill – a 'blanket' Bill – which would make all forms of sex discrimination illegal.

Although it endorsed the idea, the Six Point Group did not believe it had the resources to undertake a major campaign. But in March 1943, with the assistance of Emmeline Pethick-Lawrence, Evans persuaded the Women's Publicity Planning Association to sponsor a nation-wide campaign in support of the Bill. Since it was unlikely that it would become law if introduced as a private member's Bill, the specific purpose of the campaign was to arouse public support to such an extent that the government would sponsor it in Parliament. [101] The campaign was initiated in September 1943 with a mass meeting at the Central Hall, Westminster. Following addresses by Pethick-Lawrence, Edith Summerskill and Vera Brittain, those present contributed over £600 to the campaign. This was considered a great success, since the audience comprised mainly young working women of limited means. [102]

But almost immediately the campaign began to encounter difficulties. Several distinguished legal scholars warned Evans that the proposed Bill conflicted with current interpretations of common law rights. [103] Although she subsequently revised the Bill, legal authorities continued to express doubts about it. Rather more surprising was the refusal of many feminist organisations to lend their support. The London and National Society for Women's Service decided not to participate in rallies on the ground that the Bill was not a 'practical' means of achieving sex equality. [104] Trade union women members of the Woman Power Committee were decidedly hostile to it, perhaps in part because it would have eliminated existing protective legislation that applied solely to women. Other members of the Woman Power Committee objected to the methods by which the chairwoman of the Women's Publicity Planning Association, Rebecca Sieff, was conducting the campaign. They complained that she was constantly giving the wrong impression about relations between the Women's Publicity Planning Association and the Woman Power Committee, and concluded that it was a 'wholly impracticable matter'. [105] The Bill's prospects were further diminished in summer 1944 when Evans was unable to persuade any of the three largest political parties to endorse the measure. [106] Finally, her sudden and unexpected death in August 1944 eliminated the main driving force behind the campaign. Efforts to revive it continued until 1946 but were hampered by personality conflicts and uncertainty as to whether the campaign should continue to focus on the Bill or on specific issues of sex inequality. [107]

In her 1943 study of wartime women Margaret Goldsmith remarked:

Many women, possibly the majority of married women, have not enjoyed their new independence; they have been made miserable by the wartime interruptions of family life. As a result, many married women . . . fervently wish themselves back into their pre-war home routine. A number of wives to whom I have talked are so homesick for their pre-war way of life that they seem to have created in their imagination a glowing fantasy of what this life was like. [108]

Goldsmith's comment seems more consistent with the evidence than Marwick's claim that women were emancipated by the war. After 1945 there was a marked revival of domesticity. This renewed interest in marriage and family suggests that the war's most important legacy for women was a strengthening of traditional sex roles rather than the emergence of new roles.

Notes

1 Arthur Marwick, *War and Social Change in the Twentieth Century*, London, 1974, p. 16.

2 *Ibid.*

3 Arthur Marwick, 'People's war and top people's peace', in A. Sked and C. Cook (eds.), *Crisis and Controversy*, London, 1976, pp. 161–2.

4 Margaret Goldsmith, *Women and the Future*, London, 1946, p. 9, and Gertrude Williams, *Women and Work*, London, 1945, p. 1.

5 International Labour Organisation, *The War and Women's Employment: the Experience of the United Kingdom and the United States*, Montreal, 1946, p. 152.

6 Vera Brittain, *Lady into Woman*: a History of Women from Victoria to Elizabeth II, New York, 1953, pp. 195–6.

7   Alva Myrdall and Viola Klein, *Women's two Roles*, London, 1956, pp. 53–4.

8   Sheila Lewenhak, *Women and Trade Unions: an Outline History of Women in the British Trade Union Movement*, New York, 1977, Sarah Boston, *Women Workers and the Trade Union Movement*, London, 1980, Penny Summerfield, *Women Workers in the Second World War*, London, 1984, and Harold L. Smith, 'The womanpower problem in Britain during the Second World War', *Historical Journal*, XXVII, 1984, pp. 925–45.

9   Arthur Marwick, 'Problems and consequences of organizing society for total war', in N. F. Dreisziger (ed.), *Mobilization for Total War: the Canadian, American and British Experience, 1914–1918, 1939–1945*, Waterloo, Ont., 1981, pp. 3–21.

10   Marwick, 'People's war', p. 159.

11   Terence H. O'Brien, *Civil Defence*, London, 1955, p. 678.

12   Arthur Marwick, *Britain in our Century*, London, 1984, pp. 112–13.

13   Ministry of Labour and National Service, 'Report for the years 1939–1946', *Parliamentary Papers 1946–47*, Cmd 7225, p. 2.

14   Angus Calder, in the *London Review of Books*, VII, 21 March 1985, p. 9.

15   Margaret Allen, 'The domestic ideal and the mobilization of womanpower in World War II', *Women's Studies International Forum*, VI, 1983, pp. 441–5.

16   Richard Broad and Suzie Fleming (eds.), *Nella Last's War: a Mother's Diary, 1939–45*, Bristol, 1981, p. 255.

17   See, for example, Ann Oakley, *The Sociology of Housework*, New York, 1974, ch. 8, and Viola Klein, *Britain's Married Women Workers*, London, 1965, pp. 74–5. Even Marwick, when discussing the post-1945 period, appears to agree that the 'fundamental relationship of man and wife had not really changed since the beginning of the century . . .'. See Arthur Marwick, *British Society since 1945*, London, 1982, p. 71.

18   Paul Thompson, *The Edwardians*, London, 1977, pp. 293–4.

19   Ministry of Labour, 'Report', p. 2.

20   Marwick, 'Problems and consequences', p. 9.

21   H. M. D. Parker, *Manpower*, London, 1957, pp. 210–11.

22   Geoffrey Thomas, *Women at Work*, Wartime Social Survey, 1944, p. 9.

23   A. H. Halsey (ed.), *Trends in British Society since 1900*, London, 1972, p. 118.

24   Arthur Marwick, *Britain in the Century of Total War*, London, 1968, p. 292.

25   This view is repeated in many of Marwick's writings, and is also presented in Alan Bullock, *The Life and Times of Ernest Bevin*, II, *Minister of Labour, 1940–1945*, London, 1967, p. 255.

26   Memorandum by William Beveridge, 8 November 1940. PRO, Cab. 118/65.

27   Parker, *Manpower*, p. 137.

28   *Parliamentary Debates* (House of Commons), 392, 14 October 1943, col. 1064, and Neil Stammers, *Civil Liberties in Britain during the Second World War*, London, 1983, p. 185.

29   Parker, *Manpower*, p. 224.

30   *Ibid.*, p. 285, and Penny Summerfield, *Women Workers in the Second World War*, London, 1984, p. 35.

31   Wartime Social Survey, 'An Investigation of the Attitudes of Women, the General Public, and ATS Personnel to the Auxiliary Territorial Service', 21 October 1941, cited in Summerfield, *Women Workers*, p. 37.

32   Mass-Observation, File Report 615, 20 March 1941.

33   Mass-Observation, File Report 919, 'Female Attitude to Conscription', 16 October 1941.

34   Memorandum on 'Man-power' by Winston Churchill, 6 November 1941. W.P. (41) 258, File BBK D/77, Beaverbrook papers, House of Lords Record Office.

35   PRO, Cab. 66/20, W.P. (41) 285. Cited in Stammers, *Civil Liberties*, p. 181.

36   Ministry of Labour, 'Report', p. 31.

37   *Ibid.*

38   See the results of the Gallup poll in the *News Chronicle*, 27 November 1941, p. 2.

39   Mass-Observation, File Report 952, 'A.T.S. Campaign', 7 November 1941.

40   *International Women's News*, XXXV, March 1941, p. 81.

41   Minutes of the Ministry of Labour's Women's Consultative Committee, 5 and 26 November 1941, PRO, Lab. 8/380.

42   Minutes of the Womanpower Committee, 28 October 1941, British Library of Political and Economic Science.

43   Minutes of the Women's Consultative Committee, 26 November 1941, PRO, Lab. 8/380.

44   Edith Summerskill, 'Conscription and women', *Fortnightly*, CLI, March 1942, p. 209.

45   Mass-Observation, File Report 822, 'Tenth Weekly Report', 11 August 1941.

46   *Report of the 11th Annual Conference of Unions catering for Women Workers*, April 1941, p. 15.

47   London Women's Parliament, 'Calling all Women! Report of the Second Session of the London Women's Parliament', 26 October 1941, p. 23.

48   Parker, *Manpower*, p. 289.

49   Ministry of Labour, 'Report', p. 35.

50   *Ibid.*, 65.

51   Mary A. Hamilton, *Women at Work*, London, 1941, pp. 138–9.

52   Peggy Inman, *Labour in the Munition Industries*, London, 1957.

53   Inman, *Labour*, p. 80.

54   Summerfield, *Women Workers*, p. 167

55   Harold L. Smith, 'The problem of "equal pay for equal work" in Great Britain', *Journal of Modern History*, LIII, December 1984, p. 657.

56   Inman, *Labour*, p. 354.

57   For an example of the latter see Vera Douie, *Daughters of Britain*, Oxford, 1950.

58   Thomas, *Women at Work*, p. 14.

59   *Ibid.*, p. 28.

60   Mass-Observation, File Report 2059, 'Will the factory girls want to stay put or go home?' 8 March 1944.

61   Quoted in Angus Calder and Dorothy Sheridan (eds.), *Speak for Yourself: a Mass-Observation Anthology, 1937–49*, London, 1984, p. 181.

62   *News Chronicle*, 19 February 1945, p. 1.

63   Halsey, *Trends*, p. 118.

64   Hiliary Land, 'Women: supporters or supported?' in D. L. Barker and S. Allen (eds.), *Sexual Divisions and Society: Process and Change*, London, 1976, p. 117.

65   Louise Tilly and Joan Scott, *Women, Work and Family*, New York, 1978, p. 215.

66   PEP, 'Employment of women', *Planning*, XV, 23 July 1948, p. 39.

67   Smith, 'Womanpower', pp. 941–2.

68   Memorandum by James Chuter Ede, 6 March 1944, PRO, Ed. 136/480.

69   Cabinet minutes, 9 September 1946, Cabinet 80 (46) 6, PRO, Cab. 128/6.

70   Marwick, *Britain in our Century*, p. 122, 'People's War', p. 162, and *War and Social Change*, 160.

71   'Report of the civil service National Whitley Council committee on the marriage bar', *Parliamentary Papers 1945–46*, Cmd 6886, pp. 19–22.

72   Cited in Jane Lewis, *Women in England, 1870–1950*, London, 1984, p. 187.

73   Richard Titmuss, *Essays on the Welfare State*, Boston, Mass., 1969, p. 91.

74   Calder, *The People's War*, New York, 1969, p. 360.

75   It may be a coincidence that the birth rate soared in 1942, the year after the government announced that women with children under fourteen would be exempt from conscription.

76   Halsey, *Trends*, p. 31.

77   John Stevenson, *British Society, 1914–45*, London, 1984, p. 163.

78   Calder, *People's War*, p. 360.

79   Elizabeth Wilson, *Only Halfway to Paradise: Women in Postwar Britain, 1945–1968*, London, 1980.

80   Denise Riley, *War in the Nursery*, London, 1983, pp. 190–1.

81   Ruth Adam, *A Woman's Place, 1910–1975*, London, 1975, p. 146.

82   Norman Longmate, *The Home Front: an anthology of personal experience, 1938–1945*, London, 1981, p. 124.

83   Cited in Arthur Marwick, *Class*, New York, 1980, p. 228.

84   Richard Croucher, *Engineers at War, 1939–1945*, London, 1982, pp. 277, 299.

85   Tom Harrison, 'Appeals to women', *Political Quarterly*, July–August 1942, p. 275.

86   Croucher, *Engineers*, p. 267.

87   *Ibid.*, p. 263.

88   William Jowitt to Stafford Cripps, 9 October 1942, PRO, Cab. 117/151.

89   PRO, MH 55/695, cited in Riley, *War*, p. 119.

90   Calder, *People's War*, p. 449.

91   *Parliamentary Debates* (House of Commons), 3 August 1943, col. 2119.

92   Sir S. Vivian to Sir J. Maude, Permanent Secretary to the Ministry of Health, 26 October 1943, PRO, T 221/206.

93   John Macnicol, *The Movement for Family Allowances, 1918–45*, London, 1980, pp. 198–9.

94   Sir William Beveridge, 'Social insurance and allied services', *Parliamentary Papers 1942–43*, VI, Cmd 6404, p. 53.

95   *Women in Council*, IV, November 1943, p. 3.

96   *Report of the 16th Annual Conference of Unions catering for Women Workers*, London, 1946, p. 16.

97   Smith, 'The problem of equal pay', pp. 661–3.

98   Smith, 'The womanpower problem', pp. 928–31.

99   Smith, 'The problem of equal pay', pp. 667–70.

100   Dorothy Evans to Winston Churchill, 29 November 1941, Six Point Group Executive Papers, Fawcett Library.

101   Six Point Group, *Annual Report, 1943–44*, p. 1, Fawcett Library.

102   Women's Publicity Planning Association Executive Committee minutes, 29 September 1943, Fawcett Library.

103   *Ibid.*, 17 November 1943.

104   London and National Society for Women's Service Executive Committee minutes, 31 May 1944.

105   Woman Power Committee minutes, 28 September 1943.

106   Six Point Group, *Dorothy Evans and the Six Point Group*, London, 1945, p. 18.

107   WPPA Executive Committee minutes, 20 December 1945.

108   Margaret Goldsmith, *Women at War*, London, 1943, p. 181.

Acknowledgements

I would like to thank the following for reading and commenting on an earlier draft of this essay: Shirley Powell and Sandra Heinold of the University of Houston, Victoria and Judy McArthur, University of Texas.

III Political ideas and social change

Jose Harris

Political ideas and the debate on State welfare, 1940–45

I

For most of its history social policy-making in Britain has been closely linked to a wider context of political, social and economic ideas. Debates on social policy have often raised or revolved around some of the classic questions posed by political theorists about the nature of legitimate authority, the relation of individuals to the wider community and the 'ends' of common life. Theorists as diverse as Locke, Bentham, Green, Sidgwick and Bosanquet either wrote specific treatises on social policy questions or incorporated ideas about welfare and welfare institutions into their political philosophies. The unravelling of these ideas is a major theme of social welfare history. Historians have engaged in prolonged debate about how far political theories influenced the actual structure of social policies; and although such debate has been inconclusive, there can be little doubt that 'theory' played a significant part in policy legitimation and in imposing constraints upon what social policies could or could not do. A distinguished historiography has tracked the inter-relationship between Hanoverian, Victorian and Edwardian welfare institutions and utilitarian, natural-legal, conservative, Ruskinian, idealist, Darwinian and 'progressive' modes of thought. This vein of analysis largely peters out, however, in writing about the great national debate on the future of State, society and social welfare policies that took place during and immediately after the Second World War. Of the major social welfare initiatives of that period only full employment policies have been closely examined by historians in terms of their theoretical origins (and, even here, historians have concentrated almost exclusively on the purely economic content of the Keynesian revolution: the implications of Keynes's writings for political and constitutional thought have been curiously ignored). For the rest, the Welfare State policies of the 1940s – insurance, family allowances, National Health Service, universal secondary education, abolition of the Poor Law, fiscal redistribution – have mainly been portrayed as the fruits of compromise, pragmatism and technical adjustment. In so far as such policies had a 'philosophy' it has often been seen as a largely negative one of occupying the muddled middle ground between socialism, corporatism and free-market capitalism. Many grand generalisations have been advanced about the structural and functional implications of Welfare State policies: but few attempts have been made in a British context to view these policies as a significant episode in intellectual as well as social and administrative history.

This neglect seems strange for a number of reasons. Earlier phases of British social policy *have* been closely analysed in terms of contemporary political and social thought, as indicated above. Recent ahistorical writing by political theorists in Britain, America and elsewhere has been increasingly interested in 'welfare statism' as a philosophical problem. By any standards the Welfare State policies of the 1940s raised major issues of social, political, constitutional and ethical principle. Commentators at the time clearly expected the national and global dislocation of war to produce a major new paradigm in social and political theory.[1] And, perhaps most important from the historian's point of view, few of the advocates and framers of social policy in this period saw themselves as mere technicians engaged in compromise, horse-trading and bland incrementalism. On the contrary, many of them believed that they were building a new kind of social and political order, rooted in a wholly new relationship between the citizen and the State. Discussion of 'social welfare' and 'social policy' was seen by the writers of all complexions as inseparably bound up with 'reconstructing' a society whose traditional values and institutions had been transformed or shattered by the impact of world war. On the specific content and goals of reconstruction, however, there was profound and far-reaching diversity (a fact largely obscured by the genre of social policy studies that emphasises successful 'outcomes' in the form of legislation). Wartime thinking about social problems displayed widely varying assumptions not so much about concrete policies (though there was much disagreement there too) but about such issues as the metaphysical character of the State, individual versus 'holistic' conceptions of welfare, the 'totalitarian' implications of planning, the substantive meaning of 'freedom' and 'equality', and the logical relationship between social action and social-scientific knowledge. The following pages will attempt to map the contours of these debates, to look not merely at ideas which gained general acceptance but at those which did not, and to consider how far the crisis of war precipitated any fundamental change in perceptions of the relationship between State and society.

II

The world of social welfare in the early 1940s was of course in no sense a clean slate. It was filled with a wide variety of partly complementary and partly conflicting policies and institutions, some of great antiquity, some of recent growth. These included friendly societies and insurance companies; trade union and company welfare schemes; registered and unregistered private charities; Poor Law and Public Assistance systems; contributory national insurance and workmen's compensation; a vast range of public, quasi-public and private educational arrangements; maternity and child welfare clinics and public health. Deeply embedded in and reinforcing all these arrangements was the existence of the family, whose provision of a wide range of 'welfare' functions was tacitly assumed by social theorists and policy-makers of all political complexions.[2] The vast range of values embodied in these institutions cannot be considered in detail here; but in very broad terms all social welfare arrangements derived their basic rationale from one or both of two systems of political thought. One was the tradition of 'natural liberty' – the idea that values, rights and duties (including those relating to welfare) were private rather than public, and that the proper function of the State in the sphere of 'welfare' was merely to uphold private rights. The other was the tradition that society and/or the State was in some sense an 'organism', a body with an identity and interests larger than those of its parts, and membership of which entailed certain inherently 'public' duties and rights. The intermingling of these two traditions could be seen most clearly in the Poor Law, whose very existence conceded the organic idea, but whose practice and ideology constantly reaffirmed the model of natural liberty.

Of the two traditions, the natural liberty theme was much the more dominant in English welfare history (and in other spheres such as constitutional, legal and trade union history as well, though these cannot be discussed in detail here). At the end of the nineteenth century there had been a sustained attempt by certain reformers and social philosophers to advance the conception of the 'organic State',[3] but this was largely unsuccessful in gaining popular and public acceptance. Deeply embedded in nearly all aspects of early twentieth-century social policy was a merely instrumental view of State institutions, not as reified embodiments of shared values and identity but as useful (and sometimes dangerous) instruments for enforcing private rights. Such a view by no means precluded the growth of administrative 'collectivism' (as might be seen in Beveridge's claim that the introduction of national insurance in 1911 represented a triumph of 'contract' over 'status').[4] The First World War saw a vast extension of emergency State control but no corresponding change in ideas about State legitimacy[5] (if anything the reverse, if one may judge from the wartime and post-war vogue for syndicalism, guild socialism and various modes of 'pluralism'). Throughout the interwar years there was a continuous quantitative expansion of government social policies and a rising demand in all classes for public subsidies to the private sector: but there was an almost universal distaste for anything that might have involved a qualitative change in the identity of the State. Such a view was largely shared by theorists on the far left of British politics, who were inclined to view the State either as a conspiracy *against* the public interest or as a moral anachronism in an internationalist world order.

These attitudes form an essential backcloth to the movement for more extensive provision of public social welfare. Pressure for a comprehensive social welfare scheme – together with a full employment programme and corporatist planning – had begun in the early 1930s: but these demands had all foundered not merely on practical grounds but on the much more philosophical ground that they would require central government to play a new and constitutionally illegitimate role in the direction of national life.[6] Within all major political parties there was a sustained attempt in the mid-'30s to develop a coherent rationale for a State-managed economy; but these efforts were largely cancelled out by the residual power (among State-interventionists themselves as well as among their critics) of libertarian arguments. These arguments were eventually undermined, not by intellectual pressures, but by the growing threat and ultimate reality of war. Rearmament, bombing, evacuation, food rationing, military and industrial conscription – all gave an existential reality to the organic conception of society in a way that had never been achieved by abstract analysis.[7] This new mood was more than merely pragmatic, however, and from the start of the war it found expression in widespread intellectual and popular discussion of social and political reconstruction. It was these discussions which provided, or attempted to provide, a normative framework for what came to be known as the Welfare State. In the genesis of these new ideas academics and intellectual coteries played a perhaps excessively prominent role: yet it should not for that reason be seen as a primarily academic movement. Ideas about welfare were aired to a certain extent in economic, sociological and (very occasionally) philosophical journals: but the main forum of debate was the great cluster of 'reconstruction' committees, public and private, formal and informal, some of which dated from the start of the war but most of which stemmed from the setting up of the Churchill coalition government in May 1940.

The inner politics of these committees is a story in its own right which cannot be considered here; but to give a context to their ideas, a brief outline must be given of their institutional history. One of the first and most famous of these groups was the Keynes-Beveridge coterie of 'old dogs' and 'ancient warhorses' which met together in Bloomsbury in the winter of 1939–40 and drafted the proposals for family allowances, food subsidies, compulsory savings and post-war credits embodied in Keynes's influential little book on *How to Pay for the War*. [8] (It was the existence of this group which gave rise to the often cited but erroneous belief that there was a common Keynes–Beveridge 'philosophy of welfare' which dominated the whole reconstruction movement.) Other important private groups were G. D. H. Cole's 'reconstruction survey' at Nuffield College, Oxford; the 'Responsibility Group' of modernist churchmen convened by William Temple, shortly to become Archbishop of Canterbury; the all-party 'Ninety-Forty Council', later renamed the '1941 Committee'; and the series of social reform conferences summoned by W. G. S. Adams, the warden of All Souls. In the public sphere a Cabinet Committee on Reconstruction was appointed in 1941 and a departmental Ministry of Reconstruction in 1942. Meetings of the Cabinet committee were assiduously attended by all senior Ministers, with the conspicuous exception of Churchill, throughout the war. Central reconstruction committees were set up by Conservative, Labour and Liberal parties in the summer of 1941, and in 1942 a new party was formed, the Common Wealth Party, explicitly committed to rebuilding British society around the principle of 'organic solidarity'. A broader spectrum was covered by the Agenda group at the London School of Economics, which pursued the ambitious and not easily compatible goals of providing an open forum for the whole of the nation's intellectual life *and* of defining a coherent social policy. [9] Reconstruction proposals encompassed all areas of national life, from the established Church and the fine arts through to the turf and the breeding of bloodstock. [10] Throughout its history all branches of the reconstruction movement were explicitly concerned not merely with formulating programmes but with generating a new political philosophy. 'No thesis is too daring, no hypothesis too revolutionary, to receive some attention and credulence,' wrote a political theorist in Cambridge in 1943. 'It is a golden age of political speculation.'[11]

III

What were the ideas thrown up by the reconstruction movement and how far did they succeed in generating a coherent basis for the post-war Welfare State? One point that was often emphasised at the time is that new ideas about social policy were closely bound up with wartime propaganda and with strengthening popular motivation for the fight against fascism.[12] This was undoubtedly true up to a point, but in itself it tells us little about Welfare State theory, since politicians and intellectuals were profoundly divided about what fascism actually was – some believing that they were fighting against a perverted form of socialism, others against a deviant form of advanced monopoly capitalism. Moreover, the model of the Third Reich was not a wholly negative one: there were reformers in all parties who were prepared to adapt or borrow certain aspects of fascist social policies while rejecting others. (At the same time, theorists hostile to State welfare also drew legitimate inspiration from the fight against fascism, which could plausibly be portrayed as the logical outcome of a planned, centralised, coercive paternalism.)

An historian who surveys the wartime literature on reconstruction is soon struck by the fact that a common language of visionary patriotism and a common sense of national unity continued to mask an immense diversity of values and goals. Such diversity is not perhaps surprising in what continued, despite the pressures of war, to be a highly pluralistic and class-stratified society; but it contained some unexpected intellectual configurations that cannot easily be accommodated within such convenient categories as capitalism versus labour, individualism versus collectivism, right versus left. Protagonists of a new 'organic' social order included those who saw it as the outcome of progressive materialism, others who saw it as inseparable from the revival of a Christian polity.[13] It included those who believed that 'social justice' could be achieved only by 'just' individuals, others who believed that the virtue of a State and the virtue of its citizens were entirely separate and mutually irrelevant.[14] It included those who called for a social 'Bill of Rights', others who saw the whole idea of rights as inherently hostile to collective and communitarian interests.[15] It included those who saw the new order as predominantly working-class, others whose main concern was to rescue society from 'mass proletarianisation'.[16] It included those who saw 'compulsion' as a quintessential part of 'organicism', others who saw the two principles as deeply antithetical.[17] It included those who favoured social and industrial corporatism,[18] and those who believed that the new order could and should be contained within the vessel of parliamentary democracy. It included those who saw reform as essential for warding off (or channelling) popular post-war revolution, others who believed its main purpose was that of keeping dissident intellectuals happy.[19]

Such divergences were fully apparent to perceptive people at the time, and there were numerous regretful comments about the fact that, except for the purpose of actually fighting the war, the national consensus was an artificially manufactured myth.[20] At the level of general principle all that can definitely be said to have united the reconstruction movement was, first, a belief that social problems needed to be considered 'as a whole' instead of in piecemeal compartments; second, a belief that social reconstruction required a more extensive use of coercive governmental and legal powers than had traditionally been thought tolerable; and, thirdly, the belief that such coercion need not necessarily entail the abrogation of personal freedom – that, on the contrary the loss of 'lower' freedoms would be compensated for by 'higher' freedoms, leaving the people freer than ever before. The full range of those positions cannot be adequately treated in one short chapter, but to demonstrate them more fully I will comment on some of the ideas developed by three key groups within the reconstruction movement: the Butlerite Tories, the coterie of reformers surrounding Sir William Beveridge, and reformist intellectuals within the Labour Party. And, finally, I will look at the spasmodic critique of State welfare schemes developed during the course of the war by the 'common law' school of F. A. Hayek and Sir Ernest Benn.

IV

R. A. Butler, who became President of the Board of Education and chairman of the Conservative Reconstruction Committee in 1941, was unusual among Conservative politicians of this period in believing that ideas were important in politics, and that conservative philosophy was neither too mystical nor too banal to permit coherent formulation. In tactical terms he was a modern Peelite and supporter of empiricism and material progress; but privately he hankered after an older Tory vision, or myth, of an organic Christian hierarchy. This somewhat astigmatic outlook was reflected in his leadership of the Conservative reconstruction movement: party sub-committees were charged with the dual tasks of preparing the spadework for a possible election programme and with designing a national, supra-party social and political philosophy.[21] In the later years of the war the former goal took precedence, but from 1940 to 1942 the latter had priority. Party sub-committees drew upon the services of a large body of intellectuals many of whom were not actually members of the Conservative Party, among them Karl Mannheim, G. M. Young, Keith Feiling and T. S. Eliot. Among these non-party advisers the refugee German sociologist Karl Mannheim[22] was a key figure. Mannheim, an ex-professor of sociology at the University of Frankfurt and a disciple of Weber and Lukács seems an unlikely *éminence grise* for English Toryism; but his ideas enjoyed an unexpected vogue in the early 1940s among the kind of Conservatives who had no special attachment to free-market capitalism but who cherished the values of hierarchy and order. He had been expelled from Germany in 1933 and had fled to England, where Beveridge had found a post for him as a lecturer at the London School of Economics. As an academic theorist his most famous work was *Ideology and Utopia*, which tried to formulate a systematic 'sociology of knowledge'; but the works which appealed to English reformers were *Man and Society in an Age of Reconstruction* (1935, English translation 1940) and *Diagnosis of our Time* (1943). In these two latter works Mannheim set out a programme for using the social sciences in combination with the 'paradigmatic experiences'[23] of Christian theology to create a new rational, moral and harmonious world order. Sceptics have always been puzzled about the paradoxical certainty with which Mannheim proclaimed, on the one hand, that all ideas were socially 'predetermined' and, on the other, that society could be purposively reconstructed by the application of abstract ideas: but such problems were overlooked in the enthusiasm of the early 1940s, and the English translation of *Man and Society* was reprinted no fewer than six times within the first three years of publication.

Mannheim was introduced to Butler in the summer of 1940, and a series of conversations followed which 'cleared the ground for definite action in the field of planning'. They found that their views on reconstruction 'were in full accord'.[24] Some months later a paper by

Mannheim on 'Planning for Freedom' was circulated among Conservative intellectuals and their acolytes. This paper set out Mannheim's 'Summa' for the new moral world, in which it would be recognised that 'mass society cannot be governed by the techniques of the homespun order which were suitable for the age of craftsmanship'. Instead, values, beliefs, education, institutions, social structures and social policies would be regulated by a 'holistic' political system which would recognise and embody the ontological precedence of society over the individual ('today there are no nooks and corners which remain unaffected by the prevailing principles of social organization').[25] Such a system would, however, be crucially different from contemporary totalitarianism, in that it would draw a 'clear distinction between co-ordination in the spirit of monotony and co-ordination in the spirit of polyphony'. In other words, within the limits imposed by a 'minimum standard' of moral and behavioural consensus, the State itself would deliberately foster constructive pluralism ('gangs of youngsters', 'transient forms of group life', 'vanguard groups' and 'rolling stones'). Such a system would require a 'new form of government, which in spite of its increased power, will still be democratically controlled'. How would democracy be persuaded to accept such a system? Partly by the mediation of moral values through a new selfless, enlightened quasi-religious elite; and partly by the integrating influence of 'democratic' social policies. Such policies would include severe restriction of private property rights, economic equality combined with 'functional incentives', and the 'right to work, right to a living wage, right to a free medical service and economic security in old age . . . the principle of social justice is not only a question of morals but a precondition of the functioning of the democratic system itself'.[26]

Mannheim's ideas, or rather the language in which they were expressed, was so discordant with traditional patterns of English thought that the interest they aroused is somewhat surprising (and in itself a measure of the peculiar intellectual temper of the early 1940s). When his 'Summa' was eventually published there was some mockery in liberal organs of the press,[27] but various draft versions were widely circulated and discussed in reconstruction circles in 1940–41. Butler himself seems to have viewed Mannheim's programme as a logical development of Christian corporate conservatism, though Butler's own speeches and writings emphasised the role of the 'community' or of 'our island Volksgemeinschaft' rather than the 'aloof forbidding impersonal State'. ('Somehow that word smells wrong.') Among Conservative reconstructionists there was a varied reaction to the kind of policies that Mannheim was proposing. A sub-committee on the provision of comprehensive social services was so divided in its views that it was unable to produce even an interim report.[29] A more sympathetic response came from the sub-committees on housing and on town and country planning, both of which rejected any conception of absolute property rights and outlined proposals for communal ownership of development land in the hands of quasi-public corporations.[30] Draft outlines of a potential Conservative reconstruction programme in 1941 and 1942 all emphasised the synoptic character of social problems, the need for corporate institutions, the reciprocity of citizen rights and obligations, and the desirability of making comprehensive social welfare provision conditional upon a greatly increased degree of social discipline and social integration ('a guaranteed standard of living in return for the performance of work or certain duties').[31] It was in the sphere of education policy, however, that Mannheimian ideas were most clearly reflected. The Conservative sub-committee on educational reconstruction included an avowed disciple of Mannheim, Professor F. A. Clarke of London University;[32] but the correspondence of this committee makes it clear that in disseminating Mannheim's views Clarke was largely preaching to the converted. The Conservative intelligentsia in 1940–41 already included a large groundswell of opinion against traditional libertarian ideas and in favour of a consciously integrated organic State.

Butler's choice as chairman of his education sub-committee was Geoffrey Faber, a distinguished historian, publisher, bosom friend of T. S. Eliot and fellow of All Souls.[33] Though identifying himself as a 'conservative' in political thought, Faber had a marked distaste for the constraints of party politics; and the same was true of most of his committee, who were chosen for their intellectual combativeness or experience of education rather than for their faithfulness to the party (Butler expressed the hope that they would 'break lances with the leading knights of the Left', but in fact several members of the committee hoped for a post-war coalition with the 'Crippsite socialists' and other 'idealist' groups).[34] Apart from Faber and Clarke the most dynamic member of this group was Walter Oakeshott, High Master of St Paul's school, a man with considerable knowledge of and pronounced opinions upon many aspects of contemporary economic and social structure.[35] This trio rapidly extended the already broad terms of reference of their committee to include a far-reaching enquiry into the national 'crisis of culture'. 'What is the future of English society to be?' asked Professor

Clarke – a question which, Faber agreed, 'takes us right to the heart of everything'.[36] The answer that was given contained strong echoes of Mannheim's recipe for the blending of traditionalism and modernity, pluralism and State control – and of Mannheim's critique of orthodox libertarian perceptions of society as 'individual psychology multiplied by *n*'. The group showed little interest in the preservation of English capitalism, and clearly saw 'conservatism' as in no way inherently bound up with the defence of private enterprise and private property. (A powerful attack on plutocracy, as the vicious strain which had corrupted civic virtue and robbed public institutions of their popular legitimacy, was inserted into the committee's first interim report at the suggestion of T. S. Eliot.)[37] Nor, overtly at least, did they have an interest in retaining economically rooted class divisions.[38] On the other hand a central concern was to recover what they perceived as the lost conservative values of discipline, hierarchy, 'meaning' and common social roots. Faber explicitly rejected the doctrine (which he associated with Durkheim rather than Mannheim) that individuals were the product solely of social environment: on the contrary, there was an 'ultimate religious sphere' which escaped the meshes of any socio-political system ('individuals are citizens of more worlds than one'). Short of that ultimate sphere, however, man's 'true being' was overwhelmingly social, and the institutional embodiment of that true social existence was the State. The State had a duty to regulate and enhance collective social welfare: and the citizen in return had a range of social and political obligations extending far beyond mere contractual convenience. Moreover, although religion transcended politics, the two spheres were concentric because only religion could give social substance to moral values, altruism, group obligation: the State was therefore bound in its own interest to promote the teaching of religion. But religion could not be taught like chemistry or geography; it entailed doctrine, ritual, habit, corporate consciousness, as well as rational and factual analysis. Social solidarity and the organic nature of the State, Faber therefore concluded, imperatively required a sacramental dimension in social policy and, in particular, public support for doctrinal teaching in schools. This principle he envisaged as the mainspring of the reconstructed British State.[39]

These arguments, advanced at a time when much pressure was afoot to sever existing connections between the State and religious education, set fire to a trail of doctrinal controversy outside the scope of this chapter. What is of interest here, however, is the range of social policies that Faber and his committee saw as logically following from their political and religious ideas. These concerned particularly the future of secondary schools, technical education, philanthropic organisations, and the training of the nation's youth. Detailed proposals were framed on the assumption that educational reforms would take place within a wider context of health, social security and full-employment reforms the details of which were outside the remit of an enquiry into education. [40] Their most striking substantive proposal was that fees were to be abolished at public schools, and that places at public schools were to be opened up to able children from all social backgrounds. 'The educational race should start level and . . . no one shall beat the pistol.' [41] Public schools themselves would be taken over financially by the Board of Education, but all schools in the State sector would be given the same 'independence' in relation to curricula and staffing as was at present enjoyed by the public schools, so as to encourage experiment and diversity. [42] Such a policy, Faber claimed, would rejuvenate the nation's elite, and preserve 'all that is best in English culture' while subjecting it to 'resolute abandonment of class advantage'. [43] Secondly, in all secondary schools there should be a massive improvement in the scope, quality and status of technical education to prepare British society for its post-war economic predicament (a policy ingeniously defended as wholly consistent with the classical spirit, since the prevailing 'classical curriculum' was merely the 'technical education of fourth-century Athens'). [44] Thirdly, the existing wartime policy of compulsory 'registration' of fourteen-to-eighteen-year-olds was to be retained in peacetime, and made the basis of a new 'programme for youth'. All young people were to be required to engage in compulsory 'voluntary service', either on their own initiative or more probably through registered voluntary organisatons (which in future would be required to meet minimum standards of efficiency prescribed by the State in return for public funds). [45] Employers would be statutorily required to give time off for such service, which was to be seen as an aspect of education and citizen-building rather than leisure. The youth programme was to be an integral feature of national education policy: but, to avoid too pressing a sense of State interference, registration was to be carried out not by civil servants but by a committee of registered voluntary workers constituting a Federation for Youth. The scheme would encourage a combination of public spirit and private diversity, 'the object being to produce boys who shared the qualities of the poacher and the gangster . . . as well as having some of the more domestic virtues'. [46] The leitmotif of the committee's reports and internal correspondence was a sustained attack on the utilitarian, hedonistic and privatised goals which, it was claimed, had governed public educational policy over the previous half-century:

The nature of our national failure is indicated by the excessive emphasis placed . . . upon the ideal aim of individual happiness. To set up 'the healthy and happy life' of the 'whole man', body, mind and spirit, as the objective of education, is to presuppose a state of affairs which never has existed anywhere, does not exist now, and can scarcely take place at the end of an immensely destructive war. Disease, disablement, pain, death: inherited defects; limited capacities; misfortune, unhappiness, and the sense of guilt or sin – all these are a necessary part of any man's life . . . it must be a prime object of education to fit the child to face and overcome trial and hardship, as well as for his own sake as that of the whole community. [47]

The Faber committee's first and second interim reports – on overall educational aims and training for youth – were completed in September 1942. [48] The report on overall aims promised a subsequent more detailed report dealing with democratisation of the public schools and their absorption into the national education system. The two reports were launched by Butler in an eloquent speech to the Conservative Central Council early in October. The immediate response in both Conservative and wider circles, however, was almost uniformly unfavourable. At the Conservative Council meeting there was an outburst of indignation from all quarters of the party at the prospect of 'stark totalitarianism', 'Christian fascism' and 'the importation of the Hitler Youth'. 'The last thing we want,' declared a member of the Tory Social Reform Group, 'is to have a brass-bound sausage machine to turn out thousands upon thousands of loathsome young prigs all classed in the same category.' 'It might have been written by an earnest Young Liberal after a visit to Germany', was the verdict on Faber's *Plan for Youth*. Voluntary charities, many of whom saw their *raison d'être* as lying in resistance to the State's embrace, reacted coldly to their proposed role as agents of State incorporation. Similar comments appeared in many sections of the press, where the reports were widely interpreted as fascist in inspiration and as 'offering to Conservatism's enemies a gift almost as good as the Zinoviev letter'. The trade union movement interpreted 'registration' as a disguised form of peacetime industrial conscription, while progressive intellectuals denounced the philosophy of Christian pessimism as not merely defeatist but morally obnoxious. [49] In educational circles those commentators who favoured reform of the public schools were almost universally repelled by the youth registration proposals, while the few who favoured youth registration were generally unsympathetic to a State take-over of public schools. [50] There was widespread condemnation of the supposed threat to the Englishman's privacy and leisure (although the reports had specifically repudiated any attempt to encroach upon the citizen's leisure time). The result was that Butler, having assiduously promoted such schemes in private, now tacitly withdrew his support and transferred his confidence to the group of departmental civil servants who eventually drafted the Education Act of 1944 (an Act in which public schools, technical education and youth training programmes were largely ignored).[51] Subsequent reports of the Faber committee on public schools and on 'continuation' schooling remained unpublished and undiscussed. The initiative in framing Conservative social policy passed away from the reconstruction committees to the Tory Social Reform Group – a body of young MPs who studiously avoided the kind of 'crisis' analysis and enunciation of first principles attempted by the group of intellectuals surrounding Geoffrey Faber.[52]

V

The fate of the Faber reports presented a striking contrast to the fate of a report produced two months later by a rather similar body, the Committee on Social Insurance and Allied Services under Sir William Beveridge.[53] Like the Faber committee the Beveridge committee was an obscure sub-committee of a larger reconstruction committee (that appointed by the War Cabinet in 1941). Like Faber, Beveridge ranged widely outside his original terms of reference and was ambitious to produce, not merely technical proposals, but a blueprint for the future of national life. Like the Conservative reconstructionists Beveridge felt a close *rapport* with the ideas of Karl Mannheim, though he found Mannheim's style of expressing those ideas unnecessarily grandiose and sententious. Like Mannheim and Faber and many other wartime social reformers Beveridge saw 'social policy' not merely as an end in itself but as a means of giving moral and constitutional legitimacy to the modern interventionist State. Like the Faber committee the Beveridge report (and, even more, Beveridge's follow-up report on *Full Employment in a Free Society* of 1944) proposed a great increase in State regulation of what had previously been seen as the essentially private concerns of the individual citizen. His social security scheme encroached drastically upon the autonomy of voluntary and philanthropic organisations. Yet Beveridge's proposals were widely acclaimed as a great advance for both democracy and freedom. How did his ideas differ from those of other less successful reconstructionists, and how can the contrasting reception of the Faber and the Beveridge reports be explained?

A key to Beveridge's ideas about social welfare can be found in the fact that, throughout his long career as a social reformer, he had ridden in tandem (though never successfully reconciled) the two competing social philosophies described earlier in this chapter. There was a visionary and intuitive side to his thought which saw individual welfare, individual rights, individual efficiency as predicated upon the existence of the larger social whole. And on the other hand there was a side of him which saw such notions as pretentious and dangerous nonsense: welfare was simply a commodity which was traded between contracting parties (even when one of those parties – the State – was the body responsible for ensuring that contracts were enforced). [54] Throughout the 1930s Beveridge had been highly critical of the mounting tide of progressive thought in Britain that was trying to shift social policy in a more 'organic' direction – objecting that, without specific contractual obligations on the part of individuals, organicism inevitably degenerated into either tyranny or sentimental muddle. Unlike many collectivist liberals and democratic socialists – with whom he is often bracketed – Beveridge did not believe in the 1930s that rights to work, maintenance and a 'living wage' could be universally extended without eroding parliamentary democracy and personal liberty. On the contrary, his main contribution to social policy in the interwar years was to defend both intellectually and administratively the contractarian and essentially limited basis of the system of national insurance: [55] more extensive welfare rights, he argued, could be given only in exchange for industrial conscription and State direction of labour. He had himself no principled objection to such policies – in fact he saw them in many ways as highly desirable – but he believed that such policies had no possibility of acceptance within a non-totalitarian system. [56]

This line of argument was never entirely dispelled from Beveridge's thought; but – as was the case with many people in Britain between 1939 and 1942 – the pressures of war shifted the balance of his political ideas in favour of a more strongly étatist conception. The general, if somewhat grudging, popular acceptance of conscription seems to have dissolved Beveridge's scepticism about the willingness of citizens to accept unpalatable political obligations. And the fact that direction of civilian manpower, rationing of resources, high levels of taxation and expropriation of private property for wartime purposes all occurred with popular consent persuaded him that more collectivist social arrangements were feasible than had been the case in the 1930s. The full extent of the 'collectivism' envisaged in his two reports has often been overlooked. The corollaries of unlimited subsistence-level benefits were compulsory training schemes and severe constraints upon personal choice of employment; and Beveridge's conception of 'full employment' included a systematic policy of centralised direction of labour. [57] *Full Employment in a Free Society* clearly envisaged that economic security for all citizens might well entail the virtual abolition of private investment and public control of three-quarters of the nation's enterprise. [58] Moreover, as Beveridge's published writings and private correspondence make clear, he assumed that a State which controlled minimum standards in social welfare would also take powers to impose maximum standards on prices and incomes. [59] In other words, his vision of the Welfare State, which was derived from the attitudes and behaviour of wartime, included the perpetuation of an extensive range of wartime socio-economic controls.

Why were Beveridge's proposals, which included such strongly regulatory elements, widely proclaimed as a practical embodiment of freedom, while the much more limited Faber proposals were denounced as crypto-fascism? One obvious difference lay in their different subject matters and in the fact that a mass audience was inherently likely to be more interested in promises of cash in hand than in promises of access to elite education. But though this might explain the popularity of Beveridge's insurance scheme, it does not account for general lack of concern about his plans for directing labour. Another answer lies in style of political language: Beveridge's reports, apart from a few vague messianic passages, were couched in the language of middle-brow commonsense, while Faber's were literary and donnish. This again might explain Beveridge's popular appeal, but not his vogue among academics and intellectuals. An elusive but more fundamental factor may have been the different role of underlying principles. Faber's committee, as I have shown, sought uncompromisingly to change the social character of the British people and the metaphysical character of the British State. Beveridge's schemes, for all their far-reaching collectivism, could plausibly be interpreted as doing neither. What must be emphasised here, however, are Beveridge's eclecticism and ambiguity, and his habit of piling up arguments derived from different modes of political thought without pausing to consider whether they were mutually consistent. His stress on 'universality', on the public absorption of private agencies and on the prior existence of a communitarian framework without which social security could not be envisaged – all these factors led idealist commentators to imagine that the Beveridge plan was designed to precipitate the quantum jump into the Rousseauesque corporate polity which they themselves envisaged.[60] This view was not wholly unfounded, and certainly Beveridge himself frequently spoke and wrote as though this were his goal. But many of his proposals could also be interpreted as primarily utilitarian, or as a mere enlargement of the kind of private contractarianism hitherto so dominant in English social policy. This latter approach could be seen most clearly in Beveridge's social insurance scheme, where – for all his claim that he was making social security co-extensive with the nation – individuals continued to qualify for social welfare benefits *qua* contributors rather than *qua* citizens. (A Conservative committee which reviewed Beveridge's social insurance plan specifically welcomed its limited and contractarian basis, though fearing that it might turn out to be a 'contract of unlimited liability for the state'.)[61]

In fact nowhere in Beveridge's two reports did he put forward a reasoned defence of what many people subsequently imagined to be the central principle of the Welfare State: the principle that people were entitled to welfare because they were members of a community. Nor did he make a case for the view (which he undoubtedly shared with Geoffrey Faber and other reconstruction enthusiasts) that individual citizens had reciprocal social obligations to the State. There were similar uncertainties in Beveridge's ideas about planning. Comprehensive 'planning' was portrayed as an essential prerequisite of the war on poverty: yet he also claimed as a cardinal principle of social policy that it should reflect the existing contours of social and economic structure.[62] The result was that people could find in Beveridge whatever they chose. His 'universalist' language appealed to a mood of corporate social solidarity transiently induced by war: but his report ultimately reinforced a highly traditional role for the State as a merely instrumental protector of private satisfactions.[63] Indeed, when the dust had settled over the report, one of the most popular aspects of his social security scheme proved to be its emphasis on privacy and contractual entitlement. 'Getting what you had paid for' become a touchstone of virtue in popular post-war Welfare State ideology.

VI

Beveridge's role as the purveyor of a portmanteau set of ideas offering all things to all men could be seen most clearly in the expectations and visions of his disciples. The Social Security League which was set up in 1943 to act as a pressure group for Beveridgean ideas attracted support from Tory pragmatists like Hugh Molson, 'organicist' liberals like Seebohm Rowntree, collectivist utilitarians like Barbara Wootton, and marxisant intellectuals like Harold Laski and Joan Robinson. Public debate on Beveridge tended to focus on concrete and limited issues rather than on general principles of policy: not because there was a national consensus about principles but because different individuals and interest groups read their own idiosyncratic interpretations into the Beveridge plan. Much of the criticism of Beveridge was couched in terms of simply trying to get more for (or resisting possible demands upon) one's own particular interest group – as could be seen in the responses of the trade union movement, the Federation of British Industries, City banks and finance houses, and various women's organisations.[64] The mid-war period saw the publication of a number of rival social security schemes which tried to reconcile the conflict between libertarian and organic principles latent in Beveridge; but these made little impact in the press and the intellectual community.[65] There was a sense in which public euphoria for Beveridge tended to stifle rather than stimulate serious debate; virtue was arbitrarily defined by popular *fiat*, thus foreclosing rational discussion of alternatives. This occurred in both the major political parties. In the Conservative Party failure to agree upon principles of reconstruction in 1942 meant that the search for an organic philosophy receded into the background: Tory reconstructionists continued to use self-consciously 'organic' language, but in substance they were increasingly concerned with piecemeal adaptation of Beveridge and Keynes.[66] A similar process occurred within the Labour Party, where thinking about social policy was largely swallowed up by Beveridgean ideas. More must be said at this point, however, about Labour theories of welfare, since the Labour Party was to become so closely identified with the historical implementation of the Welfare State.

The Labour Party and its antecedents had had a social welfare theory since 1897, when the Webbs formulated their principle of the 'national minimum'.[67] The essence of this idea was that the State should enforce for all its citizens the minimum standards of wages, welfare and working conditions that skilled trade unionists had achieved for themselves by collective bargaining. Superficially a coherent and simple idea, it in fact bristled with difficulties. It presented an implicit challenge to the lateral and sectoral differentials deeply embedded in the trade union movement; but at the same time it was rooted in the 'labour' rather than 'socialist' identity of the Labour Party, and therefore of limited appeal to the party's socialist intellectuals. And, taken to its logical conclusion, it necessarily entailed a degree of centralised and coercive State power that nearly all branches of the Labour Party viewed with suspicion. Throughout the interwar years Labour's desire for redistribution of resources and for greater public control of the economy had vied with a largely hostile or negative view of the powers of the State. In many quarters there was a lurking fear that the growth of the 'social service state' was merely an outwork of advanced capitalism ('pluto-democracy' in Harold Laski's phrase). [68] All these factors had long inhibited the growth of a Labour philosophy of welfare: the 'national minimum' was retained as a vague statement of moral purpose rather than a guide to political reform.

This approach had begun to change slightly in the mid-1930s. The period of retreat into utopia which had followed the Labour collapse of 1931 was succeeded on both right and left by attempts to define an attainable economic and social policy. On the left suspicion of the State persisted, but was increasingly rivalled by a new and highly ambitious vision of parliamentary democracy as a potential powerhouse of purposive social change. [69] At the right and centre of the party, economists in the New Fabian Research Bureau set out new models for constructing a planned economy, which would pursue overall socialist goals while borrowing techniques such as price theory from neo-classical economics. [70] It was found with some surprise that there was increasing working-class enthusiasm for social insurance (a system which a few years earlier both trade unionists and party theorists had denounced as a regressive capitalist placebo). [71] A new interest in social policy was shown by a commitment to the principle of a State health service in 1934, and to a programme of pension and social security reform in 1937. This growing priority given to social welfare schemes received a great reinforcement from the outbreak of war and particularly from Labour's entry into the Churchill coalition. Labour's anti-reformist far left were temporarily silenced by the fact that their favourite foreign friend was in league with the enemy: but at the same time Labour, with its strongly internationalist and quasi-pacifist tradition, needed far more than other parties to find a rationale for fighting the war other than mere national defence. The 'price' of Labour's support for the war was to be the implementation of social justice and the 'making of a more equal society', wrote Harold Laski [72] – a goal which expressed itself throughout the party in passionate discussion of post-war social reform. As in other parties a Central Reconstruction Committee was set up in 1940, study groups were appointed in many branch and district parties, and surveys were conducted into consumer opinion among social welfare beneficiaries. Among the various Labour policy-making organisations, social welfare played a very prominent role (second only to discussions on the future of the Empire) throughout 1941 and 1942. By 1943 Labour Party activists scented future election victory in the air: a victory which they increasingly equated with Labour's ability to deliver a 'national minimum standard of living' through the redistributive medium of a centralised State. [73]

Labour's ultimate success in attracting the social reform vote in 1945 has been much discussed by historians, and need not be considered here. As was noted early in the war, however, Labour's new priorities, and particularly the emphasis on a powerful and dynamic State, involved a major *bouleversement* of earlier Labour values. How far was this change thought out, and how far did Labour theorists provide a rationale for this new approach to welfare? The answer is, scarcely at all. This is not to say that there was no shift in Labour political thought in the early 1940s; but the change took the form of an increasingly accentuated emphasis on popular democracy as not merely compatible but virtually coterminous with the achievement of a socialist society. 'We take our standard upon that faith in reason which looks to the declared will of the people as the only valid source of power,' declared Labour's home policy committee: the rational will of the people was all that was required to 'provide a highroad along which the nation can pass peacefully from an acquisitive to a socialist society'. [74] More systematic and detailed analysis of the implications of this view was conspicuous by its absence. The possibility that the popular will might opt for non-socialist perceptions of its own welfare (embarrassingly revealed by some Labour Party surveys of popular opinion) was hurriedly glossed over. [75] The likelihood that some sectors of society might resist redistribution was hastily dismissed (the war had shown that the privileged classes enjoyed the sensation of sharing). [76] Redistribution itself was justified by a rather crude critique of *rentiers* and unearned income: little use was made of the ideas about 'public property rights' and the 'social' basis of wealth creation outlined by theorists such as J. A. Hobson. [77] Delegates at the Labour Party Conference of 1942 revived the long-standing issues of how far State welfare was compatible both with trade union independence and with the long-term attainment of 'socialism'; but it was argued that the public discussion of such issues might erode confidence in Labour among an increasingly friendly electorate. [78] Private discussions on reconstruction revealed wide variations among party members on such central issues as the scope of private freedom, the status of private property rights, the balance of power between central and local government, the utility of means tests, and the degree to which welfare benefits should reinforce or ignore economic incentives.[79] But, even more than such bodies in the Conservative Party, Labour reconstruction committees singularly failed to provide a forum for resolving these issues. Reconstruction provided a superficial focus of unity, but Labour values and philosophies remained as diverse and uncoordinated as in the pre-war period.

Beyond a general assertion of altruistic values Labour intellectuals therefore provided little in the way of a coherent rationale for the reconstruction of a Welfare State. This helps to explain the party's largely uncritical absorption of Beveridge's ideas – even though these included a number of principles that might have been viewed as traditionally unacceptable. Moreover the Beveridge plan provided an external rallying point for all different veins of Labour thought of a kind that had never been found within the party among Labour's own intellectuals. The plan was enthusiastically welcomed by the National Council of Labour as a 'Charter of Security' offering a 'minimum standard' to all people by virtue of their being 'citizens of the country'[80] (even though, as I have shown, it is arguable that it did nothing of the sort). Far from criticising Beveridge's scheme for falling short of socialism or for consolidating State power, the Labour left took up Beveridge as their own special cause and berated Labour moderates for being so slow to demand immediate implementation. ('The class struggle shows itself in sharp relief . . . it is Social or State Insurance versus Private Enterprise.')[81] When voices were raised at the party conference in 1943 against Beveridge's advocacy of direction of manpower they were drowned by an extraordinary outburst of enthusiasm for what had always in the past been one of Labour's sacred nightmares. 'So far from protesting, I, who have just received a direction, rejoice in it,' declared a delegate from England's largest coalface. 'I am glad that the government has got both the guts and the intelligence to tell me what I have got to do.'[82] Among Labour's leaders there was caution about the speed with which Beveridge's proposals could be implemented, but no doubts about their underlying philosophy. The Beveridge plan marked the transition from 'conception of the police state' to the 'conception of the social service state', declared Clement Attlee.[83] And a report by Harold Laski for the party's National Executive portrayed the plan as inaugurating a new epoch in national morality and psychology:

inspired by a sense of service, of the joy and value of life, and by a living faith in man's destiny . . . if a community wants to inspire its people with ideas larger than their own selfish and personal purposes, it must itself set them a living example. . . . How can such ideas spread and take root except in a form of society which is itself based upon them?[84]

VII

It was easy to frame such rhetorical questions. Less easy to answer them, except in terms of wishful thinking, or of the kind of coercion which most Englishmen in normal circumstances claimed to find abhorrent. From the start of the war there was always an underground murmur of dissent against wartime regulation – and a much more voluble protest against the suggestion that such regulation should form a permanent model for the future of society. 'People . . . can be divided in their attitudes to Planning [into] the Busy, the Indifferent, the Bored and the Distasteful,' observed a distinguished Tory historian (not himself an enemy of extensive State regulation).[85] State power that failed to be menacing was easily portrayed as ludicruous, and the pretensions of social reformers were a sitting target for both arcane and popular wit.[86] Much of the protest was merely picaresque, such as the revolt of the Women's Institutes against public inspection of home-made jam. ('No more home-made cakes, no more of Mother's cooking as Father likes it, communal kitchens on Russian lines. . . .') Part of the reaction was resolutely philistine ('few, if any, of these reformers are able to rise above the materialism of Marx to those higher social conceptions learnt on the cricket field').[87] But at least part of the anti-State-welfare school advanced a serious critique of the underlying assumptions of the reformist movement which few reconstruction enthusiasts were able to answer. These criticisms were cultural and cognitive as well as political, legal and economic. The central objection of the anti-reformers was not to social reform *per se* (many of them supported individual reforms such as national insurance, family allowances and factory legislation)[88] but to the attempt to view social policy 'as a whole' that was common to reconstruction enthusiasts of all political ideologies and parties. Nor were they all adherents of old-fashioned *laissez faire* – indeed, a recurrent theme was that social injustice stemmed not from capitalism but from the failure to control capitalism by a powerful framework of law.[89] Their leading public spokesman was the publisher Sir Ernest Benn, who in August

1942 organised a Manifesto on British Liberties and a few months later founded the Society of Individualists specifically to resist the programmatic approach to post-war problems being advanced by Mannheim, Beveridge, Faber and others. [90] The Liberty Manifesto explicitly rejected organic political thought: 'the unit of existence is the natural human being and his or her natural extension the family, not the artificial personality of the State'. [90] Their major theorist was the Austrian economist Professor F. A. Hayek, who played a role rather similar in libertarian circles to that played among reconstructionists by Karl Mannheim. (The striking similarity in their backgrounds and careers lent some support to Hayek's claim that he was an embodied refutation of the sociology of knowledge.) [91]

Hayek's most famous work on reconstruction questions was the polemical *The Road to Serfdom*, published in 1944: but throughout the war years and earlier he had published a series of less emotive and more systematic critiques of the underlying premises of State intervention. [92] Hayek's work in this period has been widely misunderstood (and he himself subsequently made claims about its application to policy that he would not have made in the early 1940s). His central thesis in the 1940s was not a defence of the 'free market' but scepticism about the prescriptive relationship between economic theory and economic action. Thus there not merely was not, but could not be, an economic theory which told public policy-makers what to do. On more specific issues, he questioned the claim of planners to have found surrogates for the price mechanism: prices determined not by supply and demand but by administratively determined price schedules were a contradiction in terms. [93] Public expenditure, except in those few areas of social life which were by definition public, was wholly incapable of satisfying consumer choice, since the sum of consumers had no corporate existence. The 'social rationality' invoked by theorists like Mannheim was purely imaginary. Planning generally was based on false premises: to be other than arbitrary it had to be based on an infinity of variables that was both practically and logically impossible. Its arbitrariness inevitably led, even in the hands of the most well meaning administrators, to tyranny and corruption. This did not mean that social administrators and reformers could do nothing: but in Hayek's view they should proceed historically and incrementally rather than 'rationally' by the gradual extension of individual claims to welfare through the common law. [94]

Hayek's criticisms had almost no positive impact upon the Welfare State debate but his negative impact appears to have been considerable.

Few people took very seriously his suggestion that social welfare policies in a mass society could be effectively implemented solely through the common law. But many who opposed Hayek's views on specific items of policy found that they agreed with his underlying values and his cognitive agnosticism: J. M. Keynes (often portrayed as Hayek's antipodes) was a case in point.[95] Similar views were expressed in the steering committee which prepared the government's 1944 White Paper on full employment. Unemployment was seen as in the last resort an attribute of 'individual liberty' and a 'free society'; there was a 'definite limit to what the State can do'; and 'governmental machinery could be hopelessly swamped if the State came to be looked upon as an omniscient, all-provident and universal wet-nurse'.[96] *The Road to Serfdom* did not cause but it coincided with a general disenchantment with organic thought that was already setting in by the end of the war. Serious Welfare State theorists like Barbara Wootton who tried to meet Hayek's arguments were unable to do so: she found herself reluctantly forced back upon mere pragmatic assertions, e.g. that all freedom was 'relative'; that all action was based on inadequate knowledge, therefore planning and public provision were no more inherently irrational than private choice; that sensitive, popular, egalitarian planners *were* inherently different from brutish authoritarian elites.[97]

VIII

The hope of reformist intellectuals that the war would generate a new and lasting paradigm in political thought therefore proved largely unfounded. In terms of ideas and values the context of war was an inadequate launching pad for permanent social 'reconstruction'. It created an artificial sense of social solidarity and at the same time encouraged the largely false expectation that much of the emergency apparatus of control, direction and demotion of private goals would be permanently acceptable.[98] Scepticism of this latter view was frequently expressed among civil servants charged with implementing reconstruction proposals; but even in Whitehall it was widely expected that interest groups in the post-war period would continue to observe wartime standards of public spirit and voluntary restraint.[99] The atmosphere of the early war years gave great encouragement to those sectors of the intellectual community which had long been straining for a more 'organic' conception of society and politics: but loyalty to the contractarian and natural-libertarian tradition proved unexpectedly tenacious. The possibilities of developing a rigorous contractarianism as a basis for Welfare State policies (to be revived later in the twentieth century) remained largely unexplored. Progressive thought continued to wobble uneasily, as it had done for half a century, between embracing the State as the highest expression of communal life and rejecting it as morally and politically outdated. In the Labour Party particularly there was little effective attempt to justify the State's transformation from *magnum latrocinium*[100] into universal provider. However, serious debate on political thought was poorly accommodated by all the political parties. Policies, ideas and values cut across party barriers, yet (even in a period of coalition government) the existence of those barriers artificially segregated like-minded coteries. A final point that may or may not be significant is that (in marked contrast to the Edwardian and Victorian social policy debates) discussion of the Welfare State attracted remarkably little attention from professional moral and political philosophers: attempts to redefine community, welfare and social obligation occurred at a time when in philosophic circles all such debate was in fashionable eclipse.[101] The consequence was that, in spite of the profusion of ideas that surrounded its conception, the Welfare State came into being with no clearly defined perception of welfare and no coherent theory of the State. This did not affect its short-term implementation, since democratic pressures in the 1940s and '50s overwhelmingly supported extension of State welfare; but in the long term it left the Welfare State peculiarly vulnerable to changes in political and economic climate, and to attacks from more rigorous and dogmatic intellectual rivals.

Notes

1 David Thomson, 'New currents in political thought', *Hibbert Journal*, vol. 37, July 1939, pp. 626–33, and 'Political thought in time of war', *Hibbert Journal*, 41, July 1943, pp. 365–9.

2 May Ravden, 'The importance of the family', *Sociological Review*, XXXIV, July–October 1942, pp. 198–208; Barbara Wootton, 'Am I my brother's keeper', *Agenda*, III, May 1944, pp. 114–25; Lord Horder *et al.*, *Rebuilding Family Life in the Post-war World. An Inquiry with Recommendations*, 1945.

3 Melvin Richter, *The Politics of Conscience: T. H. Green and his Age*, 1964; Michael Freeden, *The New Liberalism: an Ideology of Social Reform*, 1978.

4 W. H. Beveridge, *Unemployment: a Study of Industry*, 1930 edn, pp. 288–9.

5 R. H. Tawney, 'The abolition of economic controls', *Econ. Hist. Rev.*, XIII, 1, p. 7.

6 R. Middleton, 'The Treasury in the 1930s: political and administrative constraints to acceptance of the 'new' economics', *Oxford Economic Papers*, 34, 1982, pp. 48–77.

7 Julian S. Huxley, 'The growth of a group-mind in Britain under the influence of war', *Hibbert Journal*, 39, July 1941, pp. 337–50.

8 José Harris, *William Beveridge: a Biography*, 1977, p. 367.

9 On the membership of these various groups see Bodleian Library, Conservative Party Archives (CPA) CRD 058 *passim*; and *Agenda: a Quarterly Journal of Reconstruction*, 3 vols, 1942–44.

10 E. Kemp, 'Reconstruction in the Church of England', *Agenda*, II, November 1943, pp. 358–69; Storm Jameson, 'Why not a Ministry of the Fine Arts?' *Fortnightly*, 154, November 1940, pp. 449–57; Newmarket Heath, 'The turf today and tomorrow', *National Review*, January 1945, pp. 60–8.

11 David Thomson, 'Political thought in time of war', *loc. cit.*, p. 365.

12 Victor Gollancz, Harold Laski and John Strachey, 'The L.B.C. in wartime', *Left News*, 41, September 1939, pp. 1381–4.

13 'Julian Huxley and the "religion of progress" ', *Nineteenth Century*, CXXXIII, March 1943, pp. 97–108. Archbishop of York, 'Principles of reconstruction', *Fortnightly*, 153, May 1940, pp. 453–61. F. A. Cockin, 'Christianity and reconstruction', *Fortnightly*, 157, March 1942, pp. 215–21.

14 E. L. Allen, 'Christianity, property and social insurance', *Hibbert Journal*, XLIII, January 1945, pp. 171–5.

15 H. G. Wells, 'The new world order', *Fortnightly*, January 1940, pp. 49–54; F. A. Hayek, *The Road to Serfdom*, 1944, pp. 84–6.

16 Labour Party Conference Report, 1943, pp. 137–8; CPA, CRD 600/02, Charles Grant Robertson to Geoffrey Faber, 18 November 1941.

17 CPA, CRD 600/02, W. B. Kenryck to Geoffrey Faber, 23 March and 7 April 1942.

18 Federation of British Industries, *A National Policy for Industry*, 1942; CPA, CRD 058, 'A future to work for', April 1941, pp. 10–12.

19 H. G. Wells, 'The new world order', *Fortnightly*, 152, pp. 594–604; Charles Madge, 'Public opinion and paying for the war', *Econ. J.*, LI, 201, April 1941, p. 37. CPA, CRD 058, 'Notes of a discussion held on 19 July 1940'.

20 John Armitage, 'Morale and the war worker', *Fortnightly*, December 1942, p. 394; CPA, CRD 600/02, Sir Harold Webbe to Geoffrey Faber (n.d., ?April 1942).

21 On Butler's political philosophy see Lord Butler, *The Art of the Possible*, 1971. On the background to Conservative reconstruction thinking see John Ramsden, *The Making of Conservative Party Policy*, 1980, pp. 95–116.

22 Karl Mannheim (1893–1947) born in Budapest, studied philosophy at Freiburg and Heidelberg; professor of sociology at Frankfurt 1929–33; lecturer at LSE 1933–45; Professor of Education, London University, 1945–47.

23 Karl Mannheim, *Diagnosis of our Time*, 1943, p. 134.

24 CPA, CRD 058, Margaret Godley to R. A. Butler, 29 May 1940; 'Points arising from an interview', 28 May 1940.

25 *Diagnosis of our Time*, p. 114.

26 CPA, CRD 058, 'Planning for Freedom: some Remarks on the Necessity for Creating a Body which could Co-ordinate Theory and Practice in our Future Policy', by Karl Mannheim. Parts of this paper were later incorporated into the essay on 'Towards a New Social Philosophy', in Mannheim's *Diagnosis of our Time*. On the intellectual and social provenance of the paper see *Diagnosis*,

n. on p. 100.

27 E.g. George Schwartz, 'Laissez-faire', *Nineteenth Century*, CXXXIV, November 1943, p. 216.

28 CPA, CRD 600/02, typescript draft of speech by Butler for Central Council meeting, 1 October 1942.

29 CPA, CRD 600/01, Post-war Problems Central Committee minutes, 14 April 1942.

30 CPA, CRD 600/04, 'Looking ahead. The aims and methods of a national planning policy', February 1943; CRD 600/03, 'Looking ahead. Foundation for housing', March 1944.

31 CPA, CRD 058, 'Notes for R.A.B.' and 'Further Notes for R.A.B.' by F. Gwatkin, typescripts on 'Outline of Possible Future Developments', and 'A Programme for the Future', all undated (?1941–42).

32 See Clarke's review of Mannheim's *Man and Society in an Age of Reconstruction* (*Economica*, August 1940, pp. 329–32) and F. A. Clarke, 'The social function of secondary education', *Sociological Review*, XXXIII, July–October 1941, pp. 105–25.

33 Geoffrey Faber (1889–1961), chairman of Faber & Faber, President of the Publishers' Association, estates bursar of All Souls, author of *The Oxford Apostles* and *Jowett*.

34 CPA, CRD 600/02, R. A. Butler to G. Faber, July 1941; W. Oakeshott to G. Faber, n.d. (March 1942) and 2 November 1942.

35 Walter Oakeshott (1903–   ), schoolmaster and medieval scholar, subsequently headmaster of Winchester and Rector of Lincoln College Oxford. During the late 1930s Oakeshott had acted as chief investigator of the Pilgrim Trust enquiry into *Men without Work*. Other members of the committee included three Conservative MPs, two businessmen, an ex-HMI, a classics tutor from Christ Church, a public school headmaster and two members of the National Union of Teachers. A recurrent note of dissent from the views of the rest of the committee was struck by Alderman W. B. Kenryck, leader of Birmingham unitarianism, who defended a libertarianian and pluralistic conception of society against the strong étatism of Faber and Oakeshott.

36 CPA, CRD 600/02, Geoffrey Faber to Walter Oakeshott, 27 August 1942.

37 CPA, CRD 600/05, draft report on 'Aims of a System of National Education', p. 5, ms. note by T. S. Eliot and revised draft, p. 22.

38 The maintenance of such divisions was denounced as 'treasonable error' (see CPA, CRD 600/02, typescript on 'Education', n.d., *c.* September 1942).

39 CPA, CRD 600/05, 'The Ultimate Religious Field and the State', n.d. (June–July 1942).

There was much argument, and some confusion, among Faber and his colleagues about what the doctrinal teaching was to consist of in practice. The committee included Anglicans, Nonconformists, a Roman Catholic, a Unitarian and several agnostics, so there was little enthusiasm for and no agreement among them about the traditional Conservative principle of support for the established Church. Their only common ground was that religion should foster service to the community and public spirit. (Several of them expressed admiration for the effectiveness of 'doctrinal' teaching in the Soviet Union, as compared with the effete secularism of the Third Republic in France.) But failure to agree on the substance of doctrinal teaching eventually led Faber to retreat somewhat from his original position and to support the non-doctrinal 'agreed syllabus' currently being canvassed by religious progressives.

40 CPA, CRD 058, 'Reconstruction', n.d.

41 CPA, CRD 600/02, 'A Plan for Youth' by I. J. Pitman, 8 October 1942.

42 CPA, CRD 600/02, Walter Oakeshott to Geoffrey Faber, 17 October 1942.

43 CAP, CRD 600/05, Educational Sub-committee, draft of first interim report, section on 'Privileged Children, Exceptional Children, Specialisation'.

44 CPA, CRD 600/03, paper on 'Technical Education', n.d.

45 CPA, CRD 600/05, 'Report on the 14 to 18 Age Group', n.d.; CRD 600/02, 'A Plan for Youth', by I. J. Pitman, 6 October 1942. On the wartime youth registration scheme see Kenneth Lindsay, 'The registration of youth', *Fortnightly*, 159, 1943, pp. 151–7.

46 CPA, CRD 600/02, Walter Oakeshott to Geoffrey Faber, 18 February 1942. Both Oakeshott and Faber emphatically denied that their aim was to produce a nation of patriotic conformists; Faber often cited A. N. Whitehead's view that all forms of human diversity were 'godsends' (CRD, 600/02, G. Faber to W. B. Kenryck, 13 April 1942).

47 CPA, CRD 600/05, Educational subcommittee, first interim report, revised draft, p. 23.

48 The reports were entitled *Aims of a System of National Education* and *A Plan for Youth*.

49 CPA, CRD 600/05, file of press cuttings, 1942; C. E. M. Joad, 'Tory education', *New Statesman*, 3 October 1942, pp. 215–16.

50 L. P. Jacks, S. Maxwell and J. Murray, *The New Authoritarianism in Education*, 1943.

51 P. H. J. H. Gosden, *Education in the Second World War: a Study in Policy and Administration*, 1976, especially ch. 14.

52 Hugh Molson, 'The Beveridge Plan', *Nineteenth Century* (January 1943), pp. 22–30; Ramsden, *op. cit.*, pp. 99–100.

53 William Henry Beveridge (1879–1963), social reformer, journalist, civil servant, director of LSE (1919–37) and Master of University College, Oxford (1937–44). Liberal MP 1944–45, author of numerous works on unemployment and social insurance.

54 Harris, *William Beveridge*, especially chs. 5 and 13.

55 *Ibid.*, pp. 352–7. W. H. Beveridge, *Unemployment: a Problem of Industry*, 1930 edn, ch. XIII.

56 Harris, *op. cit.*, pp. 324–33.

57 *Ibid.*, pp. 430–3; *Full Employment in a Free Society: a Report by William H. Beveridge*, 1944, pp. 170–5.

58 *Ibid.*, p. 177.

59 Harris, *op. cit.*, p. 437. See also *Full Employment in a Free Society*, Part V.

60 Olwen W. Campbell, 'Political remedy for a motiveless world', *Hibbert Journal*, XLII, January 1944, pp. 131–8.

61 CPA, CRD 600/01, 'Report on the Beveridge Proposals', 1943.

62 *Social Insurance and Allied Services*, p. 49.

63 For evidence of this interpretation of Beveridge, see PRO, Cab. 87/11, War Cabinet Reconstruction Committee, Sub-committee on Social Insurance,

meetings of 27 January and 9 February 1944.

64 Harris, *op. cit.*, pp. 400–7; *Social Insurance and Allied Services, Memoranda from Organisations* (Cmnd 6405/1942); A. H. Gibson, 'The Beveridge scheme for social security', *Bankers Magazine*, 1943, pp. 204–9.

65 Most notable of these were Lady Juliet Rhys Williams's proposal for a combination of national insurance and social credit schemes (*Something to Look forward to*, 1942); and R. F. Harrod, 'Full employment and security of livelihood', *Econ. J.*, LIII, 212, December 1943, pp. 321–42. Harrod's scheme included the proposal, extremely challenging to orthodox economic beliefs, that wage-employees should be employed on long-term contracts, and that – instead of paying insurance benefits or creating artificial employment – governments should subsidise wages whenever the 'economic wage' fell below the 'living wage'. Incentives and mobility would be maintained, Harrod argued, by the pull of high market wages in expanding industries and by 'closing' declining industries to further recruitment. Such a scheme, he suggested, would reconcile the apparently antagonistic goals of personal liberty, preservation of close-knit communities, and market efficiency.

66 Q. Hogg, 'Politics and the present generation', *Fortnightly*, 160, August 1943, pp. 84–91; A. D. K. Owen, 'The Beveridge report. I. Its proposals', *Econ. J.*, LIII, 209, April 1943, pp. 1–9.

67 S. and B. Webb, *Industrial Democracy*, 1897, pp. 766–84.

68 Harold Laski, *Where do we go from here?* New York, 1940, pp. 23, 137.

69 Aneurin Bevan, *In Place of Fear*, 1952; 1978 edn, pp. 33–52.

70 Elizabeth Durbin, *New Jerusalems*, 1985, ch. 8.

71 Ann Gross, thesis in progress on the labour movement and State welfare in the 1920s and 1930s, University of Oxford.

72 Laski, *Where do we go from here?* p. 145.

73 Harvester Microfilms, Labour Party Archives, NEC minutes, 28 July 1943.

74 *Labour Party Conference Report*, 1940, p. 191.

75 Labour Party Archives, NEC minutes, report of the Standing Joint Committee of Working Women's Organisations, January 1943. A similar reluctance to acknowledge popular preferences, if they clashed with the nostrums of planners, can be found among Conservative reconstructionists (e.g., CPA, CRD 600/03, 'Looking Ahead: a Policy for Housing in England and Wales', January 1945, p. 10).

76 Labour Party Archives, NEC minutes, paper on 'Rationing, Price-fixing and Mr. Keynes', by Susan Lawrence, June 1940.

77 'Labour's Home Policy', statement by the NEC in *Labour Party Conference Report*, 1940, p. 193; John Allett, *New Liberalism: the Political Economy of J. A. Hobson*, Toronto, 1981, pp. 195–207.

78 *Labour Party Conference Report*, 1942, pp. 134–7.

79 Labour Party Archives, minutes of the Standing Joint Committee of Industrial Women's Organisations, 16 February 1940; NEC minutes, 18 February 1943. *Labour Party Conference Report*, 1942, *passim*.

80 Labour Party Archives, NEC minutes, 20 December 1942. The National Council of Labour was a joint body representing the Labour Party, the TUC and the Co-operative Congress.

81   *Labour Party Conference Report*, 1943, pp. 136–40. A similar note was taken up by the Communist Party, which early in 1943 made one of its periodic bids for Labour Party affiliation – and cited its support for Beveridge against capitalist vested interests as proof of its common cause with labour (Labour Party Archives, NEC minutes, 24 February 1943).

82   *Labour Party Conference Report*, 1943, p. 72. This reaction may be compared with the extremely hostile trade union reaction to government training schemes four years earlier (*Labour Party Conference Report*, 1939, pp. 267–70). See also the TUC's response to Beveridge's proposals for statutory control of prices and limitation of collective bargaining, advanced when he was preparing *Full Employment in a Free Society* (Beveridge Papers IXa 15, Employment Investigation minutes, 9 February 1944).

83   Bodleian Library, Mss Attlee, dep. 9, f. 56 and following, Attlee's notes for a speech at Greenwich, 12 July 1943.

84   *Labour Party Conference Report*, 1943, report of the National Executive Committee, p. 5.

85   CPA, CRD 600/03, 'Note', by G. M. Young, n.d., p. 10.

86   George Schwartz, '*Laissez-faire*', *Nineteenth Century*, CXXXIV, November 1943, pp. 209–20.

87   Sir Ernest Benn, *More Murmurings*, Vol. II of 'The Murmurings of an Individualist', reprinted from *Truth*, July–December 1941. Not all criticism of planning was rooted in theoretical individualism. See, e.g., F. H. Knight, 'Ethics and economic reform', *Economica*, VI, 21, 1939, pp. 1–29. Knight's argument was that planning was invalidated precisely by the 'social' nature of human beings: the actual process of planning constantly modified human actions and values and thus eroded the data on which planning was based.

88   Hayek, for example, strongly supported the social policies set out by Keynes in *How to Pay for the War* (*The Collected Writings of John Maynard Keynes*, XXII, pp. 106–7).

89   George Schwartz, 'A modest proposal', *Nineteenth Century*, March 1943, pp. 109–13; W. L. Burns, 'Workmen's compensation: the new proposals', *Nineteenth Century*, January 1945, pp. 20–8.

90   Deryck Abel, *Ernest Benn: Counsel for Liberty*, 1960, pp. 99–123.

91   F. A. Hayek, *The Road to Serfdom*, pp. vi–vii.

92   F. A. Hayek (ed.), *Collectivist Planning*, 1938; and the series of articles in *Economica*, 1942–44, on 'Scientism and the study of society'.

93   F. A. Hayek, 'Socialist calculation: the competitive "solution",' *Economica*, VII, May 1940, pp. 125–49. Hayek's scepticism about how far socialist planning could make use of capitalist techniques found unexpected support on the intellectual far left (see M. H. Dobb, review of Claude Baldwin, *Economics of Planning*, and F. Zweig, *The Planning of Free Societies*, in *Econ. J.*, LIII, June–September 1943, pp. 221–3).

94   Hayek, *The Road to Serfdom*, *passim*.

95   J. M. Keynes to F. A. Hayek, 28 June 1984 (*The Collected Writings of John Maynard Keynes*, XXVII, pp. 385–8).

96   PRO, Cab. 124/204, file on the report of the Steering Committee on Post-war Employment.

97   Barbara Wootton, *Freedom Under Planning*, 1945, *passim*.

98 For an example of this assumption see *Full Employment* (ten articles reprinted from *The Times*, 27 November 1942–49, April 1943).

99 PRO, Cab. 124/204, notes on report of the Steering Committee on Postwar Employment, circulated to the Reconstruction Committee of the War Cabinet, 11 January 1944.

100 St Augustine's phrase, often cited by Laski (Harold J. Laski, *The Dilemma of our Times*, 1952, p. 92).

101 H. D. Lewis, 'The present state of ethics', *Cambridge Journal*, III, 5 February 1950, pp. 259–76.

Acknowledgement

A draft version of this paper was presented to a seminar at the Shelby Cullom Davis Center for Historical Studies, Princeton University, where I was a visiting fellow. I am most grateful to Professor Lawrence Stone and other members of the Center for helpful comment and financial support.

Index